Mr. President, Mr. President!

My Fifty Years of Covering the White House

By Sarah McClendon

With Jules Minton

GPG
GENERAL
PUBLISHING
GROUP, INC

Publisher: W. Quay Hays
Editor: Colby Allerton
Design: Chitra Sekhar

For information:

General Publishing Group, Inc.
2701 Ocean Park Boulevard, Suite 140
Santa Monica, CA 90405

Special thanks to Kristin Nelson, Eleanor Neumaier and Carolyn Wendt

Cover photo courtesy of the White House; back cover photos,
top to bottom, Lyndon Baines Johnson Library, Del Ankers
photographers, the White House, Sarah McClendon collection

Library of Congress Cataloging-in-Publication Data

McClendon, Sarah.
    Mr. President, Mr. President! : my 50 years of covering the
White House / by Sarah McClendon.
        p.   cm.
    Includes index.
    ISBN 1-57544-005-9
    1. Presidents—United States—Anecdotes. 2. McClendon, Sarah.
3. Journalists—United States—Biography. 4. Women journalists—
United States—Biography. 5. United States—Politics and
government—1945-1989—Anecdotes. 6. United States—Politics
and government—1989—Anecdotes. I. Title.
E176.1.M39 1996
070'.92--dc20
[B]   96-32780
                                               CIP

Printed in the USA by RR Donnelley & Sons Company
10 9 8 7 6 5 4 3 2 1

General Publishing Group
Los Angeles

TABLE OF CONTENTS

INTRODUCTION

by Sam Donaldson

The first presidential press conference I ever attended was one held in 1962 by President John Kennedy. I was working for a local television station, my seat was in the far back reaches of the State Department Auditorium and I wasn't called on to ask a question. But, boy(!), does that news conference stand out in my memory. A woman got up—yes, a WOMAN—and said to the president, "Mr. President, two well known security risks have recently been put on a task force in the State Department..." and Kennedy began sputtering, got red in the face and started looking for cover. I knew at that instant I had found a role model.

The reporter who upset the President so was Sarah McClendon, born and raised in Tyler, Texas, which calls itself the "Rose Capital of the World." Well, Sarah has certainly been a "thorn" in the sides of Presidents...beginning with Franklin Delano Roosevelt. She insists she is a shy person. And, indeed, when you meet and talk to her socially she is friendly, kind and polite. But get her in the vicinity of a President and the fur flies. And why does she do it?

To understand Sarah you have to remember how she rose to the rank of Lieutenant in the old World War II Women's Army Corps (WAC), how she was forcibly discharged because she was pregnant (in those days that was a "sin" in the armed services), and how she came to the man's world of the Washington press corps and cracked the barrier against women journalists. Just one example: until Sarah forced a change, women reporters could only cover a newsmaker luncheon at the National Press Club from a seat in the balcony. The men, of course, sat on the main floor.

Once Sarah clawed her way into the first ranks of the press corps, she fought harder than almost anyone else to change public policy in favor of the rights of women, veterans and disenfranchised people. And in fighting for these causes Sarah believes Harry Truman got it right...The buck stops in the Oval Office. Once she asked President Reagan such a blistering question that he responded only half jokingly, "How can you say that about such a sweet fellow like me?" Easy...if you've got Sarah's courage, tenacity and sense of mission.

It's all here in this book. Well, not quite all. Sarah is pretty much confined to a wheelchair these days, but she continues to work. Who knows how many more presidents will feel her lash before she's done? The more, the better off for the country.

FOREWORD

by Larry King
noted television, radio and newspaper journalist

She is one of a kind. She is uniquely herself. What you see is what she is. There are no dark corners. Sarah is Sarah.

She is the venerable Washington journalist…if it's happening, she is there. Her questions are on the mark. She takes no prisoners. Sarah is the Potomac…and we need our gadflies.

The first time I interviewed Sarah was when I started my national radio show in 1978. Sarah was one of my first guests. She came on at midnight and stayed until 5AM, and was just as peppy at 5AM as she was at midnight. Then that very morning she was out at the White House for a press conference promptly at 9AM. Sarah's energy is legendary around Washington. She is her own business woman, having set up her own service which feeds broadcast stations around the country while continuing to meet print journalism schedules. She is a business in and of herself. She is a giant.

It is a remarkable fact that Sarah McClendon has been both professionally and often personally close to one-fourth of the men who have ever held the office of President of the United States. From Franklin Delano Roosevelt to William Jefferson Clinton, Sarah has been a common current in Washington. Sarah knows the White House, upstairs and downstairs.

Thankfully, the divine Sarah McClendon has used her rare vantage point at the center of our nation's political activity to raise her voice as a true representative of the American people—serving us all every bit as much as have any of the presidents and congressional leaders she has known for the past 50 years.

President Kennedy once remarked, in a show of warmth and humor, that he was "not scared of Sarah McClendon—but that she was 'not scared' of him, either." In these pages, Sarah proves again, in spades, that she is not "scared" to express her strongly felt opinions of each of the presidents she has known so well.

Fortunately, after enjoying her many fascinating inside stories about the private and public moments spent with these towering historical figures, you readers will come away from this book knowing much about Sarah McClendon and her own personal life. We can only hope that it continues for another century.

ACKNOWLEDGMENTS

My special thanks to Jules Minton, who has spent months of time and hard work with me in preparation of this book.

To my Publishers, Quay and Sharon Hays, for their belief in this book and their commitment to American history...and to Mr. Jim Pinkston, my literary agent.

My heartfelt thanks to Lyle Gregory, for encouraging me to write my life story at this time and helping me make it a reality.

To the very fine creative people at General Publishing Group, Colby Allerton, Joni Solomon and Chitra Sekhar, I thank you for your artistry and dedication.

Here in Washington and out in the country my sincere thanks to Jan Du Plain, Janet Donovan, John Edward Hurley, Roberta Oster, Susan Eisenhower, Marion Norby, General Erle Cooke, Father Ambrose Smith, O.P., Rt. Rev William F. O'Donnell, Col. Vann M. Kennedy, Katy Kane, Louise Michalowicz, Dr. Donna Allen, George Boerner, Sue Mayborn III, Mary Tierney, Malvina Stephenson, Georgie Anne Geyer, Calvin Clyde, Nelson Clyde, Miss Mildred Howell, Major General Jeanne Holm, S.S. McClendon III, S.S. McClendon IV, Mrs. Dorothy McClendon, Norma McClendon, Kenneth Gunn, Marjorie and Mastin White, Ralph Hill, Grace Johnson, E.G. Marshall, Joan Schffer, Christy Bowe, Dr. Arton Dhima, Barbara Wheeler, Vicki Komer, Kathleen Hietala, Nils Shapiro, Bill Lennert, Rick Reidy, Bill Reed, Phylis Kaelin at Pacific Research and Charles Harrell at the The Muntz Library at the University of Texas-Tyler.

Thank you ever so much Sen. Bob Dole, Sen. George Mitchell, Speaker Jim Wright, Sen. Alan Simpson, Sen. Bennett Johnston, Sen. Robert C. Byrd, Rep. Ralph M. Hall, Rep. Gillespie Montgomery, Sen. Edward Kennedy, Rep. Melvin Laird, Marlin Fitzwater, Joe Laitin and Tex Easley.

To Sam Donaldson and to Larry King, I thank you so for your kind words.

Great apreciation is due to the National Archives and the Presidential Libraries of Presidents Roosevelt, Truman, Eisenhower, Kennedy, Johnson, Nixon, Ford, Carter, Reagan and Bush.

Finally I wish to express my gratitude to The Presidents of The United States themselves. What a privilege and honor it has been these 52 years ...and continues to be!

PROLOGUE

As befits a reporter's story, this is a book about "who," "what," "when," "where," "why" and "how." The emphasis, however, is on the "why" and "how."

It is, for the most part, a book about Washington DC, a few square miles on the Potomac River where laws are made for a vast country that spans a continent and half an ocean. It chronicles the life-long journey of Sarah McClendon from Texas to Washington and tells tales of many others who made Washington the way it was in the years from 1944 to 1996.

It is a story which shows that one can overcome difficulties and keep going strong for eight decades. It is an account of a life which has intersected with and affected, sometimes significantly, other extraordinary lives.

It is not a sermon. It does not vindicate nor apologize to anyone. It does not offer solutions. It may, however, illustrate some of the things that discourage us in our quest for full democracy and point out some of the things that need fixing.

This chronology of 86 years is like a clock that I have never allowed to wind down. The key has been my belief that "Nothing happens by accident": preparation and production are important words with me. The mainspring is my participation in government and my alertness to what is happening to the average American. If there is a timely message in these pages, it is that one man or one woman can make a difference for the better in the way our country works.

Sarah McClendon
Washington DC, August 1996

WASHINGTON, DC, 1944:

At the beginning of June 1944, I was flat on my back in the Walter Reed Army Hospital in Washington DC. I had just given birth to a baby girl. I was without a husband, without any nearby relatives and soon to be without a job.

My daughter's father, who'd had little to recommend him but my own loneliness, had, after a few months of our marriage, gone back to his former girlfriend. Though I'd managed to keep my condition hidden under my regulation WAC uniform for eight months, I was about to be honorably (and quite unwillingly) discharged from my commission as the first female First Lieutenant in the Office of the Army Surgeon General. Back in those unenlightened days, you could not be a soldier and a mother too. Though it upset the people at Walter Reed to no end, I had insisted on my full rights and privileges and became the first army officer to ever give birth at a military hospital. Somehow, though, I didn't feel like celebrating the fact. I missed my family back in Texas, but most of them had acted horrified when I'd joined the service the year before. Considering how they'd react to this, I knew I had to go through it alone.

By the end of June 1944, I was standing in the Oval Office, listening to President Franklin Delano Roosevelt and furiously scribbling notes. I was the newest member of the White House press corps. I had a child to support, readers to inform and a career that would last a lifetime.

Chapter I

FDR: THE EMPEROR

I was very lucky to get a White House press pass that June. I was even more lucky to meet Bascom Timmons, who became my employer, my mentor and my friend.

I had certainly not felt fortunate during my short stay at Walter Reed. The hospital's well-equipped, busy department of obstetrics had, until I came along to upset the apple cart, been available exclusively to the wives of military men. Officer's wives, in particular, treated their long stays as though they were visiting some fancy spa. The atmosphere was like a social club, one to which it was quite clear that I did not belong.

Though our name had been recently changed from the Women's *Auxiliary* Army Corps to the Women's Army Corps, the transformation from WAAC to WAC had not made that much difference in the way we were treated. Like my sisters in uniform, I had grown used to having army wives—and much of the public at large—look at me as little more than a camp follower. That sense of lonely isolation had played a big part in my ill-advised decision to marry. So, as news of the June 6th Invasion of Europe spread around the OB wards and the chatter took on the tone of "So *that's* why my husband couldn't tell me what he was doing," my thoughts were on my own personal D-Day. As soon as I possibly could, I would leave the hospital to face a life that had been, I knew, changed forever.

When I did leave, I had no one to go home to. I had planned to have a woman in my building help take care of the child, but she had unexpectedly left town. So I had no more time for bed rest. I had to get up and learn to bathe my baby.

I named my infant daughter Sally because I'd always wanted that name myself. It was a beautiful name, but no one ever called me Sally. They wouldn't even let me use it as my nickname. When Sally was nine days old, I left her with a baby sitter and visited the doctor for advice. It was so very hot that summer, living right near the Capitol, that I was afraid she was going to suffocate. To move out to

Public Affairs Officer at the Pentagon, I hadn't thoroughly read a newspaper in two years. Given the relative sophistication of the reporters about me and the President's reputation as a masterful controller of his image, it seemed best to keep my mouth shut and not show my ignorance.

Roosevelt was famous for the sarcastic wit he would unleash on any reporter—or, for that matter, any politician—who seemed uncooperative, uninformed or unwilling to play the game by Roosevelt's rules. His sly tongue lashings, backed up by an occasional publicity-conscious stunt, played well with the public. Many people thought his treatment of foot-draggers, critics, renegades and others who wouldn't get with the Roosevelt program was funny. At times, I enjoyed it, too—but I knew I wouldn't like to be the butt of it.

I had heard that FDR had once handed a dunce cap to the noted columnist Drew Pearson, who frequently criticized the New Deal, and ordered him to go stand in the corner and wear it. Then there was John O'Donnell of the *New York Daily News*, who openly opposed the President. Roosevelt presented him an Iron Cross, the kind the Germans awarded, saying he'd earned it for hurting the war effort. It was, of course, quite true that O'Donnell despised Roosevelt. But O'Donnell's wife, Doris Fleeson, also a news correspondent at that time, was a strong supporter of Mrs. Roosevelt and very good friends of the Roosevelt family. In fact, O'Donnell and Fleeson finally divorced over their opinions of the First Family.

I also had a personal reason for not asking FDR any questions. Though solidly Democrat, my family back in Texas had a bone to pick with Roosevelt, and I had this in mind when I first saw him. My enmity came from something I had learned during the Great Depression, long before I had ever even thought of coming to Washington.

Among Mr. Roosevelt's formidable bag of tools for ensuring cooperation was a tendency to disburse government funds in ways that would help those loyal to him gain power and influence. My father, S.S. McClendon, was the County Democratic Chairman of Smith County, Texas. He was naturally the head of the party in Tyler, our home town. But when FDR wanted to tell anyone in Tyler that he was going to give the community some federal money, which was desperately needed to meet the needs of the unemployed, he would notify not my father but the town banker, Mr. Gus F. Taylor. The banker, of course, had great talent and even greater experience at using this information to get more customers for his bank. He enlarged his influence, and weakened my father's, by making everybody think that if you wanted to get to Roosevelt, you had to come through him.

Well, my father didn't like this. And I, then a fledgling reporter on both the town papers, agreed with my father. We both thought that this was blatantly political and saw, even in these early years of the new administration, a definite dictatorial streak in the way Roosevelt chose to operate. But, at the same time, I was developing a grudging respect for the new President. He was bringing us all so many, many changes for the better. He understood what needed to be done to fight the Depression, and that included the smaller things as well as the big.

So there I stood in the Roosevelt press conferences, uncomfortable, conflicted and feeling out of place. I had decided it was best not to ask any questions, and I'm glad now that I showed the good sense not to. I was, I am sure, not the only reporter in that office who felt like a Christian in the Roman Colosseum, facing the lions and the Emperor himself, all rolled into one. In the twelfth year of the longest Presidency in the history of our nation, it would have been difficult not to be aware of the enormous influence and impact of Franklin Delano Roosevelt. There, in his spellbinding, awe-inspiring presence, it was impossible.

This was the man who had brought us through the Great Depression by changing the very nature of the federal government's role in the lives of the American people. This was the man whose strong hand had steered us through three years of involvement in the most all-encompassing war the world had known. This was the man who was in control of the nation in ways no man had ever been before, not even Washington and Lincoln. Like any great man, he had great detractors, but any amongst the press corps who dared to voice criticism or even seemed to lean toward doing so were soon brought to heel or banished from the charmed circle. FDR could be ruthless to those he felt got in the way of his efforts to help our nation survive.

Many people have asked me who I thought was the greatest President that I've known. I would have to say today that

Franklin Delano Roosevelt was perhaps the greatest we've ever had. Though there have been good, even excellent Presidents among the ten I've seen follow him, FDR was, I feel, head and shoulders above them all.

There is a paradox here, because in many ways, Roosevelt set the example for or, at the very least, took us a long way down the path into the problem that has most plagued the Presidency during the other ten administrations I've covered in my half-century in Washington. Responding to the perilous times through which he sailed and the unprecedented mandate we gave him of over twelve years at the helm of the ship of state, FDR changed the figurative rank of the office from that of Captain to Admiral. He seemed to have forgotten, and certainly made us forget, that we, the people, created the Presidency and, in effect, own it. We bestow its duties and honors on those we elect, but it is both our right and responsibility to insist upon accountability—and to maintain surveillance of and, if necessary, offer guidance to the person we have temporarily hired to fill this high office. A President who is secretive, less than honest or non-responsive to the Americans for whom he works has forgotten the essential nature of his job.

In the first two of these ways, Roosevelt frequently failed the test. His secrets not only made life hard for his sudden successor, Harry Truman, but still worry us as a nation. What happened, for example, at the Teheran conference when FDR, Churchill and Stalin met and talked about Southeast Asia? And as far as his honesty is concerned, why do a majority of residents of the state of Hawaii feel that Mr. Roosevelt had advanced knowledge of the attack on Pearl Harbor and chose to withhold it in order to force the isolationists to withdraw their objections to our entering the war?

Why then, do I rank Roosevelt, who set new standards in running an imperial presidency, so highly? Because in the third area, that of responsiveness to the people's needs, I think he succeeded in many admirable ways. Though he was undeniably patrician by nature and usually appeared far more ready to talk than listen, Roosevelt, through intelligence, effort and an uncanny ability to relate to and inspire the common man and woman, gave us, in my opinion, exactly what we needed as a nation during two very different, very turbulent decades.

Roosevelt had brains, nerve and a willingness to work. He was well educated. He had a fine family background, which gave him much confidence and a natural entree into many things. And he had trained for the Presidency. He had investigated it and knew what it required. From youth on, he had methodically prepared himself for the job, the first President, I think, to ever do so.

Before he left New York, Roosevelt had gone to the homes of the poor. He'd gone to homeless shelters. He'd spoken with the unemployed. He'd looked around and found all kinds of Americans. He'd talked with old men and young ones. He'd talked to blacks and other minority groups. He and his wife had made contact with the people long before he ever won the office.

One of the great contributions that Roosevelt made as president was to continue that contact by keeping up a sense of communications between himself and the nation: the little people, in cities and small towns across the country, on farms and ranches and even out in the woods. This was done by radio. He was persuaded to broadcast "Fireside Chats" by a man named Harry Butcher, who was covering the White House at the time for CBS. Butcher later became a vice president at CBS and then Gen. Eisenhower's Naval Aide during World War II. Butcher thought up the Fireside Chats, coached Roosevelt on the manner of handling them and suggested subjects, as well. The talks were given from the Diplomatic Room on the first floor of the White House, which is now used as an entryway by Presidents to and from their helicopters and for visitors who come in by car to the South Lawn area. This very important room is always pointed out to visitors as where the Fireside Chats originated.

Communications were crucial in Mr. Roosevelt's relationship with the people; he needed their confidence and support because of the great changes he was making in their government and their way of life. I remember Mrs. Tom Connally (who was, in the 1930s, Mrs. Morris Shepard; a resolutely political wife, she married first Senator Shepard and then Senator Connally, both of Texas) speak of the risks Roosevelt faced and the courage he showed in taking these bold steps. Close to the new President and his wife, she was there in March 1933 when FDR decided to declare a Bank Holiday on the first day after his inauguration into office. His quick, controversial action, which led to giving the Treasury Department the power to reopen and regulate the banks, saved the banking system and, perhaps, the finances of the country. Mrs. Connally glowed with admiration when she remembered that.

I think it is very important to point out that Franklin Roosevelt brought to government many important programs that we needed then and may well need now. We should look back to some of these to realize the wisdom of them. One that was especially helpful was the WPA, Works Progress Administration. It helped so many of the unemployed during the Depression that something similar might be useful today. The WPA helped the jobless to train—to learn how to get work and how to carry out their duties—as well as giving them a small salary while they prepared. There were also within the WPA programs for all the arts, including support for authors and journalists.

Roosevelt had wonderful assistance in making all these changes in the government. He brought down from Harvard a number of young men who were brilliant. They became known as "The Harvard Brain Trust." One of these was my dear friend, Maston G. White, of Tyler, Texas. Maston White served with the government as chief lawyer for the Department of the Army and then for the Agriculture Department and still later for the Interior Department, where he fought for our National Parks. As one of the "Harvard Brain-Trusters," he was called to Washington to help to reconstruct government and stayed on, beyond FDR's years, to help to make the government work.

Franklin Roosevelt had an amazing effect on those closest to him. I think that every man and woman on his staff absolutely adored him. They were as loyal to him as they could be. Perhaps even more amazing was the loyalty he got from his wife Eleanor. In some ways, he treated her quite poorly, but of all those who helped him during his more than twelve years in office, she was probably the most important.

The more I learn about Eleanor Roosevelt, the more respect I have for her. She set a standard that all the First Ladies who have followed her must measure themselves against. She was, in many ways, our "Assistant President." Besides handling a mammoth volume of mail from people who sought her out as a sort of legal counsel or a Mother Superior, she was her husband's eyes and ears, traveling across the nation and, during World War II, on many a long trek to see the military overseas. She was certainly an exceptional partner for FDR. With all the problems of what seems to have been a troubled marriage, she was excellent at showing him her full support, whether mixing and mingling with the public or the White House's inner circle.

President Roosevelt used to let people come to the White House and see him informally a great deal, including a number of Texans. Senator Shepard, then Chairman of the Senate Committee on Armed Forces, went there frequently to talk about defense projects. He also tried, with his wife's influence, to get more projects for Texas, which had a lot of unemployed at the time. Congressman Lyndon Johnson used to frequently go by the White House on his way to work in the morning. He had an excuse. He was taking Grace Tulley, President Roosevelt's secretary, to work. They lived near each other in the Cleveland Park area of Washington. Since Johnson lived at the Woodley Park Towers, right around the corner from Grace, who lived in Cathedral Mansions on Connecticut Avenue, he would give her a ride to work, taking the opportunity to go into the White House and try to see what he could get for Texas. It was all quite informal.

You don't see Presidents today letting people drop in on them and the White House staff as you did back then. But Roosevelt had a different way of doing many things. Take, for example, his work schedule. Besides being his secretary, Grace Tulley ate dinner with FDR every night for many, many years. She once told me it was for *seventeen* years. This was because he worked late at night, sometimes staying until midnight or 1:00 AM at his desk. Of course, he had many jobs to do at that time, helping to run the war—and the world.

Grace was a great asset to the President. She worked at all hours. Whenever he needed anything, she was willing to do it, even if it meant working late and starting early the next morning. She was well known to Mrs. Roosevelt first. She was originally hired from a secretarial service when the Roosevelts still lived in New York City. She tried out and wound up staying for as long as Franklin Roosevelt lived, becoming almost part of the family. All the Roosevelt children had great regard for her. Some time after FDR's death, she obtained a job through her old ride to work, Lyndon Johnson, who was by then Senate Majority Leader. She worked in the Policy Committee of the Senate for a long time. She was a friend of all Democrats and they all loved her back. She was a wonderful woman who, among other things, could tell many an experience of her life with the Roosevelt clan.

She was also a dear friend of mine. After FDR's death, she wrote a book about her many years with him. Her book is out of print now, but it is a wonderful source of information. I visited her in her apartment to ask if I could borrow a copy and found she had only one left. She loaned it to me, and I'm afraid to say I kept it for some time. At least I did manage to return it before she died.

Since I was a friend, she told me a few things that she couldn't put in her book. One puts a new light on the hours just before and after President Roosevelt's death.

In April 1945, Franklin Roosevelt was at his cottage in Warm Springs, Georgia, along with some members of his staff and a few guests. Mrs. Roosevelt had remained behind in Washington DC, as was usual when the President went down to "The Summer White House." FDR had two cousins visiting him, and in one of the cabins outside was Lucy Mercer, the woman who had once worked for him as a secretary and then later, apparently, became his girlfriend. Lucy Mercer was a socialite who belonged to a very fine, well-connected family. Though Mrs. Roosevelt had overlooked other incidents, she seemed quite disturbed about Miss Mercer. Franklin had once promised not to see the girl anymore, but Eleanor had found that he was still meeting her.

In the morning, the President remained in the cabin, posing for the famed Russian painter, Madame Schoumatoff. As it turned out, the portrait was to be the last image Roosevelt posed for during his lifetime. Grace was instructed to send the lady staff members down to the spa to have a swim. It was apparently to get them away from the compound for the afternoon. No one is quite sure where Lucy Mercer was in the hours that followed. But Grace was later sent for and told that Mr. Roosevelt had become extremely ill. She, in turn, called all the women together. After FDR died, Grace went down to the cottage where Lucy Mercer was staying. She informed Lucy that the President was dead and told her to leave immediately, which she did. Mrs. Roosevelt had been summoned to come from Washington and did not deserve the extra heartbreak.

Even knowing nothing about Miss Mercer's presence, the nation was, of course, stunned by the President's death. Most Americans had all but forgotten that while in office Franklin Delano Roosevelt had never been a completely well man. An adult-onset case of polio, infantile paralysis, had permanently impaired him. But his courage in overcoming his disabled legs had taught him how to give the country courage.

I remember seeing Mr. Roosevelt take his fourth Oath of Office in January of 1945. I was standing on the White House lawn and he was up on the large pedestal erected for the ceremonies. One of his sons, Jimmy Roosevelt, was by his side. Jimmy often did much to carry his father's weight, since his father could not walk, only stand. Jimmy was very good at covering up how much he was needed, acting as if he were only casually there when his father was really leaning on him heavily.

One never realizes what Roosevelt went through, how much strength he had to give to the job and how much he must have suffered physically, until one goes to Warm Springs, Georgia, as I did later in life. Here you can see the braces he had to wear to stand. I was struck by the cruelty, the harshness, the meanness of those old fashioned prosthetic pieces. Now we have much more comfortable devices, even the Seattle Shoe, with which a veteran friend of mine who lost both of his legs is able to walk comfortably.

A trip to Warm Springs is also a reminder that FDR had great moments of sadness, as well as his great moments of triumph. You can see his specially equipped car, in which he was able to pilot himself to a lonely, high place where he could look over at the mountains. He sat there by himself in weary quiet for many hours during the days before he died. I wondered why Eleanor was not with him during those lonely days at Warm Springs.

Mr. Roosevelt was obviously ill the last time I saw him at the White House, that final year. He was really too ill to assume the duties of office again, but he was running for his fourth term. His hands were shaking very badly, making me think he had some illness. Though I couldn't guess what, I thought it might be Parkinson's disease. FDR hid his hands under the desk so people wouldn't see the tremors. He won that fourth term, but was dead after serving only three months of it.

His death made it clear how great an impact he had on the people. When Roosevelt's body was carried down Pennsylvania Avenue to the White House, there was an immense mob out on the streets. It was amazing to be in that crowd. I almost fainted because we were all packed so tightly. The people loved him. The day that he died was a profound shock to the nation. I know how intensely we felt the impact in my own little office in the National Press Building. Many of the people who had formerly worked for Mr. Bascom Timmons and were now in other occupations came back to his office to work that night, just to be helpful. They were catching up on reminiscences. They were interviewing people who might remember some personal experiences with the President. We were trying to get any kind of news copy we could.

We worked late that night. Then, when the work seemed done, I went with a fellow reporter walking down Pennsylvania Avenue, just looking and thinking. And as we walked by the old War, Navy and State Department building, next door to the White House, we saw a light on upstairs. This was almost midnight and someone was still working in an office up there. We decided we'd go in. Can you believe it? With all of the security measures employed today, you can't possibly get in unless you can prove that you have an appointment. But odd as it was, we just walked into that building in the middle of the night, a man and woman, asked to go up into the office where the light was and were told the way.

The lighted office turned out to be that of the Assistant Secretary of State, Will Clayton of Houston, Texas. He was a very important man who would have a great deal to do with fashioning and inaugurating the Marshall Plan. We found he was hard at work. He admired the President so greatly that, out of respect, he just couldn't go home for the night. It was important to keep working and thinking and writing about things that were important to Roosevelt.

That's the kind of tribute the Roosevelts would have liked. That's the kind of people the Roosevelts were. His knowledge, leadership and courage and her intelligence, compassion, and loyalty changed our ideas of what a President and First Lady could accomplish. The deep flaws only made the accomplishments seem all that greater. I think that's why we still look to them, love them, and respect them today.

If reporters are born, not made, then someone had better check my birth certificate, because when I was growing up in Texas, I never once considered journalism as a career.

I knew I'd have to work for a living; though we McClendons came from old stock, including a couple of folks who came over on the Mayflower, there was hardly the kind of wealth to support any of the nine children once we were old enough to work. I thought I'd take up the law, like brothers and uncles and cousins had before me. But as I took preparatory courses at Tyler Junior College and toiled at a hatefully boring bookkeeping job my sister had gotten me at the local bank where she worked, I grew restless and impatient. When a drama teacher who'd come from out of state suggested I attend journalism school at the university in her home town, I jumped at the suggestion. With my small savings and what I could borrow from my older brothers and sisters, I entered the University of Missouri School of Journalism in 1929.

Founded in 1908 by Dean Walter Williams, the school had been the first of its kind, and it is still often rated the best. I was lucky to be there the last year Dean Williams taught, to hear his words before he moved on to be president of the entire university. Because of his guidance, my education was not only practical, but based on ethics. His "Journalist's Creed," which calls reporting the news a public trust, still hangs on my wall. We were encouraged to crusade for good causes. I campaigned for a better standard of quality for the local milk supply— and, when I succeeded, had my first taste of my stories making a difference. It was a taste I liked.

The school published a daily newspaper, not just for the students but for the town of Columbia, Missouri, filled with world and local news as well as the usual campus chatter. The offices were open all week, on weekends and holidays, and we'd work at all hours, getting the kind of experience we would at a professional paper. I was at the copy desk the day the stock market crashed and learned just what this would mean for the country from an expert instructor on turning out editorials, Roscoe Ellard, who went on to teach at the Columbia University School of Journalism. When, two years later, I went to work at both my hometown papers, I felt secure in my skills. I'd already served my apprenticeship. In fact, there was only one thing about my training that wasn't realistic: it was the one extended period in my career when I was not discriminated against simply because I am a woman.

I did not, however, come away from my college years with the same glowing opinion of the state as I did of its university. Though I had several life-altering experiences, including my first truly passionate relationship and, even more importantly, the spiritual awakening that led to my becoming a Catholic, I found little encouraging about Missouri in my day-to-day life.

The state was hot in summer and cold in winter. And since my family didn't want me to join just any sorority, I wound up joining none and living alone in a room without good ventilation or a working heater. The rest of the building got heat. I got soot all over the floor and the furniture, in my closet, everywhere.

Even living on the tightest of budgets, I had to work. My mother had made me promise when I left home that I would never be a waitress. When I couldn't find other work, I followed the letter if not the spirit of the promise and took a job as a restaurant receptionist. I lived on sandwiches for a month at a time.

I was, for the most part, lonely. It seemed to me that the locals were sharply divided into two kinds of people: some very nice but most rather crude and outspoken. Missourians would say and do just about anything. It was the first time (though hardly the last) I ever saw students going to college in overalls. I thought that Missouri's nickname was all too appropriate: we Texans didn't have to go around braying "Show Me"...because we already knew.

I guess that, being young, I was too "sophisticated" to realize the virtues that come with Missouri's lack of affectation, which I merely took as a lack of polish, and too aristocratic to see the straight-forward values that come with plain sense and plain speaking. Working on local Texas papers taught me to understand and identify with the common American, but it took Harry S Truman to teach me, and most of the nation, about the hidden strengths his state bred into its native sons and daughters.

Chapter 2

HARRY TRUMAN:
WHERE THE BUCK STOPPED

In the midst of the most desperate war the world had known, some ninety days after becoming Vice President, former Senator Harry S Truman, Democrat of Missouri, suddenly found he had become Chief Executive of the most powerful nation on Earth. I wonder how that felt.

There was a little room on the first floor of the House side of the U.S. Capitol, just outside the House chamber itself. It was here that Sam Rayburn, Lyndon Johnson and others used to meet after 5 o'clock over a bottle of bourbon. One day when the new Vice President dropped by as he often did to have a drink and talk shop, Sam told him, "Harry, you'd better call the White House at once!" Roosevelt was dead and Truman was to take the place of the man who'd been President longer than anyone else in U.S. history. When he arrived at 2400 Pennsylvania Avenue, Truman immediately asked Eleanor Roosevelt how he could help. "How can I help *you*?" the widow answered. "You're the one in trouble now."

Like most of the nation, I underestimated Harry S Truman at first. Though FDR was dead, the new President still stood in his giant shadow. Truman seemed small, ordinary, rural and unsophisticated in comparison. He wasn't an intellectual. He didn't even have a real middle name. The S, it's claimed, was a compromise by his parents, so one side of the family would think he'd been named for grandfather Anderson Shippe Truman while the other side was sure it honored grandfather Solomon Young. But it was just an S, without even a period, and really stood for nothing. Truman's critics, and there would be many, said he just stuck it in there to make him sound more dignified.

It didn't help that Roosevelt, in his authoritarian, often covert fashion, had not kept his Vice President up on what was going on. Roosevelt had been involved in many secret negotiations, and getting information about them made Truman's early weeks especially difficult. With less than three months' experience in the Executive Branch, Truman found it hard to earn the trust of many in the government, in the country and in countries overseas. Hostile staffers hampered his work at first. Career State Department men would brief him as if he knew nothing at all. He got tired of people assuming he was ignorant, but he didn't make a fuss about it. The fact that he was able to sort out the threads and act decisively was much to his credit.

This was a President who surprised us all, political insider and ordinary citizen, not once but many times. He was a man who, amidst continuing opposition, made decisions and initiated programs that profoundly affected the history of the United States and the world. Besides the controversial judgment for which he is best known, to drop atomic bombs on Japan to end World War II, Truman logged an amazing number of lasting achievements.

In world affairs, he picked up Roosevelt's fallen reins by establishing the Truman Doctrine to aid countries in their fight against Communism, the Marshall Plan to help rebuild Europe, the North Atlantic Treaty Organization (NATO) to enforce the peace, and the astonishing Berlin Air Lift. To avoid the post–World War I mistakes that impoverished Germany and led to the rise of Hitler, Truman even helped the economies of our former enemies and allowed Japan to keep its Emperor. He oversaw the birth of the United Nations and helped form the Organization of American States. He recognized the state of Israel, which gave it the credibility it needed to exist. He became the first President ever to make an official state visit to our northern neighbor, Canada.

Domestically, Truman reorganized our defense resources with the National Security Act, which created the Department of Defense with its component Departments of the Army, Navy and Air Force and also authorized establishment of the Central Intelligence Agency. He formed the Council of Economic Advisors. He sent the first civil rights message ever to Congress and desegregated the Armed Forces. After deciding to intervene in Korea, he upheld civilian control over the military by firing General Douglas MacArthur, who had all but declared himself independent of Presidential control.

Not all these monumental decisions sat well with the American public. Truman began his presidency as a "nobody" and wound up the last of his almost eight years in office with one of the lowest approval ratings the Gallup poll had ever shown, only 26%. His own party tried to dump him as its presidential candidate in 1948. His final years in office were spent under fire from General MacArthur's supporters and the Communist conspiracy ravings of Senator Joseph McCarthy of Wisconsin. Truman once said that he received more abuse than any other president, and, with the possible exception of Abraham Lincoln, he may well have.

Yet one now frequently hears comments from politicians, journalists and citizens alike that they had never realized how Truman exemplified much of what is best in the American national character. His mottoes, "The Buck Stops Here" and "If you can't stand the heat, get out of the kitchen," have become part of modern folklore. In the past twenty years, since Gerald Ford hung Truman's portrait in the Cabinet Room, U.S. Presidents (and presidential hopefuls), Democrat and Republican alike, have scrambled all over each other to praise Harry S Truman, to identify themselves with him, and to put him on the pedestal as one of the greatest of their predecessors. Bill Clinton understood the irony of this when he joked that he came from a family that was for Truman "when he was alive."

This re-evaluation of Truman reached its climax in 1995, when the nation formally honored the fiftieth anniversary of Truman's coming to office. Though Truman had already become a rather salty, colorful, outsider hero in our popular memory (partly thanks to books and plays like Merle Miller's "Plain Speaking" and James Whitmore's "Give 'Em Hell, Harry!"), this official canonization came about through the efforts of his daughter, Mrs. Margaret Truman Daniel, a former concert singer now turned successful mystery novelist.[1]

To raise $16 million from private sources to expand the Truman Library in Independence, Missouri, Truman's daughter conceived the idea of having a great celebration in Washington and several other cities. Her efforts brought forth ready volunteers from all over, including almost all the living ex-Presidents and the Clintons.

---

[1] Like her father, Margaret, too, had been surprised by the announcement that he had become President. She was at her apartment on Connecticut Avenue, dressing, when there was a knock at the door. It was the Secret Service, telling her she was now to live at the White House as First Daughter. "I will never open the door again for anybody who wants to knock!" she told me.

Unfortunately, Margaret became so ill at the last moment that she couldn't participate in the festivities personally. But the gala, which brought together celebrities, citizens and current and former officials of every political stripe, was an enormous success.

President Clinton's words about President Truman at that event were, I think, both interesting and true. He said that Truman once remarked that America was not built on fear, but on courage, imagination and an unbeatable determination to do the job at hand. Clinton continued, "Today we draw strength from this unforgettable lesson and from the life of a decent, honest Missourian who ascended to the highest office in the land and set our nation on a course of peace, prosperity and leadership."

In a way, Harry S Truman set my career back on course, as well. Uncomfortable at and disappointed by the intimidating Roosevelt press conferences, I had begun to attend the Presidential briefings with less and less frequency. I concentrated on Congress, where I could cover the Congressmen who most directly represented my readers. I found the House and Senate fascinating and hoped to make the workings of government more meaningful and under-standable through my Congressional reporting. I decided to leave the "larger issues" that were dealt with in the White House to the wire ser-vices. It was in the halls of the Capitol that I began to make my clos-est friends and most trusted contacts. I felt more at home among the "grassroots" politicians and was keeping quite busy getting out the news on the often frantic activities. Then events conspired to make me even busier, as worries appeared about my job security.

When peace came, first in Europe and then in the Pacific, the men who had left Bascom Timmons' employment to fight in the War began to return. Timmons reluctantly told me that he'd have to give them their jobs back. "You should start your own news bureau, like May Craig has," Mr. Timmons suggested. But this was not a clear cut, finely tuned or easy to accomplish goal. One did it the best way one could.

I had been allowed, while still with Timmons, to represent a few other newspapers on the side, like my former employer in Texas, the *Beaumont Enterprise*. With these as a start, I also began to write for my friend Frank Mayborn's three Texas papers and with the help of the late Claude Wootten and his improbably named assistant, Edgar Allen Poe, was able to add enough income to make a go of it. I picked up other newspapers through friends, from folks hearing about my service, and from visiting editors who suddenly decided they wanted Washington representation but could not afford a full-time correspondent.

I got my first client up in New England from a colleague who furnished a specialized column for the notorious William Loeb, who owned several papers in the region, including New Hampshire's *Manchester Union-Leader*. Loeb, an outspoken archconservative who was often viewed with a combination of hatred and fear, had asked her to cover politics for him. Feeling more than a little trepidation about this request, she suggested me, instead. Since I actually enjoy controversial people, I welcomed Loeb's accounts. In fact, I had to fight for them, but won out over the competition.

I always remember Mr. Timmons' warning that I should forever keep looking for more newspapers because I would never know when an established client might pull out, merge with a rival paper, be bought or simply die. Running a news bureau is a bit like juggling, but since 1946, this circus act has made a living for my daughter and myself.

For baby Sally's health, I had managed to move, renting an apartment house in the more climatically temperate suburbs of Southeast Washington. But with the added responsibilities of running my own business and the increased, more irregular hours it took me away from home, child care went from being a concern to being the problem that ruled my life. It sometimes seemed as complicated as running my business. Oh, for the modern-day convenience of daycare centers! With the war-time economy and post-war boom pulling workers into the factories, hired help was hard to come by. So I made alliances with every mother I could find—married, divorced, house-wives, part- and full-time workers—to share lists of housekeepers. When I rode with a cab driver who had his baby sitting beside him on the front seat, I got him into my network.

I finally found a child care worker who seemed to meet my needs. Lillian Stensland was perfect, except for one rather troubling element in her past job history: she was the nursemaid of Charles Lindbergh's son, Charles Jr., at the time the infant was kidnapped and eventually killed. She assured me, however, that it had not been her responsibility to be by the sleeping Lindbergh baby's side. Given my natural inclination to side with the underdog—and the fact that I really needed the help—I hired her. My daughter still shakes her head (half-jokingly, half in earnest) about my choice of nursemaids, but if you want to know the truth, this woman was actually one of the better picks in my decades-long mixed bag of domestic helpers. She and her six-year-old son slept in the apartment's one bedroom, with Sally in a crib beside the bed. I slept in the dining room alcove. Later, after she had moved on, I had other housekeepers who, when I got home, would already have their hats on and be out the door in seconds! Lillian has kept in touch with Sally and me through the years.

With my new business and new clients, I began to feel pressure to start attending Presidential press conferences with greater regularity. To be an effective bureau chief, I would have to cover both the White House and the Hill. Fortunately, Mr. Truman's choices, his personality, and his way with reporters made this far easier than facing FDR on a regular basis would have been. Like the best of those in Congress, Truman had not lost touch with the folks at home and seemed to want to keep government as open and non-mystifying to them as it could be.

The Washington Press Corps were all looking to see how Truman would handle his press conferences. He lost no time in giving us a pleasant surprise. He said he had noticed how crowded the Press had been at FDR's crowded conferences in the Oval Office. So he had decided to move the press conferences to the old War, Navy and State Department Building which sat just west, across the street, from the White House. The three Departments were actually housed in one building back then, which would be an impossibility today. Truman held his press conferences in the Indian Treaty Room, where we could all sit down and thus take better notes. It was a relief indeed to sit in this relatively spacious historic room where most of the treaties with the Indians had actually been signed.

I found Harry Truman's personality quite likable, if a little shocking from time to time. He was a man of few words—direct, plain, realistic and understandable. His answers were usually short and blunt, never mincing words. Though he sometimes seemed to speak out on things a little too quickly and without sufficient thought, he did indeed cut through the veneer and red tape in an economical fashion. His approach to a subject was never circular. You felt he was being honest, no matter how much or who it hurt. This was one man who, when he told you that he was telling the truth, actually made you believe it.

This no-nonsense approach could keep you on your toes. At one early morning conference, when I was sitting in the second row, there was a lull right after the questioning started. I guess our brains weren't working too fast that early, so we sat, thinking what to ask. Truman waited in silence for a moment, then said, "Well, I guess that's all, boys," and left. He seemed to think if we could not come up with a question quickly enough, we did not deserve to be taking up his time. He'd ended the conference after just six minutes. Disappointed, somewhat embarrassed, shocked and surprised, we reporters talked it over and agreed that we would try to do something to see that this wouldn't happen again. A volunteer committee was sent to the President to ask him in the future to please let the press conference go on for at least half an hour. He agreed, and that is why Presidential press conferences these days are generally timed to be 30 minutes long.

Truman always had great rapport with the press. Unlike Roosevelt, he seemed to meet us on an equal footing. He had played poker with the boys who covered the Senate before he was Vice President, and he kept those relationships even after he was President. As he entered his car on Connecticut Avenue, getting ready to go to the White House for the first time since having been sworn in as President, Truman looked over the crowd of reporters standing by and saw one of his old card-playing chums, Tony Vocarro. He said, "Come on, Tony. Let me give you a ride." Tony hopped in and, from that moment on, became *the* source of Truman's thoughts for the wire services and everyone else.

Every now and then a reporter would simply run into Harry Truman. He was not like some presidents who kept their distance. Once, during Truman's second term, I went down to the White House for a reason which, even at the time, seemed rather inconsistent with that complex where decisions were being made that would change the world. A White House guard I had become friendly with had, upon hearing I'd never eaten a Chincoteague oyster, a local delicacy, promised he'd bring me some from his next fishing trip. Well, one Saturday, my friend called to say that he had a half gallon tin of oysters waiting for me at the White House gate as a gift. After I had picked up the oysters, I decided that while there, I should check out the day's happenings. Hiding my treasure under a bush, I headed to the residence. (In today's world, I'm sure the Secret Service would have swooped in to check for a bomb.)

Normally we do not cover news at the White House on weekends unless there is something extraordinary going on. On this day, just as I put my head into the front door of the west wing lobby, I ran into Vice President Alben Barkley of Kentucky, whom I had met on numerous occasions. Until Truman had been elected on his own accord in 1948, he had gotten along quite well without a Vice President, so Barkley had few illusions about what back then was seen as a largely ceremonial office unless a President should happen to die. He was a delightful man, and everybody liked to hear his good stories.

As we chatted, a tiny, almost scolding voice came from the back of the room: "Barkley, Barkley, where are you?" Then Harry Truman peeked around a narrow column at the other side of the foyer and spotted us. "Might have known you would be talking to a pretty girl!" As Barkley scurried off to his business with Truman, I got to thinking, "It isn't every person who can be talking with the Vice President and have the President of the United States interrupt them."

Having grown up in eastern Texas, I was used to the courteous manners and flattery of the Old South. But the brutally frank, sometimes crude but always truthful way of speaking that I had so disliked among the Missourians I met at the university seemed, after the initial shock, somehow refreshing in a President. My underestimation of Harry S Truman did not last for long.

One of the reasons he could so quickly take on the problems left hanging by Roosevelt's death, I came to realize, was that he had actually served under fire in World War I as a captain in the infantry. He knew firsthand from combat that life-and-death decisions sometimes had to be made quickly. Truman's decisiveness is in sharp contrast to that of some other presidents who delayed or never made up their minds on a question, much to the annoyance of affected individuals.

Truman was also better prepared for the job than he was usually given credit for. He came to the vice presidency from nearly four years chairing the Special Senate Committee to Investigate the National Defense Program, more often referred to as the "Preparedness Subcommittee." Truman handled it with such skill and authority that most people wound up simply calling it "The Truman Committee." This unique panel, which examined all our defenses and defense industries and not only streamlined our war effort but saved the government millions, was a surprisingly good training ground for running the country and a major reason why FDR picked Truman for his running mate in 1944.

Truman's wide experience in both military combat and military preparedness surely helped when, within four months of taking office, he had to make the biggest decision of his administration, one of the most important, controversial and morally significant choices that any President has ever had to make. Of all the affairs of state that FDR had neglected to let Truman in on, the greatest was the Manhattan Project, the United States' high-priority, top-secret, enormously costly program to create an atomic bomb. As it turned out, Truman would be the man forced to decide if and how to use it.

I have gained some insight into what Truman went through while making this decision through my conversations with India Edwards, a former vice chairman of the Democratic National Committee. She was a close friend of the Trumans, a newswoman from Chicago who came to Washington to become active for the Democratic Party. She talked to Truman practically every day. It is amazing how many conversations they had and what an influence she had over him. She and I discussed Truman on several occasions and one time, while on a panel with me at Hofstra University on Long Island, she publicly revealed an amazing story.

When, out of genuine concern, she asked her dear friend how he felt the night he'd ordered the bombing of Hiroshima, Truman had replied, "I slept like a baby." Seeing her puzzlement, he continued, "I spent a lot of time looking at all the angles and making up my mind. But once I decide what I am going to do, I stick with it." Many men would never have known a good night's sleep again after such a fateful choice. But like the famous sign on his desk said, Truman felt the buck stopped with him, and he was always willing to accept the credit or shoulder the blame.

Books have been written about the impact of Truman's decision to unleash the Atomic Age. But I'll bring up only two points from all the facts and analyses I've read, heard or seen.

The first concerns the television miniseries "Hiroshima," a Canadian-Japanese co-production shown on U.S. cable on the fiftieth anniversary of the bombing in August of 1995. This nearly five-hour film told half the story from a Japanese point of view. Neither the Canadians nor the Japanese had any reason to whitewash the action the United States took in dropping the bombs. But in sequences written, directed and acted in the Japanese language by Japanese film makers, it is made clear that the leaders of the military had Japan firmly in their grip, stifling the Emperor's and diplomats' attempts to respond positively to the demand for surrender which Truman, Churchill and Stalin had issued at Potsdam. The terrified population was armed (if, in many cases, only with bamboo spears) and most of them were willing to lay down their lives to stop any invasion of their beloved homeland. If the Allies had tried to take Japan by landing troops, millions on both sides would have been killed, including many more Japanese citizens than died in the bombings of Hiroshima and Nagasaki.

The second observation is something that Margaret Truman recently told me—that she is still approached almost daily by some veteran who says, "I am alive today because your father dropped that bomb on Japan."

Another important decision that Truman "spent a lot of time looking at all the angles" happened in May, 1948, when the United Nations agreed to let the Jews establish Israel. There was much speculation as to whether other countries would recognize it as a nation and open diplomatic ties. It was clear that any country doing so would damage its relations with not only the Islamic countries which surrounded Israel but the oil-rich states further east, as well as much of North Africa. Israel desperately wanted our approval. If we didn't recognize it, it would be almost impossible for it to exist. Many nations in Europe and other parts of the world were looking to the United States, ready to follow our lead.

I was watching this closely for one of the papers I was covering for at the time, the *Houston Chronicle*. Federal Judge Hutchinson of Houston was on the commission named by Truman to study and make recommendations on U.S. recognition of the new state of Israel. I was not sure what Judge Hutchinson would do. In the end he went along with the other commissioners in recommending to Truman that the U.S. endorse the new state, which eventually was what we did.

But Truman was trying to make up his own mind, as well. He therefore deliberately stayed away from his close Jewish friend from

Missouri, Eddie Jacobson. After he came back from fighting in World War I, Truman and Eddie had been partners in a men's clothing store, or haberdashery as they were called back then, in Kansas City. Eddie was a dedicated Zionist and Truman knew that if he spent any time around his old friend, Jacobson would convince him to go along with recognition. So, because he loved Eddie, Harry avoided him until he could be absolutely positive that he'd make the right decision for the right reason. Jacobson understood and applauded him in the end.

It may have been a good thing that Truman liked to make up his mind on his own, because during the times he had to make many of these heavy decisions, he was quite literally alone. His beloved wife, Bess, refused to have much to do with the workings of the Presidency. She despised politics and stayed away from the trappings of public office as much as she possibly could. This meant that, for surprisingly long periods during his presidency, Bess went home to her family in Missouri, ignoring the important role of supporting her husband through the hard choices and harsh criticism that seemed to dog his heels. There were many times, I have been told by some of Truman's close friends, that he literally pined for her warm presence, deeply missing the extra strength and comfort she might have offered. And she could, indeed, be quite cordial and charming. On the few occasions when she and Margaret would attend parties at the American News Women's Club, they both seemed comfortable and talked easily with us.

As the 1948 Presidential Elections approached, it became clear that Truman was going to have a fight on his hands if he wished to return to the White House, elected this time on his own merits. And not just from his loving but highly reluctant wife.

A lot of anti-Truman grumbling was being heard from around the country. Even many folks who liked the fact that the President was an honest, down-to-earth person who said exactly what he thought were bitterly opposed to his efforts to continue the New Deal. His continued support for the Office of Price Administration was an especially contentious issue in my home state of Texas. Besides enforcing price controls on oil, the OPA had put government regulations on how certain things could be done—in some instances, things that people had been doing all their lives. Outsiders should know better than to tell Texans how to do, or not do, things.

Take, for example, the growing of black-eyed peas, a staple crop in East Texas and much of the South. My father tipped his hat (or at least claimed he did) every time he passed a field of black-eyed peas because they had kept so many people in the South from starving to death after the Civil War. Many Southerners eat them every New Year's Day for good luck. Well, the OPA came out with regulations telling everyone how they could and could not can black-eyed peas, all neatly printed in a brochure probably written by some man from California who never even tasted one. Reactions ranged from scorn to rage.

Another issue working against Truman was a shady political practice that had been uncovered and got much play in the papers. The subject of "Five Percenters" got tongues wagging and tempers up everywhere. The Five Percenters were greedy lobbyists, special representatives who were trying to make money off the government. Their name came from the 5% of a government contract they would demand if they managed to get such a contract for any of their clients. This payment, of course, inflated the bidding, which meant that the taxpayer was ultimately the one to foot the bill.

There were ugly stories of how these lobbyists were bribing people with any connection to the administration in their efforts to get White House decisions from which they could profit. One White House staffer, the wife of one of Truman's attorneys, told me that she, like several others, had indeed accepted a bribe. Though she never revealed what, if any, services she performed to get it, she was quite frank in showing off the fur coat she had received to her table companions at a Woman's National Democratic Club luncheon. The Five Percenters knew no shame. One sent a huge electric refrigerator, quite a luxury at the time, to the White House. When the First Lady met the delivery men, they merely said they had a gift for the White House. Unaware of the criticism growing amidst the grass roots, Mrs. Truman told them, "Take it around to the mess hall," and had it installed in the staffers' lunch room. Truman's old World War I buddy and White House military aide, Major General Harry H. Vaughn, told me about this later.

Truman despised dishonesty in those who had been given a public trust, but having entered public service through the machine politics of Kansas City's notorious Boss Pendergast, he was enough of a pragmatist to understand trade-offs and compromises. In reality, much of this was just the way politics was played back then—and is often, though with greater sophistication, still played now. (In today's Washington, the Five Percenters call themselves consultants and charge more.) But without the blindingly charismatic FDR in the White House, many took the political wheeling and dealing to be a new phenomenon. Others were all too willing to demonize the legacy of strong federal control that Roosevelt had left behind and which Truman sought to continue. One of my own brothers asked me how I could live in "that horrible city" and have anything to do with "lying, crooked, sneaky big government."

Add to this the fact that Truman was constantly locked in battle with a hostile Congress, and the stage was set for a turbulent confrontation at the Democratic Convention in Philadelphia. It was to be not only the first national convention I had ever attended, but the first experience most of the newspaper women from Washington had at being treated like equals by the men in the profession. Though the National Press Club in Washington continued to deny women membership and to restrict their access, the Philadelphia Press Club let us share the facilities with no restrictions. That made our political coverage far easier.

Since Truman was so unpopular, practically no one thought he would get the nomination. The floor was buzzing with rumors of potential tickets as politicians tested the atmosphere and scrambled for alliances. But with all the maneuvering back and forth, the other candidates canceled each other out and Truman finally received the nomination, with Alben Barkley as his running mate. The disappointment of the professional Democrats was written all over their faces. Weighed down with knowledge of Truman's unpopularity and his vulnerability due to the infamous Five Percenters, they were sure he couldn't win.

There were perhaps only two people who left that convention utterly convinced that Harry S Truman would win. One was India Edwards. With Bess Truman away in Missouri so much, India had often found herself supplying Truman with important insight into how he was regarded by the female half of the American population. In her frequent conversations with the President, she had continued to encourage him that he was not nearly the political pariah the "common wisdom" saw him to be. Her own surveys had convinced her he could win the election. And so, despite Bess' continuing opposition, India had talked her friend Harry into believing in himself—and into attending the convention with the intention of coming away the nominee.

The other solid Truman supporter was Leslie Biffle of Arkansas, secretary of the U.S. Senate. Like India, he had taken a grass-roots poll and was convinced that Harry S Truman could win. But Biffle had his own unique way of doing things. He had traveled through Ohio and other Midwestern states, dressed in overalls and a beat-up old hat and driving a well-weathered truck. When he'd spot a farmer, he would stop and talk to him about crops and prices. Then he would slip in, "Not meaning to be nosy, but who are you going to vote for for President?" Time and again, the answer would be "Truman." He returned to Washington to tell Truman not to worry. The farmers were all going to vote for him. "And, oh, by the way... farm prices are going up."

News of this stunt circulated around Washington. Sometime later, at a dinner of the capital city's Gridiron Club, a member acting the part of Truman in a sketch sang, to the tune of "Jesus Loves Me," "The people love me, this I know, Leslie Biffle told me so."

What both India's and Biffle's surveys, far different from the usual Washington insider's, had shown was that the very down-to-earthiness of Harry Truman was his main asset. People wanted a people's man.

And so the legendary Whistle Stop Campaign was launched. Truman crisscrossed the land, stopping at small towns and large, rein-forcing his image as a man who was clear in both thought and expres-sion. He turned his battles with Congress into a major campaign issue, skillfully turning his negatives into a portrait of an outsider with strong ties to the common man. This was done despite almost daily discour-agement from his beloved Bess. She did not think he could win and hated for him to put so much into his run only to lose, so she prepared him for the worst. That is, every day up until the evening before the election—when she finally admitted that she thought he had a chance.

Truman's victory, coming amidst widespread predictions of his defeat by the big Eastern establishment press and the *Chicago Tribune*'s premature announcement on election night that he had lost, provided one of the most dramatic events ever in American politics. It greatly enhanced Truman's standing with the American public and gave him more confidence to continue making those enormous decisions.

But in some ways, that election night would be the high-water mark of the Truman presidency. Though he would use his newfound power to push the establishment of NATO, Truman's second four years would be haunted by the Korean War and the twin specters of MacArthur and McCarthy. The personal attacks returned, as bad as before, and on November 1, 1950, came an attack that literally threatened his life and that of his family. Living at Blair House as the White House underwent repairs, Truman became the target of a pair of Puerto Rican nationalists. At the time when the two radicals attempted to storm the temporary Presidential mansion, I was having lunch at the Washington Hotel, a block away. I went to the scene shortly thereafter and saw two dead bodies on the ground, one of the would-be assassins and that of a loyal presidential guard, Leslie Coffelt. The other gunman and two more guards had been wounded.

Though the nation all experienced great shock at the attack and great sorrow at the death of Truman's guard, we didn't seem to realize the devastating significance of this, the first lethal force directed against a president since six shots had been fired at President-elect Roosevelt in Miami, Florida, early in 1933. Barely an hour after the attack, Truman went back to work, attending a scheduled dedication ceremony at Arlington Cemetery. It was not until after the Kennedy assassination, thirteen years later, that presidential security finally became the intense concern it is today.

Security never seemed high on the list of Harry Truman's worries. Through his morning walks in public and his attendance at many functions, Truman continued to remain available to the people who had elected him. Truman was probably the most humble president in history. He knew that all the fuss, all the trappings, were for the office, not the man. After being sworn in as president, many men become haughty and think that they have been divinely sent to fill the job. I believe that Harry S Truman never lost touch with the people back home.

The last two times I saw him are testimony to that. In October of 1959, ex-President Truman returned to Washington to attend the funeral of his former Secretary of State, Secretary of Defense and good friend, General George C. Marshall. I learned that after the ceremony Truman had returned to his suite at the Mayflower hotel. I went down to the hotel to see him. That was rather nervy on my part and, in fact, would not be allowed by the Secret Service today.

He came out from an inner room where he had been visiting with friends to greet me and talk for a while. As I sat there, he went to the suite's small bar and poured himself a full four fingers of bourbon. It was the first time, though hardly the last, that I had ever seen a government official drinking anything but a cocktail at a reception or on an airplane. I should have been shocked, but in a strange way, I was complimented. Harry had always said he liked bourbon. He didn't apologize for it and was honest enough to drink it straight while talking to a newspaper reporter. That was the last time I saw him in Washington.

My very last memory of Truman is of something remarkable he did on a regular basis that summed up his attachment to and consideration for the people. Sometime in the 1960s, I was being shown about the Truman Library at Independence, Missouri by the librarian and Truman family friend, Miss Gentry. There were many tourists that day, people of all ages, come to learn about Truman's life and to see his photographs and displayed papers. Suddenly there was Truman himself, on a landing overlooking the throng. He spoke to the people and told them to ask him any questions they wished.

He did not have to arouse himself from his well-deserved retirement to meet the crowd. But, as Miss Gentry told me, he felt that as long as he was still alive, there could be no more educational exhibit at the library than himself. The people deserved to learn from him. They were, after all, the ones he had worked for, the ones who paid his salary. So as long as he was able, he regularly gave his library's visitors the chance I've been privileged to have so many times...to be at a press conference with a President of the United States.

President Truman once said, "I have tried my best to give the nation everything I had in me. There are probably a million people who could have done the job better than I did, but I had the job—and I always quote an epitaph from a cemetery in Tombstone, Arizona that read, 'Here lies Jack Williams. He done his damndest.'"

Though I doubt one in a million could have brought the dedication, skills and strength of character he did to the job of U.S. President, I must agree with the rest of Truman's self evaluation. It's a shame that most of America never truly appreciated his legacy until after his death in 1972. It shouldn't have taken a tombstone to make us all realize that Harry S Truman done his damndest.

BEAUMONT, TEXAS, 1941-1942;

FORT DES MOINES, IOWA, 1942;

FORT OGLETHORPE, GEORGIA, 1943;

WASHINGTON, DC, 1943-1944:

In 1918, I swore that I'd someday be a soldier. As two of my brothers left home to serve their country in World War I, I pledged, with a seven-year-old's seriousness, that if there was ever another war, I'd go too.

In December of 1941, when the United States entered another war, I was a reporter for the Beaumont Enterprise in Beaumont, Texas. Lt. Colonel Eisenhower was training troops in Louisiana, only a few miles across the state border, so I asked my editor to let me cover the maneuvers. Instead, he told me to report on the local Women's Army Auxiliary Corps. Next to Ike and his men, they looked silly and inefficient—and my stories did not disguise my disdain. Thinking myself too good for the WAACs, I applied to join military intelligence. When I found out the program accepted only lawyers and those already in uniform, I finally, reluctantly signed up for the very corps I had called a joke. The day I appeared to take the oath, a colonel who had read my perfectly wicked stories looked at me in amazement and said, "What, you?" I feared I'd be rejected as a troublemaker and return home disgraced.

I'd already burnt bridges with my decision. My relatives' reactions ranged from half-hearted approval to serious objections. My boyfriend was disgusted with the idea. Under the circumstances, I had turned down offers of financial support, saying I wouldn't need it—the Army would take care of me now. I even sold all the civilian clothing I wouldn't be wearing any more to pay off my department store accounts. With a $21 one-month advance on my Army salary and a ticket to Fort Des Moines, Iowa, I left Texas in September 1942 to keep my childhood promise.

Childish dreams seldom get things right. At an overnight stop on the way to Fort Des Moines, I washed my hair. The hard water made it stand out straight from my head. And there were no uniforms for us yet, so I had to wear my nice blue suit and a pair of high heel pumps to drill for the first two weeks in the Iowa mud. The Army did supply "lingerie"—when we recruits opened our foot lockers to find khaki underpants, the homesickness really set in. They moved us from the first temporary barracks into the old horse stables. These huge buildings, which had previously held ninety head of horses, held cots for 125 women in "open bay" formation, with no walls or partitions. I guess that made each of us worth a little less than 3/4 of a horse.

Living conditions soon got worse than merely 125 women per room, all snoring in a different key. In late September, the earliest snow in Iowa since 1878 blew in, and the barracks climate began to alternate between first absolutely no heat and then far too much. Despite the 25-year-old WWI wool overcoats our director, Oveta Culp Hobby of Texas, managed to requisition out of storage (and which dragged in the snow on most of us), we froze beneath them in the cotton seersucker, fatigue bloomer suits the quartermasters had finally issued us.

I was older than the rest of the girls and a bit less physically fit. What was more, nearly all of them had become familiar with Army procedures as volunteers for the Civilian Air Observers Program, watching for the enemy planes we were sure would eventually come. Southern gal that I was, I had much to learn about making a bed faultlessly and scrubbing floors. In fact, at the end of basic training, my commanding officer looked at the orders assigning me to base headquarters to work in public information and said out loud, "Who, you?" She thought there must have been some mistake. She did not know of my reporting experience, but Col. Vann Kennedy, the former Texas newsman in charge of WAAC public relations, did.

It was fascinating work, telling the world about women in the service, building our image, setting respectable rules of behavior and protecting us from vicious, untrue rumors about our purposes in joining the Army. Among us were Catherine Falvey, a former Massachusetts state legislator, and Morgan Winant, a relative of the tycoon J. Pierpont Morgan. There was also, I admit, one girl who worked at a bar downtown as a belly dancer until one of our officers, Lt. Jane Stretch, "persuaded" her to drop the off-duty extra work. But despite this choice assignment, I had to take my turns in the kitchen. I separated garbage by hand to escape scrubbing pots and pans. The food was awful at first, cooked by men. Then the WAACs took over the mess halls, and things changed. It was "women's work," but the difference in the quality and taste was worth it.

Thanks to Colonel Kennedy, I was admitted to the first Officer Candidate School class drawn from our ranks. I found to my surprise when I went that first night to store away my golf clubs (yes, they had told us to bring them), that there was, housed on the top floor adjacent to the attic, a platoon of black candidates, kept together and separate from us. But the very next OCS class was integrated; the blacks had rightfully complained and Director Hobby met the challenge, years before the Armed Services were fully desegregated by Presidential order. In another way, however, discrimination continued. Because of it, one of my fellow class members was gone by Christmas. Not knowing she was headed for OCS, she had secretly married and then found herself pregnant. Finally, she told the Commanding Officer, who sweetly arranged for us all to give her a baby shower and then sent her home. I had no idea that, with variations, this was a preview of the end of my own military career less than two years later.

I do not know how I passed OCS. I cannot read a map decently to this day and I still remember trying to keep up as we marched through 21-degree-below-zero weather, singing "Praise the Lord and Pass Me My Commission," with a Philadelphia snowbird in front of me who could put an extra beat in her step and land on the correct foot. When Col. Kennedy called to ask if the newly promoted Lt. McClendon wanted a transfer to the WAAC Training Center at Fort Oglethorpe, Georgia, I almost screamed, "You bet!"

I was to be in charge of the public relations office there. But by the time I arrived, another WAAC officer, Madeline Hawes, former secretary to the publisher of the Boston Herald-Traveler, had arrived, and had by chance been handed the papers setting up the office. So some bright junior officer said to her, "Well, since you've got the papers, you head up the office." As it turned out, Madeline actually was better equipped to handle the administrative responsibilities, so it was fate at work—in more ways than one: when a telegram eventually came in specifically requesting either Madeline Hawes or Sarah McClendon to relocate to WAAC headquarters in the Pentagon, Madeline was so vital to running the office that I took the transfer. And that's how I wound up in Washington, DC, my home from then on.

The office at Fort Oglethorpe had a staff of 22, both male and female. The bottom line of our job was to get more women to join the military to relieve men who were needed to go from desk work to combat. To accomplish this, we did some pretty odd things. Once we helped the ladies of Chattanooga, Tennessee put on their debutante ball—which they assured us would honor the WAACs. It turned out that at the last moment they didn't come up with the promised escorts for our girls, and I had to scramble to get four hundred enlisted men who were getting ready to ship overseas to escort them in the "grand march"—as well as a group of married officers to accompany the WAAC officers. About once a month, a crew from one Hollywood studio or another would come through, and we'd supply them with a pretty face or great personality in uniform to put on film, portraying the "glamour" of military life. One time we prepared a giant birthday cake to celebrate the anniversary of the founding of the Women's Army Auxiliary Corps. We put the mess halls on the base to work and got a cake so big, we had to take the double doors off to move it outside. There's a clipping about it in the display case about the WAACs in the Pentagon.

In Washington, I became a liaison between WAAC headquarters and the War Department Bureau of Public Relations—and the first WAAC ever on orders to the Army Surgeon General's office. The Major in charge was Munro Leaf, the famous writer of humorous children's books. (I also got to know an officer who reviewed reports from field surgeons operating on battle casualties. He was Dr. Michael DeBakey, later renowned as the guru of heart surgery.) We furnished pictures and story ideas to magazine and newspaper editors. We also kept watch over the press to make sure their information was accurate and non-classified. I once decided to make the American Medical Association scrap a publication which contained material we had told them not to print. It cost them $10,000, I was told.

Army medical officials did a great service to their country and humanity when they decided we would "sell" the concept of accepting back into normal living those scarred by the war: the maimed, the blind, the burned, the amputees. After WWI, crippled veterans were left to beg on street corners with a tin cup. We were determined that this would not happen again. We pushed for magazine articles, news articles, books and movies that would help families face up to the return of the war wounded. We called attention to developments in prostheses and training. I traveled to hospitals, interviewing patients, families and staff, stressing heroism and readaptation, not victimization and hopelessness. It was one of the most valuable things the Army could have done, the forerunner of greater acceptance of the handicapped by society and of government legislation to accommodate them, like the Disability Act. Every time I see someone with a new leg or arm, I know he or she got it and the training to use it as the legacy of military medicine.

It was there, on assignment to the Pentagon itself, that I was sworn into service once again, as the WAACs became the WACs, dropping the "Auxiliary" to become the Women's Army Corps. I would have been glad to spend my career as part of the new, more respectfully named corps. But the baby growing within me—and short-sighted regulations about military women having babies—said otherwise.

While I had been down at Fort Oglethorpe, a large group of women reporters from Washington had visited to see what the WAACs were all about. After we had described success after success, one reporter, Lee Carson, whose journalistic instincts "told" her we must be hiding something, slipped out after dark to nose around and was promptly picked up by the military police. They called our public relations office, and we got her out of custody. Some of these women became my close friends. Once I came to Washington, they let me, in uniform, have a visitor's membership in the Women's National Press Club. That is where I started my professional associations and got the idea to approach Bascom Timmons after Sally was born.

And now, as a full-fledged member of the Washington Press Corps, years after I had been turned down by a sexist editor who told me to file a story on the WAACs—I finally got my chance to cover General Eisenhower.

Chapter 3

IKE: THE GENERAL

One of the great ironies of my life is that Dwight David Eisenhower, the first President I was ever accused of showing disrespect to, was, and continues to be, one of the Presidents I most thoroughly respect.

There is a special place in my heart for the men and women of the Armed Services. I treasure not only my time among them but my continuing connection with them through the American Legion and my position as Vice Chair for Site Advice on the Advisory Board to The Battle Monuments Commission.[1] I revere the guardians who have sacrificed their energies, their well-being and, all too often, their lives to defend the noble principles around which our government was formed. War may be hell, but those who shoulder its duties sometimes gain the fierce nobility of angels. Among our nation's warriors, Ike stands high.

It is true that I developed my pushy, sometimes confrontational style of questioning during eight years of press conferences with President Eisenhower. It is true that I sometimes caused him to go so red with anger that some of my colleagues accused me of causing his heart problems. But it is also true that I have always thought the country owes Ike a greater debt than they have paid him so far, not only for handing us the greatest victory in the longest war we ever had, but for his underrated service as our President.

The reassuring, quietly heroic image Eisenhower presented to the world made him a perfect candidate for the 1952 Presidential

---

[1] I was named to the 12-member Advisory Board by President Clinton to help create a long-overdue National World War II Memorial here in the District of Columbia. Can you imagine that until now we have not had one? I have advocated that the memorial be not merely an allegorical sculpture and grounds, but a viable expression of what I feel was our most important participation in any war, fought and, in large part, won by American youths between 18 and 21 years of age.

elections. We were in the midst of a war in which our leading general had challenged and disobeyed his Commander-In-Chief and had been fired for it. A Congress hostile to Truman had allowed MacArthur to give a "farewell address" in the Capitol that had captured the country's emotions and intensified the widespread mistrust of the President. And then there was Wisconsin's Senator Joe McCarthy. Whether you thought he was pointing to a cure or was part of the disease, his cancerous ravings convinced many citizens that our country was in a battle for its life, or at least its soul. He said the enemy was internal Communism. His opponents said it was demagoguery disguised as patriotism.

Both parties scrambled to have Dwight Eisenhower head their ticket. The Republicans got him—and Adlai Stevenson didn't really have a chance. But the nation had not always been so eager to "Like Ike." After the war was over, General Eisenhower had still been under the gun. He had a loud and persistent critic in Congress, Senator Brewster of Maine, who attacked him for the way he had conducted the campaign in Europe. There had been deep differences of opinion between Winston Churchill and Eisenhower as to whether and how to invade Europe. Eisenhower had wanted to invade France across the English Channel, while Churchill felt a Mediterranean invasion would cost less lives. Eisenhower prevailed. As it turned out, there were great casualties on D-Day and much of the criticism centered on that.

When this came up in the Senate, the Republican Senator from Kentucky John Sherman Cooper, a close friend of mine (and eventually, more), came to Eisenhower's defense. Cooper had been a foot soldier stationed in England. He was there in one of the camps where Eisenhower addressed the men on June 3, 1944, the night before the invasion. Eisenhower went to as many Army units as he could and talked to the men as a father. He sat down with them or put one leg up on a foot locker and spoke to them about what they were going to have to do. The soldiers accepted him as "just one of the boys."

Ike knew that many of these men would be dead the next day. As Eisenhower spoke, John Sherman Cooper was indelibly impressed by the man and his sincerity, his deep devotion and his feeling for humanity. So when, years later, Senator Brewster called for an investigation into Eisenhower's conduct of the war, Senator Cooper defended Eisenhower from personal experience and made his listeners believe in not only the General's leadership, but his concern. There was to be no investigation of Eisenhower.

That John Sherman Cooper played a role (however small) in Ike's history and a role (however large) in mine is but one of several odd ways in which the President's life and mine intertwined. One happened before either of us were even born. It seems that the Eisenhower family once lived about a block from my home in Tyler, Texas. At that time, his father was a supervisor of a section of the Cotton Belt Railroad. They lived in a little company house near my own, but my family did not know them then. In 1890, shortly before Eisenhower was born, the family moved from Tyler to Denison, Texas, where Ike's father went to work for the Missouri, Kansas and Texas Railroad. By the time I came into the world, Dwight had graduated from high school in Abiline, Kansas, where his family was living then. But Ike apparently thought that he was born in Tyler; when he was at West Point, he put down his birthplace as Tyler. And, still later, when he was sent to command our troops in North Africa, the Associated Press wires carried the information that he was born in Tyler. I can tell you I jumped, just looking at it! Later the Tyler newspapers checked it out and learned that Ike was *almost* but not quite a native son.

Texas continued to figure in Ike's life. His first commission after West Point was in San Antonio. And then there were the World War II maneuvers he conducted near Beaumont, Texas as our nation prepared its soldiers to fight in Europe. Since isolationism had run deep, we were not particularly prepared for war. We were low on weapons, and some of the recruits had to train with broom sticks. But I was interested in military affairs, and the operation fascinated me—despite my editor's refusal to let me cover them. The maneuvers had spilled over from Louisiana into our section of Texas, and we had a large contingent of troops at the local airport, but I was the only reporter on the *Beaumont Enterprise* who seemed to have any interest at all in what was going on. I would work from 2:30 in the afternoon until 11:30 at night and then go out the next morning to find out what I could. There were a lot of young men from such far away cities as Brooklyn. Many were absolute strangers to nature and wound up having unexpected adventures among the streams and dams of Texas and the woods in Louisiana.

Then Eisenhower was suddenly summoned to Washington by General Marshall and left by train. Trains at that time were terribly crowded and there was no seat for him at all. It looked as if he was going to have to stand up all the way, for two or three days, but he was not complaining. On the same train, there was an oil man, Sid Richardson, who happened to have a business connection with a family associate, Clint Murchison. Richardson was from Athens, near my home town, and was always terribly interested in public affairs. When he noticed this career officer standing there, Richardson invited Eisenhower to join him in his compartment for the trip. It was the only place the soldier could sit down or sleep, and, as they rode to Washington, the two became fast friends.

One result of this chance meeting was that years later, after the war was over, when Eisenhower was at European headquarters in Paris, Sid Richardson would visit time and again, urging him to run for President. How much influence he had in Ike's final decision is open to question, but it wasn't for lack of trying. Sid continued to come to Washington frequently, and I got to know him fairly well. Obviously interested in promoting his oil interests, he often had contributions to dole out, as well as a card he gave to many Members of Congress. Its motto, which could have, but unfortunately didn't, change the way Washington operates, read: "You ain't learning nothin' if your mouth's open."

Sid Richardson was hardly the only one to be keeping an eye on Dwight David Eisenhower. I, for one, noticed that when he was Chief of Staff of the Army in the Pentagon, Ike's appearances before Congressional committees were superb. He was also being watched, and watched over, by Sam Rayburn. Sam's district included Denison, where Ike was born, and Rayburn considered himself more or less the General's Congressman. He had great respect for the man, as did Lyndon Johnson. Since Lyndon was head of the Senate Democrats and Sam was Speaker of the House, these two had a lot of power.

Once it was clear that Ike would be our next President, the pair decided (though I'm sure it was mostly Rayburn's idea) that it would be good for everyone concerned to help him in his Presidency. A lot of the conflict and contention that usually appears between a President and Congress was thus avoided. Although Eisenhower was a Republican, there was a sense of understanding between him and the Democrats who ran the House and the Senate. They cooperated frequently and on many things.

Eisenhower did not extend this cooperation as readily to the press. Unlike FDR and Truman, Ike usually seemed ill at ease around reporters, though most of his experiences with journalists during the war had been good. Many publishers, editors and reporters from around the country had volunteered their services to help with public relations at the European Headquarters in London during the months before the Invasion. And they were a great help. My friend and employer from Texas, Frank W. Mayborn, was among those working on the Eisenhower staff under Major General A.D. Surles, who, although a career military man, had a keen sense of how to communicate with the public. I've heard many say that the good sense of public relations and open communication that Surles and his staff provided were important in keeping the war effort coordinated and on track.

Although he didn't enjoy being around the press, President Eisenhower made himself have a press conference at least twice a month. He felt he owed it to the American people to make reports to them on a regular basis. By the end of 1953, he became the first President to allow his press conferences to be recorded and, after editing, broadcast on television. In a way, this was the birth of the modern-day press conference. I think that he deserved a lot of credit for doing all this.

Why, then, did I get a reputation for baiting a President whom I generally—and genuinely—admired? By the time Ike moved into the White House, I had been reporting on Washington politics for nine years. With a new President about to hold his first press conference, I felt it was high time to push my career to a new level of prominence. I had noticed that other female reporters gained attention by developing a distinctive sense of style: May Craig with her trademark hats, Esther van Wagoner Tufty with the aristocratic ways that had Washington calling her "the Duchess." It was time for me to not just attend the conferences and ask an occasional question, but to make my presence known in an ongoing way. I did not intend to be confrontational, merely heard. But it did not work exactly the way I had planned.

Ike was so popular that an unexpectedly large number of reporters showed up for his first Presidential press conference. I was not early enough to get a seat on the main floor of the Indian Treaty Room and had to go up into the balcony. At the top of the steps, I was told that no one was allowed to ask questions from up there. I argued that I had a question to ask. They said, "You can't do it from up here. It's never been done. Just forget about it."

Eisenhower came in and read a very long, rather stultifying statement covering four different subjects. Then he said he would take questions on only these four topics. Well, that eliminated the question I had planned. Three male reporters managed to come up with questions on the subjects we'd been allowed, and then a silence descended on the room. People were startled by the new, awkward format and put off their stride. Though I'm sure everyone felt restricted, they held back out of respect. Afraid that Eisenhower might simply leave (as Truman had after a similar lull), I said to myself, "It's now or never!" I shouted down from upstairs, "Mr. President, are the press conferences in the future going to follow along this form, or will reporters be able to ask questions on matters of public interest?"

Well, Ike looked up, startled, as though someone had taken a shot at him. He finally seemed to notice first the gallery and then me standing there amidst a group of horrified colleagues. Not only had I sent the President a challenge, I had done it from the balcony! Stumbling a bit over his words, he said,

> "Ladies and gentlemen, there are a lot of you that know me, and you know I am rather apt to change a habit at any time. Let's don't take this one as a necessary pattern. If we find some method among us that would be more convenient...I am certainly open to suggestions...So I should say as time goes on we will see what happens, and I would hope that they at least will be friendly..."

I had stepped out of line, but I had made a good point. And the style of his press conferences did change after that. I had begun to make a name for myself. I just wasn't sure it was the name I wanted.

From then on, I arrived early and usually got a seat near the front. I tried to ask clear, hard questions—and I tried to ask at least one every press conference. I felt I was fighting for my readers, fighting for information, trying to cut through all the bureaucratic words and phrases. These inquiries, which some started to call "THOSE questions," soon became synonymous with Sarah McClendon.

I must have been doing something right, because a few months later, Eisenhower's Press Secretary, Jim Haggerty, a wonderful, professionally experienced reporter, came up to me at a reception and said, "Sarah, we will always take your questions." I asked, "Whatever do you mean by that, Jim?" Haggerty replied, "Well, at one Cabinet meeting a couple of Cabinet officers got up and told Ike that whatever he did, to quit taking any questions from you, to simply stop recognizing that woman who asks all those sharp questions. 'She's from west of the Mississippi,' they said. 'Don't have anything to do with her.'"

But then, Haggerty continued, a hand was raised in the back of the room. A second- or third-level member of the staff, I. Jack Martin, a young Jewish fellow who had worked on the Hill and who later became a federal judge, wanted to speak. "Mr. President," he said, "I know this woman. She used to come into my office covering news when I worked for Senator Harold Burton of Ohio. She knows what's going on at the grass roots, and she'll ask questions that reflect what those people are concerned about. And, Mr. President, you need to know what the people are thinking and doing."

Those words, which I have always considered a fine compliment, turned the thinking of the Cabinet around 180 degrees. Not only was a decision made to always take my questions, but they began to invite me to attend other press conferences. "You stir things up," one of the Cabinet members later told me. I took that to be praise, as well.

It turned out that one of the reasons Eisenhower's people had mistrusted me at first was I confused them. With the McClendon News Service representing papers in small cities and towns in far-flung areas across the country from New Hampshire to Orange County, California, Administration officials couldn't get a grip on just who I worked for. Since Ike was giving wider media exposure to the press conferences than Presidents before him had, reporters were instructed to identify themselves and who they represented before asking a question. So in fairness to my many clients, I would identify myself as working for a different one of my newspapers each time I was called upon. Every local area would have different industries, different issues and different reasons for questions. If I asked about a tin smelter on the Texas Gulf Coast, I couldn't very well tie it to a paper in Maine, even if the plant did help set the world price of this scarce metal. So I identified it with the *Port Arthur News*, the paper I represented that was nearest to the subject at hand. I can see how it may have been a little bewildering.

After they felt they'd figured me out and decided they might actually like me, someone on Ike's staff decided to put the President up to a joke. One day, as I started asking Eisenhower a question, he interrupted with, "Now just a minute. Before you go on, I want to ask you a question. Do you get fired every week and go to work for a different paper?" He got a big laugh at my expense, but I didn't mind. It was just part of the game, and I usually tried to play by the rules.

But like others in the press corps, I soon discovered that some of the rules had changed. When you asked Eisenhower a question, you had to ask it a certain way—not because he wanted you to but simply because he was not yet familiar with government. He had been a military man, and military men usually know one thing and one thing only. That's why I think Colin Powell has a lot to learn before he should be considered a viable Presidential candidate. If the comparisons to Eisenhower are accurate, he might some day become a fine Chief Executive, but I would prefer military men, no matter how able, to learn the job before they go for it.

Eisenhower did not really know just what all the agencies were. Considering how many of them there were (and there are more of them now), that may have been expecting too much. But he could certainly have been clearer on the issues—and on the complexities of the way the government worked. So, when the President would call on me, I would ask the question, explain the issue, define its status, point out where in government it was or wasn't being dealt with, and then ask what he was going to do about it. Other reporters would find they had to follow that same menu. I must admit that Ike always tried his best to answer these carefully structured questions. But sometimes his volatile temper would get in the way.

May Craig and I came up with an early warning system to monitor this. After hurrying to an Eisenhower press conference, we would take our seats, one to each side of where he'd stand. By then May was an elderly woman but still a great reporter, with a lot of common sense and great journalistic instincts. May and I would try to sit close enough to see if the President was getting angry. If someone or something disturbed Ike—and he had a low boiling point—we would see these veins in his forehead, one on each temple, begin to throb. Then it was time to watch out for an explosion.

During his two terms, I made Ike blow his fuse more times than was my share. One of the first times was over a question I asked regarding the direction in which the continuing development of the Department of Defense was proceeding. Until Truman had authorized the DOD, the different Armed Services had been quite independent of one another. As the way in which the Army, Navy and Air Force would be coordinated became clearer, it looked to me as if the plans put a lot of power under the control of one person—the President. When I asked about that, Eisenhower became very insulted. He said of course not. The idea was not meant to concentrate power in the hands of one person at all. It was meant to add efficiency to the defense of our nation. Ike reacted as though I had accused him of trying to set up a military dictatorship.

Another question I asked that raised the President's temperature came in mid-1958, when I asked why he had sent troops to Lebanon without asking Congress. Under the Constitution, shouldn't Congress be the one to decide where and when our troops would be used? And, I added, exactly how were they going to be paid without authorization from Congress? Eisenhower resented these questions very much. He said he believed that he was fully justified in sending troops to protect Lebanon from infiltration from the United Arab Republic. As a man who had always respected Congress and its authority, he wanted to make it clear that he wasn't trying to sidestep the balance of power. He merely understood more about the military than most in Congress did, felt he had their confidence and knew he had to move with speed. Many Presidents far less qualified than Ike have used the same dubious reasoning. I have called several of them on it—and have usually had the same, explosive result.

Some people, even among my fellow journalists, thought the questions I asked Eisenhower were a deliberate, publicity-seeking attempt to get a rise out of him, a stunt that would backfire if and when I caused him to have another heart attack or stroke. This could not be further from the truth. Every question I ask has a single aim in mind: to dispel the fog, clearing the air so the public can see not only the issues but what their President intends to do about them. I believe that the Presidential press conference is among the greatest institutions we have, a shortcut to accountability. I remember the old Army rule about requests: put them in letter form, type them in triplicate and put them through channels. Well, at a Presidential press conference, a reporter can, in the people's name, ask a question that doesn't have to go through channels and that stands a better chance of being answered than if it showed up a thousand times in the White House mail bag. It's an end run around the President's staff, and, if necessary, a chance to give the Chief a little "hail."

Ike almost always responded to my questions in thoughtful ways. I once asked if he was in favor of building dams high upstream, where the rain fell, or near the mouth, just before the water poured into a larger river or the ocean. For many years the practice of the Army Corps of Engineers, who have jurisdiction over navigable waters in this country, had been to build large dams down near a river's outflow, but there had been a lot of discussion in the mid-west and west as to whether this practice was best for all the uses a dam could be put to: water storage and distribution, irrigation planning, flood control, recreation and hydroelectric power. I wanted to alert the President to the importance of an issue that affected far more Americans than almost anyone in government could guess. The Washington Press Corps, which had no idea what I was talking about, scoffed at it as a trivial, rural concern. Mr. Eisenhower said that he could not even hazard a guess as to which location for building a dam was best.

At a press conference a few months later, he mentioned that he had just read a book called "Big Dam Foolishness." He wanted us to know he had studied up on my question, found it a valid concern and intended to discuss it with the appropriate authorities. I was pleased he had taken me seriously and gratified that, unlike many in Washington, he could grasp that the nation's water concerns went well beyond the banks of the Potomac. I knew then, that this President was not afraid to learn. And if my questions could help that learning occur, I would gladly take the anger or laughter they sometimes caused.

There is, in fact, just one question I can remember regretting having asked Eisenhower. At the time, I had an awkward feeling that should have warned me. Concerned over his lack of attention to a proposed public works project, I asked why the President spent so much time out of town, playing golf in Augusta, Georgia. Well, later on that day, it was pointed out to me that he was playing golf for his health. I knew, of course, that he'd had a heart attack back in 1955 and a minor stroke in 1957, and I realized I'd been unfair. I immediately wrote him a letter of apology for having put the question the way I did.

Ike wrote me back that same day as kind and understanding a letter as you ever saw, on pale green stationery. He said that I had every right to ask the question, and actually thanked me for my continued interest in making his press conferences useful. I was grateful for the letter and still have it, a prized possession.

Despite the understanding that developed between the President and myself, rumors continued to circulate that I was out to make a name for myself by goading him and dogging his heels. There were a few times he might just have agreed with the rumors. I still remember the expression on Ike's face when he came across me while on a trip to observe Army maneuvers in the woods near Uniontown Gap, Pennsylvania. I was there to observe, too. The President came around a corner, his mind a long way off from Washington. Then, all of a sudden, there I was, standing by the side of the road. Eisenhower jumped, then covered his surprise with a smile. But his eyes were easy to read, and they said, "What—are you up here, too?" It was all very funny—at least to me.

A few people even thought I was deliberately trying to put Ike back in the hospital. Some seem to have felt the First Lady was among those who considered me the President's enemy. I learned this when I was invited to attend a luncheon by Mrs. A.D. Surles, wife of the public relations advisor who had served General Eisenhower so well back in World War II. Mrs. Surles came from El Paso, Texas and the *El Paso Times* was one of the newspapers I worked for. She had been a good source of information for me on several military personnel matters. The luncheon she was hosting would bring together a number of high-level military wives. I was delighted to be invited and wanted very much to go. Then Mrs. Surles called to "dis-invite" me. She said that Mamie Eisenhower was going to attend, and when certain parties found out I'd be there, they saw trouble ahead. They thought that Mamie would be offended if she saw me at the function. Therefore, would I please stay away? Well, sad as I was about this, I agreed to. There was nothing else I could do. It was just one of the things that a reporter has to endure in connection with her work.

Actually, there were many things I liked about Mrs. Eisenhower, though I really never got to know her. She held only one press conference that I know of, but she seemed to be a sweet, charming and caring person, if a bit unusual. For example, she loved pink and she used the color in everything she could. I had sympathy for her, as well, since I knew she had been the victim of rumors, too.

Some of these concerned the relationship Eisenhower had with a female British military aide assigned to help him while he was serving in Europe during the war. Kay Summersby was, by all accounts, a marvelous, efficient chauffeur. She knew London so well that, even in the blackout, she could speed Ike swiftly to any part of the city. She was always polite, courteous, accurate and on time. As they drove around together, they became warm, personal friends.

Though practically every Army officer I knew who was over there was quite aware of Eisenhower's and Summersby's mutual fondness, none of them would commit to actually saying it was an affair. At one time, Kay Summersby lived with several WAC officers assigned to high positions around Eisenhower and they, too, refused to speculate; they liked Kay very much, and they supported and defended her. They admitted there was obviously a deep attachment. "But this was wartime. Nearly everybody had some unusual friendship or relationship," I was told by Mattie Pinette, who was Eisenhower's secretary during D-Day. "If you didn't, that would be surprising, because that was the effect that war had on people."

At any rate, when Kay Summersby came to America and visited Eisenhower in the Pentagon, while he was Truman's Chief of Staff, it became clear that the friendship was over. I've been told by other officers who were there that it was sad to see her realize how Ike had changed. He was aloof, avoiding any chance remark that might be used to confirm the notion that he'd been unfaithful to his wife. It was said that President Truman had told the General that if he divorced Mamie, he would have no future as part of the military high command. Eisenhower realized that the war, and its attachments, were over, and he put the past behind him.

In at least one way, Eisenhower had always shown a streak of loyal devotion to Mamie. As I've been told by his secretaries, he wrote to Mamie at least once a week throughout the war. He would have them address envelopes to her and place them in sight so that he would not forget to write. He was very diligent about it. These letters were read by Eisenhower's wife and her friend, Ruth Butcher, who roomed with her at the Sheraton Washington Hotel. Mrs. Butcher, wife of Eisenhower's Naval Aide (and the man who thought up FDR's "fireside chats"), was very close to Mamie until a question of alcoholism arose and Ruth and her daughter left. Mrs. Butcher's daughter, who finally became a Member of Congress from the Sixth District of Maryland, remembers, as a child, hearing these letters that Ike sent back from the Front read aloud.

The Eisenhowers seemed close throughout his Presidency. Mamie was devoted to keeping Ike calm, and they both loved to get away from Washington and spend time "alone together" at their farm in Gettysburg, Pennsylvania. This special place, which was a great joy to Ike's heart, is now open for public tours.

There were quite a few gifts made to him to supply the farm. One oil man from my home town of Tyler, for example, presented him with some fine cattle. One of Mamie's responsibilities was to decide the right thing to do whenever a gift arrived for the President. She would ask, "Is this for the President himself, or is it for the White House?" There was a difference. If it was for the White House, it was public property. Most of the things that were for the President, himself, eventually wound up at the Eisenhower Library in Kansas.

Though Kay Summersby was but a memory, Mamie did, at least at first, have a determined rival for the President's attentions— Sherman Adams, who as Assistant to the President, was very close to him. When they were on the campaign trail, Adams always made the advance arrangements. He would book himself a room right next to Ike's or into the Presidential suite itself, putting Mamie in whatever accommodations were left over, often a room on another floor. Finally, Mrs. Eisenhower got tired of this. The next time that they stopped, Mamie had her bags placed in Ike's room and forbade her husband to meet with Adams in *their* room. I admired that kind of spunk.

Sherman Adams eventually presented Eisenhower with a far greater problem. The way Ike handled it shows his strength of character. Adams, a former governor of New Hampshire who had also worked in the State Department, was a highly respected man. As the President's top assistant, he was one of the nation's most powerful men. Everybody thought that he was the soul of honesty and integrity.

Everybody, that is, except for William Loeb of New Hampshire's *Manchester Union-Leader*, the most contrary—and controversial—editor for whom I've ever worked. Loeb mistrusted anyone who smelled, to his highly developed right-wing sense of smell, of The Establishment. Though he was nice to me, he was terribly disrespectful to most of the government officials that it was my job to cover. Luckily, I rarely had to do anything but deliver news to Loeb. He had his own agenda, and if he had anything special to work on, he usually came to Washington and did it himself.

Loeb sent me a query that turned out to be a land mine. He wanted me to ask Press Secretary Jim Haggerty if Sherman Adams had, in fact, taken the gifts of a rug and a vicuña coat from the Boston-area industrialist Bernard Goldfine. Was it true, Loeb inquired, that in exchange for these, Adams was making telephone calls from the White House to various government agencies requesting favored treatment to this industrialist in removing regulatory roadblocks? When I approached Haggerty, he was even more skeptical than I was. This was not the case of some low-level staffer under the influence of a "Five Percenter." Why would a man of Adams' prestige risk everything by going "on the take" for a few gifts? In his typical calm and trustworthy way, Jim said he'd look into it.

The next thing I knew, Jim had found out the entire story was true. Everyone in the Administration, from the President on down, was shocked beyond belief. A Congressional committee was quickly formed to investigate the matter. Faced with scandal and the loss of his most trusted aide, Eisenhower reacted with a General's sense of honor. Many Presidents stonewall to defend their staff, insisting that they are innocent and didn't do anything wrong, even if the facts clearly show otherwise. But Ike, sad, hurt and angry, simply told his friend, Sherman Adams, to go to the Hill and tell the truth. I was in the House Office Building when Adams, accompanied by his beautiful wife, went into the hearings. I felt sorry, but I had nothing to be ashamed of. Exposing Adams had been a public service. Adams resigned and then faded from the scene, back to New Hampshire and the obscurity he'd earned.

Some time later, I was in New Hampshire, speaking to a business and professional women's club. We were at an inn, an isolated place far to the north. I thought the women would be interested in hearing how I had asked the question that so affected the life of one of their state's former governors. But as I spoke, a woman who had once worked for Sherman Adams stood up from the audience and defended him, to the cheers of many of the others. It turned out that he was still very popular up there. After the speech was over, one kindly listener advised me to go to my room, lock the door and not come out until I was ready to leave. The scheduled question-and-answer session might just be replaced by a lynching party.

Oddly enough, Eisenhower's running mate, Richard Nixon, had battled accusations resembling those against Sherman Adams during the 1952 election campaign. Accused of accepting question-able campaign donations as well as gifts, Nixon was, it was rumored, about to be dropped from the ticket. But the young Senator from California pulled off a shrewd political miracle: he took his case to the nation by going on television. In living rooms across the country, he apologized, maintaining his finances were clean and his lifestyle frugally middle class. The only gift that had not been sent back the second he realized they were questionable was a little cocker spaniel to which his two young daughters had grown attached—a puppy named "Checkers." Nixon's speech worked so well he was turned from a political liability into a vote-getter overnight.

The Vice President's continued usefulness to the Eisenhower Administration seemed open to question, however. When Ike had his 1955 heart attack, he was out in Colorado. Washington was worried and full of rumors. But when Richard Nixon came to the White House to take over the incapacitated President's duties, Press Secretary Haggerty would not even let him in. Jim thought it best to act as though Ike was still in charge, physically well enough to func-tion. He didn't want the public to think their President needed to be relieved of his responsibilities. Luckily, Eisenhower improved quickly enough to prove his press secretary right.

With that fumbled attempt at doing his duty, Richard Nixon faded back into a Vice President's usual obscurity. Many people felt that he had never been allowed much part in government affairs. In fact, by the next spring, there was some question as to whether the Republicans would put him back on Ike's reelection ticket. I could tell they needed to stress—or at least point out—Mr. Nixon's part in government if they intended to run him again as Vice President. So at one press conference, I asked, "What policy decisions did Mr. Nixon participate in?" Eisenhower's reply, "I can't think of any," shocked the press corps. Just before the conference was over, a reporter for the *New York Times* rose and repeated my question: "Mr. President, can't you think of any decision that Mr. Nixon has participated in?" The President hesitated, then said, "Give me a week, and I'll think of something." The Democratic National Committee printed up the two questions and answers and distributed them widely during the campaign, ensuring that, this time around, Nixon would not be the asset he'd been in the last election.

This brings up an important question. Had Ike actually been unable to come up with an example of Nixon's worth—or was he merely having a sly laugh with a group of reporters at his Vice President's expense? It was all too easy to underestimate Dwight Eisenhower's intelligence, disguised as it was behind a deceptively bland exterior. Like most, I had poked fun at Eisenhower's supposed shortcomings, repeating jokes like, "*Did you know Ike is quite a reader?*" "*Sure—he reads each night until his lips get tired.*" But as historians study the record and researchers pore over his private papers, there is an ongoing upward reevaluation of Ike's judgment, his values and his political skills.

In my opinion, one technique of Eisenhower's that deserves further study is his use of ambiguous statements. As bright as we reporters liked to think we were, there were answers Ike gave to some of our questions that we simply couldn't figure out. I know of at least one question that he must have answered a dozen times over his time in office. Each time he gave an answer, it was consistent with the last, which, in this case, meant it was as ununderstandable as the time before. I have finally come to the conclusion that this was deliberate. Some presidents waffle back and forth on issues. Ike merely let his answers be like those ink blot tests psychiatrists used to use: what you read into them reflected who you were and what you wanted to see. In this way, he could use the public record—and the press—to give the impression that he was on the side of both the corporations and the consumers.

I have two unambiguous memories of the man which especially convince me that there was far more to Eisenhower than met the eye. One memory is of the lovely paintings that this soldier could produce. As he waited in England for D-Day to occur, General Eisenhower was taught to paint by a fellow artist-statesman, Winston Churchill. While recuperating in Colorado from his heart attack, he captured the loveliness of a snowbound meadow. At his farm in Gettysburg, he caught the look of a weather-beaten barn. He copied, with some skill, a Gilbert Stuart portrait of our first President. And as a tribute to a tribute, he put on canvas the grand landscape surrounding Lake Eisenhower. Reproductions of these paintings were given to reporters as White House Christmas cards. Four of these prints hang framed on my apartment walls. When I tell visitors that Ike painted them, they are astounded and impressed by his near-professional skill.

The other memory is of an eloquent, passionate warning. On the night of January 17, 1961, Dwight David Eisenhower broadcast his farewell address to the American people. He gave a rather short, thoroughly remarkable speech. It was as though, after two terms of playing the game as he knew it had to be played, Ike finally wanted to leave the American people with an unambiguous message that summed up his principles and observations. The farewell address was no longer than the statement he read at his first press conference eight years before—which nearly put a roomful of hardened journalists to sleep. But what a difference eight years had made!

Rereading the five-page speech today, I am impressed by not only the grace of its words but the elevation of its thoughts. There is no confusion here, no puzzling needed to figure out exactly what Ike meant. What stands out on these pages is the spirit of bipartisan cooperation so sorely lacking in today's politics of division and spite. What stands out is an understanding that America's debt to the world is to be paid in progress and peace, not authority and war. What stands out is the knowledge that America is an ongoing adventure that is forever our right and duty to shape.

Perhaps the most impressive thoughts that Eisenhower chose to share with us in his last "goodnight" to the nation are those that echo and update the farewell address of the only other great general to become a great President, George Washington. Both men of war left warnings about the growing infrastructure and authority of the military and the industrial system that feeds it. From their experience in leading armies in defense of the country, they both knew how necessary it is to plan ahead for a strong defense. But both also warned against the power and influence of a huge war machine. They warned that the combination of profit and might could become disastrously powerful.

Take a look at the way in which Ike chose to tell us how the "military-industrial complex" was invading the life of our nation:

"American makers of plowshares could, with time and as required, make swords as well. But now...we have been compelled to create a permanent armaments industry of vast proportions... We annually spend on military security more than the net income of all United States corporations...

"Today, the solitary inventor, tinkering in his shop, has been over-shadowed by task forces of scientists in laboratories and testing fields. In the same fashion, the free university...has experienced a revolution... A government contract becomes virtually a substitute for intellectual curiosity...

"The conjunction of an immense military establishment and a large arms industry is new to the American experience. The total influence—economic, political, even spiritual—is felt in every city, every statehouse, every office of the federal government... The potential for the disastrous rise of misplaced power exists and will persist.

"We must never let the weight of this combination endanger our liberties or democratic processes."

Are these the words of a man who, as I once heard someone say, "stumbled through two terms in the feel-good fifties and some-how managed not to do much harm"? Even if they may have come from the hand of a speech writer, you can sense that they reflect the speaker's heart. And how could anyone not respect a heart—and a mind—like that?

A few years after President Eisenhower's death, I ran into his son John at a military ceremony on Memorial Day, at Fort Myers. I thought, at first, that John would resent my being there and not want to talk to me. On the contrary, he was most cordial. And of all those around his father over the years, John Eisenhower gave me the great-est compliment of all. When I told him who I was, he said, "Yes, I know. My father liked your questions. They made him think."

TYLER, TEXAS, 1936-1942;

WASHINGTON, DC, 1943, 1946:

Any woman lucky enough will have at least one charmer in her life. Any woman unlucky enough will have at least one charmer in her life.

A charmer is a very special kind of man. He's the one your heart can't resist, though your head keeps sending out warnings. The one that can call you any time of day or night, and, despite your best intentions, you'll go. The one who turns your judgment to jelly, who keeps secrets and tells lies and makes you ignore the fact he does. He can make your emotions soar or crash, nourish your intellect or send it out to lunch. And when it's over (and you know it will be over from the moment you let it begin), you will always smile, albeit a little sadly, when you think of him. You remember the promise and the pleasures, not the pain.

I had a charmer who breezed into and out of my life for a decade. He was not one of the flirtations of my girlhood. He was not my first true passion, the tall, self-assured, half-Japanese, half-Belgian youth who was a big part of all the growing and finding myself I went through at the University of Missouri. He was not one of the select group of "boyfriends" I have had among the Washingtonians it's been my job to cover. And he certainly wasn't my husband.

If anything, John Thomas O'Brien, my ex and the father of my daughter, was an anti-charmer. A paper salesman hustling a living for himself in wartime Washington, O'Brien was simply someone friendly who I and another WAC who roomed with me had met at a restaurant late one night. As service women, we felt isolated, accepted by neither the civilians nor our fellows in uniform—and especially not their wives. O'Brien, who had just fallen out of a love affair, went after my friend at first, but she was hesitant. An alcoholic, she would drink a quart of liquor to give herself courage and then wind up dragging me along on the dates. Eventually, she dropped out of the picture. And not long after I married him, so did O'Brien, back to his original lover.

No, the charmer in my life was a man named J.W. Milam. I met him in 1936, when I was reporting for my two hometown papers, the Tyler Courier-Times and the Morning Telegraph. After five years of working my way up, I was covering the Federal Courts and bureaus. Milam was special agent of the Alcohol Tax Unit, the organization that eventually became the Bureau of Alcohol, Tobacco and Firearms, better known as the ATF. Originally from Kentucky, he was an intelligent man, a lawyer grooming himself to be a Federal judge—but what really attracted me was the sense of mystery, daring and danger that surrounded him. As a field agent, he carried a gun and was directly involved in everything from cracking conspiracies to tracking down moonshine stills.

Since my editor would gladly have kept me covering society news if I hadn't taken the initiative to find causes to fight and stories to cover, I found in Milam a way to exercise my journalistic muscles—and get some other exercise, as well. One day J.W. took me with him to a little town named Malakoff to check on a still. He had discovered the illegal operation by checking the sales of sugar. If there were excessive purchases from the wholesalers by a rural storekeeper or a settler, the Alcohol Tax Unit would investigate. Then, as they traveled the highways, they would look for a sudden break in the forest, a driveway with no apparent reason for existing. These questionable trails sometimes led to a still.

J.W. was checking to see if an illegal distillery he had discovered was still up and running. Since there was more evidence to obtain and the possibility of a wider conspiracy, he didn't want the bootlegger to know the Feds were watching him. So we sneaked in like a couple of thieves ourselves. This particular operation was in a small cave. We checked out the equipment and were about to leave when we spotted a car turning in from the road. As soon as it went behind some trees, J.W. said "Run!" and we took off as fast as we could toward our own car. He had given me a gun to wear, and as I ran, it bounced against my hip. With every step, I was sure the pistol would go off and shoot me in the foot. We made it to the car and escaped discovery. From J.W.'s reaction, I think we also escaped some real trouble.

Special agents come and go, and I saw Milam at irregular intervals. But the comings and goings were often dramatic—and in the broadest sense of the word, deeply romantic. Take, for example, the night of the New London School disaster, when a natural gas leak caused a horrible explosion which demolished a school and killed over three hundred people, almost all of them the children of oilfield workers. I rushed to the site, and after covering the story, stayed to help. Suddenly, J.W. was there beside me, and we worked for hours there in the darkness, doing what we could to ease the confusion, pain and sorrow. It was one of those times when you feel as though life has turned into a Hollywood movie.

It was not, however, a movie I ever really expected to have a happy ending. Milam was secretive about everything, including our relationship, which he kept from his superiors at work. It didn't take me very long to figure out that, somewhere in Louisiana, he had a wife, but by then I really cared for him, perhaps more than any other man I've known. He had helped me to believe in myself and encouraged me to pursue my dreams.

But my pursuit of those dreams didn't always please him. As a law-and-order man, J.W. was appalled when, as happened on more than one occasion, I would show sympathy for a criminal. He didn't like the fact that I'd bring hamburgers to some of the men awaiting trial in the courts I covered. One of them was a fellow named Ray Hamilton, Clyde Barrows' bosom buddy from high school. Another was such a sad case the guards would "forget" to feed him. He was a medical student who had performed an abortion for a friend, was thrown out of school, and had gone downhill so fast, he robbed a bank. He wound up in Alcatraz, and I wound up in trouble with J.W.

As the 1940s began and I moved south to work on the Beaumont Enterprise, I saw even more of Mr. Milam. Once U.S. entry into the war seemed inevitable, he had joined the Army. Now stationed in Louisiana as a Judge Advocate General, he would frequently come over to Beaumont to see me. But when I told him my intention of joining the service as well, he was furious. Like most of my family did, he felt I was wasting myself.

Ironically enough, I eventually concluded that most of the wasting I'd done so far in my life involved him. From the time I entered the WAACs, I heard nothing from him, though, through others, I knew he was in England, involved in military intelligence. Then, in 1946, like a bolt out of the blue, his bags arrived at my apartment, direct from overseas. Two months later, he followed. He seemed to think we could pick up right where we had stopped four years before—but he was wrong. I had not only gotten a telephone call from a woman in Britain, not his wife, who had questions about her son, but had started receiving mail for him, the envelopes addressed in assorted handwriting, mostly female. Though I was still wild about him—and in some ways, always will be—I sent him on his way. I later found out that within a year he drank himself to death.

That's another thing about charmers. Their stories frequently have abrupt, unsatisfying, even tragic endings. Part of their charm is that elusiveness, the way they always leave you hanging, wondering "What if...?" The memories we have of them are like photographs taken in the golden light of a warm, September afternoon.

John Fitzgerald Kennedy was a charmer.

Chapter 4

JFK: THE CHARMER

I have a very special memory of the White House that goes back to the first party I ever attended there. It was the winter of 1944, and I still felt inexperienced as a member of the Washington Press Corps and intimidated by the President. Franklin Delano Roosevelt had just been reelected for his unprecedented fourth term, and the Executive Mansion seemed more than ever like his personal imperial palace. After receiving the invitation to the party, I had gone to a place where they sold used clothes and bought myself a red taffeta evening gown. I arrived in my second-hand splendor and was shown up the stairs. As I passed the verandah above the front door, I asked the staff if they would open the door. There was snow on the porch, but it didn't matter. I needed the fresh air—and, just as importantly, I wanted to see what it was or looked like out there. They let me out, and I just stood there for a while, taking in every sensation I could. If anyone was driving by at the time, they would have seen this woman out on the porch in the snow in her red dress. They would have thought I was crazy. But it was at that moment that I felt my first true connection to that unique place and to the men and women who had lived there for 150 years.

Many Americans I have spoken to got that same feeling when John and Jacqueline Kennedy moved into the White House. Despite the aristocratic, moneyed backgrounds of the First Couple and for all the talk of Camelot, with its overtones that once again we had royalty living at 1600 Pennsylvania Avenue, the average American suddenly felt involved with the Presidency in a way that he or she had never felt before, not even during our years of devotion to FDR. Jack and Jackie were young, vital and easy to identify with, not actually like us but like the way we wanted to think we could have been. If they were a king and queen, it was the King and Queen of the Senior Prom, all grown up.

It seemed a picture-perfect Presidency, the kind that we had been waiting for since Franklin Roosevelt's sudden, shocking death.

And though the picture was wrong, it was wrong in ways that paralleled, and in some cases even duplicated, the problems in the Roosevelts' personal lives. Whether by manipulation or choice, we ignored the evidence of illness, infidelity and physical and emotional pain that lay just below the surface. We had needed the strength Roosevelt brought, and now we needed the promise this boy President and his beautiful young wife could bring. The mythologizing of the Kennedys—and their continuing popularity—show we still need that promise.

Although we were "fooled," we were not fools. Both individually and as a couple, John and Jacqueline did, in fact, have many of the qualities the perfect picture showed: leadership, charisma, intelligence, wit, trend-setting tastes and an ability to overcome those problems they could not keep us from seeing, like his bad back and the loss of their third child. Even if JFK had accomplished nothing else, he and his wife, as symbols alone, touched the national spirit in ways that many Presidencies have been unable to accomplish. They gave us a chance to reimagine a brighter, bolder, more idealistic America and to reaffirm our own connection to it.

After the Kennedy assassination in 1963, I could look back upon the impact of his brief administration from two very different perspectives, that of a 53-year-old, veteran political journalist and that of the mother of a 19-year-old "political kid," who'd grown up in Washington with the children of politicians, officials and journalists as her best friends. I saw that in life and death, JFK had, despite a mixed record in international politics and a hardly impressive list of legislative accomplishments, a profound effect on Americans of many ages. To a lot of people in my daughter's generation, JFK will always be THE President. And many in my generation adored him. I was among them.

From my very early acquaintance with Jack Kennedy, I found him charming. We would pass each other in the corridors of the Capitol, first the House and then the Senate. He knew I was raising a daughter by myself and he would inevitably come over, lean down to me and inquire, "How is your little girl?" That, of course, endeared him to me. Throughout the early and mid-1950s, my path continued to cross with that of Jack Kennedy as he became a Senator, was sidelined by back surgery, and then campaigned to be

Adlai Stevenson's running mate in Stevenson's second try against Dwight Eisenhower.

Over the years, I began to realize how the Kennedy family and their close circle of friends and advisors were working as a team toward a single goal—and that the goal was nothing less than putting John F. Kennedy in the White House. While recovering from his spinal operation, Jack had written, aided by Jacqueline, Ted Sorenson and a group of history experts, a book designed to increase his visibility nationwide, pushing his image as a patriot, an intellectual and someone deeply aware of, and impressed by, leadership and fortitude. The book, *Profiles in Courage*, about famous Senators who took unpopular stands out of moral conviction, would go on to win a Pulitzer Prize in 1957. But by January 1956, Kennedy had personally delivered a copy of the book to each of his Senate colleagues. It was a declaration to one and all that here was a man who was going places and that their choices were to join the parade or step aside. The publication date was timed for maximum impact on the 1956 Democratic Convention in Chicago.

Even I felt the direct impact of the Kennedy machine as it made its attempt to secure the second spot on the Stevenson ticket that August. Stevenson had made it clear that he would let the convention choose his running mate, so a floor fight was inevitable. The Kennedys had made some strong political allies, such as Senate Majority Leader Lyndon Johnson, who would deliver Texas' votes, and Jack had been picked to nominate Stevenson, with the opportunity to give a rousing, attention-getting speech. But there were still serious roadblocks in JFK's path, and the Kennedy clan continued to furiously work the floor.

For one, Jack's own home state's votes were under the control of House Majority Leader John McCormack, a serious rival to the Kennedys for control of Massachusetts' Democratic party. For another, there was clear opposition to having a Catholic on the Presidential ticket. Jack had fought to turn this prejudice around, arguing that Stevenson had lost a lot of Catholic Democrats to Ike in 1952 because he was a divorced man. Putting a Catholic on the ticket would be a way to get their vote back. But the Convention Chairman, Speaker of the House Sam Rayburn, was not convinced—or at least not convinced as far as a certain Catholic named

John Kennedy was concerned. And it certainly didn't help that Stevenson's mentor, Eleanor Roosevelt, was angry about the Kennedy clan's soft spot for the now-discredited and formally censured Senator Joe McCarthy.

The Kennedys were looking for anyone who might have some influence on either Mrs. Roosevelt or Speaker Rayburn. Because I was a Catholic and quite familiar with my fellow Texan Sam Rayburn, I was approached by 24-year-old Ted Kennedy for my help. I explained that I had little clout with and no influence over the Convention Chairman: "You know Sam Rayburn. Whatever Sam's decided to do, he'll do." I was just there covering the action, circulating near the Texas delegation to report on their experiences for my Texas papers. I said I'd do what I could, but I didn't expect I would be able to do much, if anything.

On the first two ballots, Lyndon Johnson delivered Texas as he had promised. Kennedy was second to Senator Estes Kefauver of Tennessee on the first ballot, but took first place on the second. Just as it seemed that his momentum was building, though, several things happened to snatch the nomination out of his grasp. Rayburn called on Tennessee Senator Al Gore Sr., who shifted his support to his fellow home-stater, and refused to call on several states that had shifted their votes to Kennedy. And somehow, the Texans got into a real wrangle over how to vote on the third ballot. By the time they finally decided to keep supporting Kennedy, it was too late. They had missed the vote, which Kefauver went on to win. Devastated by this narrow, politically manipulated defeat, the Kennedys would always feel, with a certain bitterness, that Rayburn, Texas and perhaps even Johnson had let down the son Papa Joe was determined would some day be President of the United States.

Being part-Irish by birth, Catholic by choice, and political by upbringing and profession, I took a natural interest in the ongoing soap-opera saga of this fascinating Massachusetts family. I had heard, of course, the story that the one on whom Joseph Kennedy had originally pinned his dreams was his eldest, Joe Junior. It was only after Joe Junior's death in an airplane accident in England during World War II that Papa Joe refocused his hopes on his second-born child, John—with a reluctance to match his sorrow, if you take William Loeb's word for it.

Loeb, the notorious New England editor who was one of the clients of my news service, was having lunch one time at the Kennedy home when Papa Joe pointed up to a picture on the wall of Joe Junior. "That's the boy who should have been President," he told Loeb. "He would have made a great President. He had the capabilities." But even if JFK lost to a ghost in the battle for his father's confidence and affections, he had use of his father's wealth and political savvy. Joseph Kennedy was determined that a Kennedy would someday occupy the White House, even if it had to be his second-choice, second-best, second son.

Losing the number two spot on the 1956 Democratic ticket would be the first and last time Jack Kennedy tried for a political office and lost. Even before his reelection as Senator in 1958, the family machine was pursuing its game plan for the 1960 Democratic Convention. This time, they weren't about to take "no" for an answer—and the goal was now the top of the ticket.

I've always felt an offhand remark I made may have had an influence on how the 1960 ticket eventually did turn out. In a decade and a half covering Washington, I had grown increasingly close to one of Kennedy's fellow Senators, the Majority Leader, Lyndon Johnson. Though Lyndon frequently got riled that I wouldn't let our familiarity bias the way I reported on his activities (to Lyndon, there was no such thing as a "friendly disagreement"), he and I had a mutual respect that went beyond mere friendship. So, when Jack Kennedy invited the Majority Leader to come up to Boston and speak at Faneuil Hall, I was the one reporter Lyndon asked along. For the trip to Massachusetts, he'd been loaned a plane owned by Westinghouse. At that time, it was considered all right for corporations to lend their planes and some of their staff to government officials. The Westinghouse plane wasn't all that big, so I was the only reporter accompanying Lyndon and his wife (and most avid political supporter), Lady Bird.

The trip had been most interesting. This was in April of 1959, and we could soon be expecting announcements from various politicians letting us know their availability for next year's Presidential nomination. It soon occurred to me that Jack Kennedy had probably invited Lyndon up to his turf to show this important Democrat how well-oiled a machine and how strong a following the Kennedys had at home.

At one point, for example, in the hotel in Boston, Lady Bird had needed a seamstress to help her with her dress. I put my head out the door and said, "Lady Bird needs some help. Could you send someone who sews to the room right away?" There was a long line of local politicians right outside the door, on either side of the aisle. All these minor Boston politicians were just standing there at the beck and call of the Kennedy family, and when I came out and said, "Lady Bird needs help," they passed the word down the line: a chorus of "Lady Bird needs help, Lady Bird needs help, Lady Bird needs help." She finally got the help that she needed. But it was so funny to me because it looked like a musical comedy chorus.

When the speech had been given and we were ready to reboard the Westinghouse plane, Jack Kennedy, at the last minute, decided he wanted to go back to Washington with us. So they passed word that Jack needed his luggage—"Where's Jack's luggage?"—down along the line in the same way that they had about Lady Bird's seamstress. It was really funny to see the Boston politicians behave like that. It was clear that they were always ready to supply anything that the Kennedys or the Kennedys' guests wanted.

After we'd taken off, Lady Bird, who was tired, went up front, laid down and went to sleep. I stayed sitting in the back. On any trip I took with Lyndon, I remained awake as long as I possibly could because the talk was always so fascinating.

We were crowded into a little area of the plane in the back: Lyndon, Jack Kennedy, Claude Hobbs of Westinghouse, O.B. Lloyd—a UPI man then on Lyndon's press staff—and myself. As the two Senators, Jack and Lyndon, talked and talked, back and forth and back and forth, nobody else could even get a word in, even to ask a question. Finally, they came to a halt. There was a moment of silence. And then I piped up and said, "You know, you two would make a great ticket!" Now there was dead silence. No one said a word. They just looked at each other in a cagey way. And you could almost hear each of them thinking, "Kennedy-Johnson or Johnson-Kennedy? Would he take the second slot?"

O.B. Lloyd and Mr. Hobbs would always recall this incident to me with a laugh when we saw each other in the future. I don't know if I was the first to think about JFK and LBJ teaming up or if I was just the first one to say it aloud in front of both of them, but either way, it seemed sort of prophetic.

Of course, with the resources and organization the Kennedys had behind them, Lyndon never really had a chance for the top of the ticket. Kennedy had had an office full of political professionals and volunteers about a block from the Capitol for two years before the campaign began. Combined, the Kennedy charm and the Kennedy fortune won primary after primary. By the time Lyndon put up a real fight, it was too late. In Colorado, I saw the state's top Democrats turn out to meet LBJ—but it was clear they were already committed to JFK. I recall the big Texan shaking his finger, reprimanding me at the Democratic National Convention in Los Angeles by saying "Sarah, sometimes I think even *you* are for Kennedy."

By fall, the Johnsons were just another part of the team. I accompanied Lady Bird, Ethyl Kennedy, Jean Kennedy Smith and Eunice Kennedy Shriver on a campaign trip through the Southwest. It was clear as the Kennedy women spread the gospel, they were, in many ways, as charmed by Jack as the voters were becoming. We wound up the trip with some R & R back at the LBJ ranch. It was odd to see Eunice, who I regard as perhaps the smartest of the Kennedys (she gave JFK most of his good ideas concerning health care), deliberately slide into the swimming pool fully dressed. I remember her swimming around with a diamond on her finger the size of a bird's egg.

Though they actually got along together as well as most Presidents and Vice Presidents do, the sense of rivalry between JFK and LBJ never really went away. Each had too large a personality and too fragile an ego to mesh well with the other. Even after he became President, Lyndon would always feel in Kennedy's shadow, like the second husband of a widow who knows she still pines for her first. And I always suspected that Jack felt just a little put off by the long-standing relationship I had with LBJ. When a President-elect is picking his Cabinet, reporters typically keep a vigil outside his home to see who comes and goes. One Sunday night in the winter of 1960-61, I was among the group huddled together waiting outside JFK's Washington townhouse. It was freezing cold with about a foot of ice and snow on the ground. When Lyndon Johnson, who had been on a trip out of town, drove up in his limo, Kennedy came outside. Instead of going to greet his v.p.-to-be, Kennedy came over to me and said, "Sarah, there he is. Go get him!"

During the 1960 campaign, the issue of Jack Kennedy's Catholicism raised its head once more. As he had back in Chicago in 1956, Kennedy courageously faced the fears and prejudices that were being voiced. I believe that one of the most influential actions he took to turn the question of his religion into a non-issue was to set up a highly publicized meeting in Houston with a large group of Protestant ministers. This was done in coordination with a friend of mine, a Methodist cleric, Dr. Luther Holcomb. The ministers had many difficult questions for Kennedy, especially about whether he would be unduly influenced by his allegiance to the Vatican. But JFK answered their questions so forthrightly and so well that many of the ministers came away from the meeting as Kennedy supporters. Their example set many worried minds to rest.

Years later, I met a woman who was the niece of the Papal Nuncio, the Apostolic Delegate in Washington. She had lived in her uncle's home during the Kennedy administration. She told me that while JFK was in office, he did indeed call her uncle to get information on international affairs from the Vatican and for spiritual guidance. She was astounded at how frequently the calls came in, but realized that the Vatican was only being used as a resource, a thumb on the pulse of a huge group of people spread all over the world, most heavily, of course, in Latin America. Though Kennedy was an observant worshiper, never missing a Holy Day at St. Stephens, the church closest to the White House, no matter how busy he was, I am convinced that while his religion may have informed his decisions, it never directly influenced them. When we elected JFK, our country broke through a religious bias, as we will someday, by our future Presidential choices, break through racial and sexual barriers.

JFK was the first President to understand television well enough to use it to his advantage. He always believed that the televised debates to which he challenged Richard Nixon made the difference in the general election. Nixon, perhaps made over-confident by his memories of the successful, televised "Checkers" speech, accepted the challenge, but it was Kennedy's good looks, his way with words and his charisma that came across most strikingly over the tube.

So it seemed natural that, even before he took office, the President-elect would announce that, unlike Eisenhower, he would hold a *live* televised press conference. The networks were not too crazy about this. They and their sponsors liked knowing just how long an event would last—or at least how long it could be edited down to. Spurred on by their bosses, the TV reporters began following Kennedy around, asking questions designed to make him think again about his plans for live press conferences. While Jack was down in Florida for a last Christmas at the Kennedy compound before taking office, one reporter came up with a new way to threaten him—me! "Don't you know that sooner or later Sarah McClendon will make you sorry?" he asked. "She'll ask you an embarrassing question in front of the whole country." JFK got a smile out of that. "I know Sarah McClendon and she knows me," he answered. "I'm not a bit scared of her. And she's not scared of me."

I wasn't there at the time, but when I heard about the question later, I smiled, too. Jack Kennedy was right—but, as it eventually turned out, so was the reporter.

JFK worked hard for good press, and he got it. Though I was never one of the favored few who, due to wide viewership or circulation, get special treatment from a President's staff, I felt "courted" by this President nonetheless. I got a first-hand example of how he could win any of us over when I was among the reporters accompanying him and Jackie on their state visit to Mexico City. After a large, crowded reception, a private dinner party was thrown for the Kennedys by Manuel Tellos, who, as Minister for External Affairs, was in charge of Mexico's foreign relations. Since it was an exclusive affair, we were told no reporters would be admitted, so the rest of the pool reporters departed for the hotel.

I stayed. I didn't expect to get anything, but I was going to try, so I positioned myself right outside the door to the dining hall. There was still a huge gang of people left from the reception milling about, plus the guards at the door. But I wormed my way through the crowd in hopes of looking inside if the door opened. When it did, I got a surprise. Since I am short, I could see—and be seen—through the tangle of arms and legs. I looked in and President Kennedy was looking right at me; I was directly opposite his place at the table. He pointed and said to his aide, General Ted

Clifton, "Isn't that Sarah McClendon out there? Well, bring her in here."

With that, the men at the door stepped aside to let me in, and the surge of people behind me literally projected me right into the middle of the room—I was propelled! There I stood, out of breath and disheveled, with all the people at the dinner party looking and thinking, "What in the world is going on?" I wasn't even dressed in dinner clothes. But I just quietly made myself as inconspicuous as possible and stayed for the rest of the evening, listening to what was being said. I wound up with a good story. It was fun to be picked out by the President, especially when no other reporter could get in. I imagine JFK thought he'd scored some points with me. And, in a way, he had.

JFK took many of my questions and handled them with intelligence and charm, even when we found ourselves sparring. Once, when he had missed calling on me during a press conference, he motioned for me to come down front and ask my question after the conference was officially over. When he found out it concerned his United Nations ambassador, Adlai Stevenson, issuing statements about Red China that did not jibe with the President's, Jack shook his head in exasperation and said, for all to hear, "I should have just let this conference end." He indicated he hoped for better coordination in the future, and concluded, "With that vague and soft answer, I will leave you." As he headed to the door, he flicked me on the wrist and whispered, "You and your soft little southern voice—!"

I did, however, eventually ask a question that left John Kennedy stammering, so embarrassed that his press secretary, Pierre Salinger, maneuvered to end the press conference five minutes early. It was not my intention to embarrass the President or cause a crisis. I had something important to ask about, and I did. I wound up being accused of everything short of treason. Many of my colleagues turned against me. I lost friends, contacts and a few clients. It shook up my personal life as well as my career. But I survived—and overcame. Because, as even the government would eventually admit, I was right.

Whenever I ask a question at a press conference, I have always first researched it thoroughly and checked it out. In this case, my interest and research had started almost two years before. It involved what I consider to be one of the greatest flaws in and potential dangers to our government: the fact that there is a government within our government, a group of long-term career men who remain as administrations come and go with their elected and appointed officials. A hidden government within the CIA, the FBI, the NSA and many of the Departments, especially State. A government with its own motives and its own secrets to protect. A government that protects its own deeply-entrenched clique of well-protected workers who have little, if any, accountability to the White House, Congress or the American people.

On the day I asked this particular question, the President's press conference was being held in the State Department auditorium. Since the Kennedy press conferences were so well publicized and well attended, a room larger than any available at the White House was often necessary. I went in, put my things down on my seat and went outside to grab a telephone and make one last call to my source at the Senate Judiciary Subcommittee on Internal Security. I had to be sure of my facts.

The press conference began. And when I was recognized, I stood up and dropped what proved to be a bombshell. I asked the President why two long-time State Department officials who were at this moment being seriously investigated by Congress as security risks (and also by, so I'd heard, Attorney General Bobby Kennedy) had been assigned to the task force to reorganize the Department's Office of Security—a position which gave them access to intelligence files containing the names of our spies and agents throughout the world.

Kennedy, stunned that I had brought up such a sensitive issue, stumbled, "Well- now- who?" and when I supplied the name of William Arthur Wieland, continued, "You are- the thing- I think that- would you give me the other name?" As soon as I named J. Clayton Miller, Kennedy gathered himself and launched into a defense of both men and of the government's decision to use them for such a security sensitive task. He said both had been thoroughly cleared to the highest levels and ended by scolding me, "....and in my opinion, Mr. Miller and Mr. Wieland, the duties they've been assigned to, they can carry out without detriment to the interests of the United States, and I hope without detriment to their characters by your question." It was clear that he was uncomfortable and that he wanted this press conference to be over, which Pierre Salinger soon arranged.

My question created a sensation. Not only did it involve national security, always a hot button topic in those days, but I had done something reporters just didn't do—I had embarrassed the President. As soon as the press conference was cut short, I was surrounded by reporters with questions about my sources, which, due to confidentiality, I could not give. Then a good friend of mine at the State Department, a wonderful man who had worked there in Public Affairs for years, took me aside. He told me to go right away to one particular room. I went—and walked into a press conference they were holding about me!

The State Department's Public Affairs spokesman, Lincoln White, was telling a group of reporters that he'd already met with the wire service people and warned them not to repeat the names I had mentioned in any publication. He said that if any of us mentioned the names in our stories, we would be sued. Lincoln White was doing his best to make me look like the villain here: irresponsible—or at the very least misinformed. I knew I had done nothing wrong. I had only named names when Kennedy had asked for them directly, first one and then the other. Now here was a high State Department official denying that these two known security risks were in the position to have access to any Top Secret files at all.

Though I had already refused to reveal my sources, Lincoln White happened to be one of them—and he had gone too far. So I decided to embarrass him. "Linc," I asked. "Do you remember my calling you at home last night at ten o'clock?" His face reddened, and he said, "Yes." I said, "Remember what I asked you? Do you recall that I asked you if these two men were on the task force and you said yes, they were?" And his face got even redder.

I went back to the Capitol and went to work at my desk in the Senate Press Gallery. But I could barely get any work done. Before I realized it, it was after midnight. I kept being interrupted by the telephone and visitors. The *New York Times* and a score of other papers called. Reporters from newspapers around the country dropped by, asking why I had brought up the issue and who were my sources of information. I did not know that my daughter was undergoing the same ordeal.

I had moved to the suburbs all those years before to give my daughter Sally a chance for a more normal life. After living in apartments for a while, one of my brothers had helped me purchase a little house, even further out, in a nice neighborhood. It was quiet and safe, with a park nearby and plenty of families that would take Sally along with them whenever they went places. We had made some lifelong friends out there. But this good life was a long way from where I had to be in order to do my work. I would walk three or four blocks at either end to catch my bus. At 11:00 PM in downtown Washington, four blocks can be a little frightening. Sometimes I'd be so exhausted I'd fall asleep on the bus, but some sixth sense would always wake me up just in time to catch my stop. I went through years of this until I finally managed to buy a second-hand car. Then, as the 1960s approached and Sally grew old enough to handle life in the heart of Washington, I sold the house and bought a townhouse near Capitol Hill. A lot of Sally's friends lived nearby and it seemed she was ready to become a full-fledged "political kid." But I know she was not ready for what happened that day.

My 16-year-old daughter was at home by herself. Throughout the evening she stayed there, listening to knocks on the door and watching reporters gathering out on the sidewalk for me to come home. She took calls on two telephones, one right after the other, until I dragged myself in at 1:00 AM. When I had called and asked, "How's everything?" she'd said, "Well, I don't know what this is all about, but you're sure getting a lot of these telephone calls." I was worried how all this was affecting her until she told me about one call in particular: "One man who called said he was a writer named Eddie Hunter. And he said, 'Honey, do you know what your mother has done tonight?' I said I didn't. And he told me, 'Well, she was trying to do a job for her country.'" Sally seemed comforted by that, and so did I. It was nice to know some people understood.

The reaction to my question continued to grow—and get worse. I took a lot of abuse, personally and professionally. Politicians who had been my sources told me they couldn't even be seen talking to me now. The New York *Herald Tribune* branded me a "gadfly" and *Time* magazine called me a "president baiter" and said my question was a trap for Kennedy. Truckloads of mail took me to task for making things rough for our charming young Chief Executive. I did, however, get grateful letters from Cuban exiles—who knew that one of the men I had named was strongly suspected as a potential leak to Fidel Castro—and a not particularly welcome following among the extreme right wing.

What hurt most, perhaps, was that the Women's National Press Club, a group to which I belonged, held a program on "How Far Should a Reporter Go When Questioning a President?" (it was clear to everyone that you could just as well substitute the name "Sarah McClendon" for the words "a Reporter"). The main speaker was Louis Nizer, the famous New York libel lawyer. I went prepared to defend myself—and found I had to. But, interestingly enough, he was the only scheduled guest who actually showed up. Some of my so-called "friends" were disappointed at the turnout, but the issue was beginning to turn my way at last.

Bobby Kennedy had even announced from his Attorney General's office that he would conduct an investigation into what limits should be involved in a reporter's questioning of a President. I wasn't the only reporter who found that announcement chilling, threatening to our basic First Amendment rights. But, in the long run, Bobby never followed through on such an inquiry at all—because, in truth, my concern had been warranted.

Jack Kennedy was among the first to know that. On the way back to the White House from the press conference, he learned some shocking things—right in his car. First of all, the two men had not been given the necessary security clearances. Secretary of State Dean Rusk had ordered, some months before, that they be cleared but, for various reasons, they had not. Wieland was under intensive investigation by the Senate Judiciary Subcommittee on Internal Security. Miller's name had appeared in the investigative files of the House Un-American Activities Committee in connection with membership in several organizations in which HUAC was interested. Though Wieland's friends among those deeply entrenched in the State Department bureaucracy had tried to put him into a number of interesting new assignments, he would always get pulled back. I was told that Bobby Kennedy had seen to it that he was kept away from any sensitive posts. Yet these two, despite the fact they had apparently been red-flagged, had somehow been given highly placed positions on a highly sensitive task force. Pierre Salinger later told me that Kennedy blew his top over the incident. People on his staff were actually afraid of him.

My reputation had been damaged because the government had made a mistake and I had dared to point it out. I should have had Louis Nizer on my side, because I was, to all intent, libeled by the harsh criticism I received, especially in some of the more liberal newspapers. As it turned out, it was only by hints and whispers that I received any apologies at all. Lincoln White came up to me at a function and kissed me on the cheek. Roger Jones, the Deputy Assistant Secretary for Management at the State Department, who lost his job in the flap that followed my question, approached me at a luncheon and said, much to my surprise, "I want to shake your hand. Because of you, we found out about a lot of things we never knew were going on in government." [1]

Jack Kennedy avoided my questions for quite a while after that conference. Even though he knew I hadn't tried to embarrass him, it was some time after that before he had the desire to take me on again. Some of my fellow reporters advised him that he should never call on me again, but most of them knew Kennedy—and me—better than that. They began taking bets as to when he'd start calling on Sarah McClendon again. Finally, JFK said, "I'm so curious that I have to take a question," and things got back to normal. Or at least as close to normal as they can be when a President and I are in the same room.

One outcome of this affair was that, according to Vice President Johnson at least, I had achieved a rather high degree of fame—or notoriety. Lyndon and I were both guests of Senator Alan Ellender of Louisiana at a small luncheon in a private room at the Capitol, feasting on a gumbo over which the Senator was justifiably proud. Lyndon announced to the group that the Kennedys had taken a poll on the impact of my questions and had gotten an interesting result: "Sarah, your name is now a household word." Strange the Kennedys never told me.

---

[1] Oddly enough, after over three decades of silence, I have in recent months not only received a letter from J. Clayton Miller but was approached by William Wieland's daughter at a banquet at which I had helped honor my colleague and friend Sam Donaldson. Both politely told me I was wrong in the impression I gave the nation that Wieland and Miller were in any way subversive. Wieland's daughter said the incident has impacted on her whole life. I told her I would be pleased to have her come to my home and tell me more, and, according to others she spoke to that evening, she seemed pleased and surprised that I am always ready and willing to hear the other side of any question I ask or story I write. I look forward to our meeting.

Interestingly enough, an incident that happened early in the Kennedy Administration foreshadowed the Wieland-Miller problem in several ways. It, too, involved the State Department and security clearances. Upon assuming the Presidency, Jack Kennedy was aghast at finding how long it would take to get his friends and associates investigated by the Secret Service and FBI to see if they were "secure" enough for the jobs he wished to give them. With so many coming on to work at the White House from Massachusetts, this was embarrassing. So Jack and Bobby took things into their own hands and put the names of 150 people on the rolls at the State Department. It was speculated that they did not think anyone would find them there.

But Otto Otepka, the top guardian of security when it came to investigations of State Department personnel, discovered this and raised the matter with the Kennedy White House. I was told later that the economic expert Walter Rostow was one of those not properly cleared for security, but he was already prominent before it was realized. For his diligence, Otepka received severe treatment. His investigations were stopped and he was assigned to a room where he was expected to spend all day reading the Congressional Record. Word went out at State that no one was to speak to him or have anything to do with him. He spent months under those circumstances.

This wonderful man who received such poor treatment told me about this years later over the dinner table at my home. Otto Otepka also told me that he knew who killed JFK but would say no more on that subject. But Otepka's mentioning the assassination got me thinking once again how Jack Kennedy was always in a hurry, as though he felt a shadow at his back. I suspect one reason President Kennedy had been in such a rush to get all those officials cleared was because, from the very start of his administration, he seemed to feel there were never enough minutes in an hour, days in a week or months in a year.

I always felt Jack possessed the qualities of true leadership and had many good ideas, but he was weak on follow-through. Time and again, he would launch some promising program, but shortly after, turn his attentions to another, before he'd made sure the previous one was functioning properly. I had a feeling that he always felt a sense of urgency, perhaps even a premonition that he would never be able to finish things because he did not have much time left. Unfortunately, that turned out to be all too true.

I would have liked to have known and understood him better, but he ran too fast for me. I like to think he wanted to know me better, too. He seemed to have the idea that I should travel with him everywhere he went. He couldn't understand why I didn't go. One time he actually called out to me from the door of his plane, the *Caroline*, shouting, "Aren't you going with us?" He didn't understand that I have always been a small operation, often just a one-woman office without assistants or even interns.

It is very expensive to travel with the President. You pay first class airfare plus about another third for ground transportation and incidental expenses. Usually you need to have a telephone hookup all to yourself, as well. If there is a paper I represent in the area to which the President is going, it will often choose to send a local reporter to cover the visit. Even if my paper could afford it, it would be a duplication of staff and expenses to bring me in from Washington.

That is the basic reason I was not with the Kennedys on that final, fateful trip to my home state, Texas, in November, 1963. My Texas papers had merely asked me to find out about preparations and schedules for the trip, but try as I might, I couldn't get the routes for the motorcades in San Antonio and Houston. Ironically, maps of the route for Dallas had been widely circulated. Frustrated that I was not going along and puzzled why they were holding back the information for the other two cities, I asked Pierre Salinger again and again how he expected to have cheering throngs turn out if they were so tight with the information. He avoided the question. Finally, standing there in his office I said, "Then you can take your bloody trip for all I care and..." Cut off with an angry look, I left.

The "bloody" was an unlucky choice of words. After the assassination, I went to Pierre in tears and apologized for my unintended dire prediction. He comforted me, "I know, Sarah, I know." He was brilliant in the days that followed, keeping a stunned press corps supplied with the news for a stunned America.

As I drove out to meet *Air Force One*, bringing the new President and the body of the slain one back to Washington, I knew I had to bring Sally, too. The entire nation would be there in spirit to meet that plane. I picked her up at Georgetown University, where she was now a student, and continued on to Andrews Air Force Base, where the plane would land. I was afraid the guards might not let her enter the press area with me, but they knew the young had a special right to grieve for their fallen hero.

I know neither my daughter nor myself will ever forget the sight of Mrs. Kennedy, her clothing stained with blood, climbing into the front seat of the gray military hearse which would carry her husband's body to be autopsied at Bethesda Naval Hospital. I learned later that she and the President had seemed especially affectionate and at peace with one another on the way to Texas.

When the Johnsons came down the ramp arm in arm, it seemed all Washington was there to greet them. But the only time I saw the deep grief etched into Lyndon's face lift for even a moment was when he nodded to Sally, his daughter Linda's very good friend. After LBJ spoke, he left to write a letter to the Kennedy children. I tried to put my emotions aside and get to work.

I interviewed three Texas congressmen who had flown back on board *Air Force One*. One of them, Rep. Jack Brooks of Beaumont, had been on the floor of the House of Representatives on March 1, 1954, when Puerto Rican nationalists had fired from the Spectators' Gallery and wounded five of the 243 Representatives present. I had been there that day as well and, having actually moved over from the Press Gallery to see and hear something better, wound up almost directly in the line of fire. "The first thing I thought of was Puerto Rico," Brooks told me about the nightmare in Dallas. "I heard a boom, boom, and then later another boom. I shall never forget that sound." Texas Senator Ralph Yarborough, who came in on the next plane, seemed speechless at first. "It is an outgrowth of a campaign of hate," he finally said. "This is the saddest day I've ever known in American history."

I buried my own grief in work, but the memories are never far from the surface: how first I and a few others, then the entire press corps, fell in behind the dignitaries as President Kennedy's body was taken from the White House to the Capitol rotunda to lie in state; how, dressed all in black, I stood on a hill above the grave site at Arlington and watched the lighting of the eternal flame; how Jacqueline, Caroline and John-John were heartbreaking models of dignity throughout. And I remember writing, less than a month later:

> My woman's intuition tells me that Lee Harvey Oswald could not and did not do that by himself. He was just a diversion. It could have been the work of the underworld, using Oswald, with his peculiar background, as a smoke screen, or it could have been a national or an international plot...I always had the feeling Kennedy might die in office, but I thought it would be the result of one of his chronic ailments.

I feel that Kennedy's death was more than just a great loss to the nation, more than a loss of all the new changes, new ideas and new life he was bringing to the country. I feel it is a symptom of something that could destroy our country, because I feel strongly that his death may have been brought about by people in government.

I have spoken about this with Colonel Richard Prouty of Virginia, who had 30 years' experience with the Air Force. He was the liaison between the developing CIA and the Joint Chiefs of Staff. He had a chance to watch what was going on in the CIA and in the communications among many branches of government. His theory is that several different agencies in the federal government came together in a cabal to assassinate Jack Kennedy. He feels that this happened shortly after Kennedy told his Cabinet and others in his office that he was going to tear apart the Central Intelligence Agency, stop the war in Vietnam and bring home the troops. There were certain people who didn't want any of this to happen, and, shortly after this, a plan began to be considered for his death. I think it is a shame that a country that's as great, as important, as noble as ours, can't—or won't—find out exactly who killed John Fitzgerald Kennedy.

The Warren Commission was immediately put together by Lyndon Johnson to investigate the Kennedy death. This was done for vital national security reasons. A great question mark was hanging over our people, and foreign countries, both our allies and enemies, needed to know what we would do. Johnson was, I am sure, afraid that there'd be much more trouble if he did not have Kennedy's death investigated. But the Warren Commission, if not intended as a cover-up, became one through the need for quick answers. As we found out later, it was apparently poorly staffed. It had only a few attorneys and their small staffs did not dig deeply for evidence. They simply ignored troubling evidence which did not lead to a simple solution. One of the people on the Warren Commission was my very close friend Senator John Sherman Cooper. A thoroughly honest man, John always maintained that the Commission had done a good job. I knew him well enough to know this was the truth as he saw it, and this confuses me. Also on the Commission was Representative Gerald Ford of Michigan, who later became President. He also defended, and continues to defend, their work. A third member of it I knew was Senator Richard Russell of Georgia, who had no desire in the world to serve on it. I learned that when Johnson asked him to serve he said emphatically, "I don't want to do it." The next day Dick Russell picked up the newspaper to read that Johnson had announced to the public that Senator Russell was on the Warren Commission.

After the Warren Commission there were at least two other Congressional Investigations of Kennedy's murder. For some reason or another, they never seemed to get anywhere. There was always something or another blocking their paths. Before it even began its work, the House Committee threw out their Chairman, Henry Gonzalez of San Antonio, Texas. Gonzalez, an extremely sharp man who had been in Dallas that day and gave me a moving description of the blood-drenched Jacqueline Kennedy waiting outside the operating room to which they had rushed her husband, once told me that he, too, knew who killed Kennedy. He was interrupted at that time and has never chosen to reveal it to me since.

None of the official investigations into JFK's death have given the people of our country answers that ring true. So we continue to exist as a nation of doubters. In the meantime, there are hundreds, if not thousands of people in this country putting their time and energy into studying this, not obsessed conspiracy theorists, but credible scientists, college professors, doctors and forensic experts, many of whom testified, or offered to testify, before the sanctioned investigations and were ignored or refused. About three years ago, I was among the group founding an organization called the Coalition on Political Assassinations. I'm on the board of COPA. It meets once a year in Washington and once a year in Dallas. It provides a forum for theories about Kennedy's death. Papers read by well-qualified researchers have produced some alarming information and evidence. COPA is beginning to have quite an influence on a unique organization within the National Archives, which is authorized by Congress to declassify the government papers concerning the Kennedy assassination. This organization, the Assassination Records Review Board of the Archives, has recently brought forth some very fascinating information about activities in New Orleans before and after Kennedy's murder. I think that between them, this outside/inside approach to uncovering the truth may well eventually get close to the real story. Nothing could be of greater service to the nation than shining the light of truth on a mystery which, in many ways, keeps us rooted in the past and hampers our moving forward.

I frequently think back on Jack Kennedy's boyish good looks, his winning smile, his quick wit and captivating manner. When I do, it is with a little sigh. He was a young man with oh-so-much to do who worked like he was fighting for time. He—and we—ran out of it on that awful day in Dallas.

My sadness, however, is always tempered with hope. At a party a few years back which celebrated my being in the Senate Press Gallery for 50 years, Ted Kennedy approached me and said, "Sarah, I guess you've been covering the Kennedys longer than anybody." I hadn't thought about it, but it was true. Since the family knows I like them, Ted went on to remind me that, as far as politics is concerned, "there are five little Kennedys coming along, and we're going to be around here for a long time."

That thought makes me smile. Though it's been a while since we've seen the last one, there *have* been political dynasties that have put more than one person in the White House. Who says a family can only have one charmer—or one President?

TYLER, TEXAS, 1910-1917;

WASHINGTON, DC, 1940s:

I was born the youngest of nine children, five boys and four girls, into a family that was idealistic, politically active and committed to public service. From the eldest son, Whitaker, down to myself, we grew up in an atmosphere where politics was as natural a topic of conversation as my mother's literary interests, my father's oratorical skills, or whatever we children were learning at school that week. As natural, in fact, as discussing the weather.

My mother taught me the importance of communication, especially with so many different personalities living under one roof. My father taught me to "make contacts," which he said often led to better things, to champion the underdog, and to respect everyone, despite differences in religion, race and level of wealth. Whitaker was an example of responsibility, writing often from his engineering jobs on the Rio Grande, his letters filled with parental respect and brotherly concern and suggestions. Charles, to whom I was perhaps the closest, taught me how to fully breathe the rich political air which surrounded me. Sidney taught me generosity, which he continued to demonstrate to me throughout his life, helping me to buy my first house in the Washington area, and then later, move into the city. Annie Bonner, my oldest sister, taught me to speak early by having me recite poems—and I've rarely stopped speaking since. Patience taught me to read before I ever went to school, so I entered into the second grade, not the first. She also showed me how to endure, working at a job she hated to help the finances of our aristocratic but sometimes struggling household, then seeking solace by writing poetry. Robert encouraged me to learn to type, the skill with which I still earn my living. Martha got me my first job—which taught me great sympathy for Patience. And Frank, who, as the next youngest to me, is my only surviving sibling, told me what to expect as I grew up in his footsteps. Eventually, they all helped to put me, the baby of the family, through college. It was a wonderful childhood in a huge old house that is now one of Tyler's historical landmarks.

I loved my mother and my sisters, but I was drawn to my father and my brothers. Like most Southern women, I had an instinctive understanding of the ways to empower a man. As a child, I was taught to get up and give my seat to my older brothers. When, at preschool age, I would go with my mother from one women's suffrage meeting to another, it was my brothers who first made me stand up on the dining room table and recite the fiery speeches I'd memorized from hearing so many times. And when, as a girl of seven, I watched first Sidney, then

Charles march off to fight the Great War, I knew that if my country called when I was old enough, I would answer with the same bravery my brothers had.

World War II was the great divide in my life, between Texas and Washington, between youth and maturity, between being part of a family at home and creating one of my own. I never really lost my first family, whether they stayed in Tyler, like Patience and my father (and my mother, who'd been resting in the ground for a decade), or moved on to other places like I did. But I developed a new family, in part to make up for a missing husband and in part because I was simply used to having a crowd around. Many of them were transplanted Texans, like myself. One of them became President of the United States.

Chapter 5

LBJ: BIG BROTHER

The first time that I ever saw Lyndon Baines Johnson, he shook his huge fist in my face and shouted, "Take it back, take it back!"

He was a member of the House of Representatives at the time, and when he'd spotted me in a corridor of the Longworth Building, he'd rushed over and demanded I retract a story I had written about problems with the oil depletion allowance among independent petroleum operators in Texas. But my story was fair and accurate, so I just shook my fist right back at him and said, "I will not, I will not! I know I'm right!"

That fight was the beginning of a long up-and-down relationship with Lyndon Johnson. With his hound dog face towering more than a foot above mine and our voices raised in a loud Texas twang, we must have seemed like a big brother and little sister airing the family problems in public. And though his intimidation and my defiance would bump heads again and again over the years, we did indeed admire each other in a way that was almost a kind of love. I certainly got to know the good and bad in him in a way I never have with any other President.

Lyndon thought that everybody who knew him should write only nice, sweet things about him. But I just covered him as news—which wasn't always nice and sweet. I always wrote about him as if I was seeing him for the first time. It was good reporting, newsworthy and, to the best of my ability, always the truth. Because we were friends, he couldn't understand that. He felt our friendship meant that I should always portray him as perfect, or at the very least a great leader and great man. He saw my journalistic ethics as a roadblock to our relationship.

Lyndon Johnson was not used to having people say "no" to him. He possessed amazing powers of persuasion. No one, he thought, could stand up to "The Johnson Treatment." That I continued to do so in my writing infuriated and, I think, fascinated him in a way.

His devoted sister, Josefa Johnson, tried hard to protect him

—and me—from his temper. She once said, while she and I were having lunch at the LBJ Ranch, "Sarah, I sometimes get your stories from the Austin paper and hide them from Lyndon for weeks at a time. We don't want him to get mad over something you said." But despite Josefa's efforts, he was often angry with me. Of all the Presidents I've covered, he was the most difficult—and made life the most difficult for me.

From the start of his political career, Lyndon Johnson believed in, practiced and, to some extent, perfected the art of news management. This was disastrous at times, for other reporters as well as me. Before he ever came to Washington as a Member of Congress, Lyndon had set up a system with a number of Texas editors and publishers. When any story unfavorable to him reached their offices, they were to call him right away and not print it until he called them back. He would then get in touch with the reporter who wrote it or the syndicate that sent it and try every way in the world to have the disagreeable parts rewritten or cut out. If that didn't work, he'd pressure the editors back home to use their blue pencils. So, in many Texas papers, it was hard for anything about LBJ that LBJ didn't want to see to ever see the printed page.

This early warning system with editors and publishers gave him quite an advantage. While he was Senate Majority Leader, he developed another way of managing the news that proved every bit as effective. Lyndon noticed that newspapers had very little political news in them on Monday morning. So he came up with a way to fill that vacancy. He would have his press secretary, George Reedy, saunter into the Senate Press Gallery on Saturday morning. George had been a wire-service reporter himself and knew how the game was played. George would whisper to whatever reporters were around that there might be something important coming up. He would be very mysterious about this, getting their curiosity all aroused and making them go after it. That would increase their interest considerably. Finally, he would give them the story, just after the deadlines were over for the Sunday morning news sections, but in plenty of time for Monday. This was a great gimmick. By filling the Monday morning newspapers with a lot of news they otherwise wouldn't have had, Lyndon was able to get what he wanted into the news, whether favorable to himself or critical of his enemies.

There was another, more underhanded way in which LBJ was able to manage the news. One that destroyed more than one career. If a reporter wouldn't do as Lyndon wanted, he would use his considerable influence and far-reaching connections to get him, or her, fired. I know about this first-hand—because as he climbed from Congressman to Senator to Vice President to President, LBJ was personally responsible for getting me fired from at least four different papers at three different times.

The first was the *Abilene Reporter News*, because I wrote a story about his opponent for office, Coke Stevenson. Lyndon had cautioned all the Texas reporters that Stevenson was not fit to be a candidate and we should not even cover his appearance when he came to Washington. But I thought he should be covered, so I went to his press conference and wrote an article about it. The *Abilene Reporter News* immediately fired me. When I made them put their reasons in writing, they said it was because I'd written about Coke Stevenson in a way which was unfair to Lyndon Johnson. As I found out much later, the Abilene paper was one of those which Lyndon had an arrangement with. The story I was fired for never ran there.

Another paper that he had me fired from was the *San Antonio Light*, a Hearst paper to which I had supplied articles on issues affecting Texas for nearly 17 years. Since my news bureau specialized in strictly regional coverage, I didn't interfere with the coverage of the Hearst Bureau at all. Lyndon, who was Vice President at the time, had undergone an operation, and I'd heard a rumor that it might have been to remove a cancer. I went to the hospital to cover the story.

Bill Moyers had just begun handling the press for Lyndon at that time. Moyers, who'd graduated from Southwest Theological Institute in Fort Worth, had been brought to Washington because of another rumor: there had been speculation that LBJ's relationship with his top secretary Mary Margaret Wiley had become an intimate as well as a professional one. Concerned, Lyndon had secretly asked his good friend Harry Provence of the *Waco Tribune* and several other Texas editors to look for someone to prevent that kind of talk. And who better to give the Vice Presidential staff a more "sanctified" appearance than a young man headed for the ministry? So Moyers was hired on, ostensibly to deal with policy concerning religion and to answer letters that had a religious tone. In actuality, he was a chaperone who would travel with Lyndon and Mary Margaret to show that all was on the up-and-up.

Bill came over to me after the press conference and asked me, "Sarah, why were you asking so many questions about Lyndon's operation?" I said, "Well, Bill, the *San Antonio Light* told me that they'd heard it was a serious operation and they wanted me to give it close attention in my coverage. So I did." Well, that afternoon I was fired from the *San Antonio Light.* It took some detective work to find out why. The editor of the *Light* said he thought I was doing a fine job and had not been the one to fire me. I went to the Hearst Bureau in downtown Washington, but they didn't know a thing about it.

The only explanation left was that this must have happened because of Lyndon. Moyers had apparently told Lyndon about my particular interest in the operation, and Lyndon, always wanting to appear healthy and on top of things, had not taken well to my special attention to the state of his fitness. I knew that Lyndon was very close with a man named Berlin, a top executive for Hearst in New York, with whom the Vice President often talked and conferred. And so, though I loved covering for San Antonio, I was unceremoniously fired, with orders from the top, because, by trying to find out the truth for my readers, I had once again gotten Lyndon's temper up. The *San Antonio Light* had been a fascinating paper to cover for. I had written lots of copy for it over those 17 years, and I was sorry to see it go.

The worst incident took place almost immediately after Lyndon became President. About two or three days after he took office, LBJ called several Texas editors of mine to Washington. Making it seem as if it were a matter of the survival of a nation still reeling from JFK's assassination, he told them that he could not do his job if he had to take my questions. Therefore, according to what I later learned, he wanted them to relieve me of my duties of covering the White House. I was not even informed the editors were in town. Together, they decided that they would give the job to Les Carpenter, a Washington correspondent for a number of Texas papers, who had seldom covered the White House under previous Presidents and had not been there at all in the short time Lyndon had been President. I, of course, had been there every day.

Les Carpenter's wife, Liz, worked for Mrs. Johnson as her Press Secretary. Les told the editors that if they took me off of the *Port Arthur*

News and the *Lufkin Daily News* as well as the larger *Waco Tribune* and the *Austin American Statesman*, that I would know that the President was at the bottom of this. He explained that I would go around town and tell everybody that I got fired at Lyndon's request. Therefore, he thought it was much smarter if they would leave me with the two smaller papers, Lufkin and Port Arthur, and continue to pay me the small amount that they were paying me for the four papers. And that's what happened, though I didn't find out why till much later.

I was dismayed and bewildered that I had been fired from the Waco and Austin papers, which were essential in letting the people back in Texas know what Lyndon Johnson was doing in Washington. I was finally told the whole story by one of those who had been called to the capital, the Austin editor Dick Brown. The relationship between Johnson and the Texas editors centered around the Marsh/Fentress chain, which was headquartered in Waco. Dick Brown was a nephew of Marge Fentress, one of the publishers, but he didn't like the way Lyndon was being handed so much control of the news media in Texas. I think he also resented the power this was giving LBJ's friend, Harry Provence, over in Waco, who'd been another of the editors at the secret conference to decide my fate.

So, there you have it. Two days after he suddenly became President, at a confused and perilous time when there were so many more important issues that needed his attention, Lyndon Baines Johnson arranged to have Sarah McClendon thrown off two more papers. If I had not had other newspapers from outside of Texas as clients, I might well have lost my White House press pass altogether. Why did I put up with this? Why did I, and still do, consider that Lyndon was a friend?

It has become very stylish to bash Johnson and his presidency. But I never did—and I never will. It has also become stylish to analyze him. And how he hated to be analyzed! He wanted to be simply accepted and understood, so much so that he could not understand why anyone would try to question his motives. I probably would have enjoyed being able to relax my guard and simply take him on his own terms, but I never could. Even so, I believe that Lyndon Baines Johnson made the most realistic contribution of any American president to civil rights, to education and to the advancement of women, both in civilian life and in the military. He was often every bit as remarkable as he wanted to be. In my admiration of his extraordinary, and now often overlooked, achievements, I am proud to claim him as a friend.

Don't forget that Lyndon and I were born and grew up in the state of Texas. And though Texans, in our ornery way, sometimes play by cut-throat rules, we do stick together. Even here in Washington, I always find it easier to get information from a fellow Texan. There is a sense of group identity that goes beyond what you'll find in most other states. In a very real way, we are like a large family. We can fight and fight and still make up. As family, we all knew that Lyndon could be scheming and spiteful. But we also knew that he had greatness in him. He was the most vital, hard-working man you could meet. His iron will, though misdirected at times, had but one goal: to serve his country and help it fulfill its potential. And frankly, we were proud to have a Texan in the White House, even though the event that put him there was a national tragedy. To put it simply, I didn't hold it against Lyndon. I wrote it off as a lesson: "Never get a man mad at you just before he gets to be President."

Besides, by the time most of this had happened (or I'd found out exactly *what* had happened), I'd been around LBJ a long time and gotten to know him very well and like him very much. There were a lot of good qualities to like. He could be gracious and charming, thoughtful and generous, considerate and witty. Johnson had a tremendous desire to be loved. This came, in part, from the same insecurity that made him want to control everything that was ever said about him, but I also think that he genuinely liked to give people pleasure.

He could be very sweet at times. Once I had a car accident and was feeling so very stupid and guilty. I had run into somebody from the back. When he heard about it, Lyndon said, "Well, McClendon, I'm not surprised. You have so much to do and so much on your mind that I don't think it was your fault. I'm amazed that you get done all you do, with a child to take care of and all these things."

Lyndon was always concerned about family, his friends' as well as his own. For many years Sally and his daughter Lynda Bird had been best of friends. Just after LBJ become Vice President, Lynda Bird was named queen of the President's Cup Regatta on the Potomac. She had asked Sally to be one of her two attendants. Lyndon went out of his way to make me feel even better by assuring me that Lynda had done this "not because you're a newspaperwoman but because she likes Sally."

On more than one occasion, LBJ showed how much *he* liked Sally, too. One day, she was called at her school and told to come to his office. She didn't know what it was all about. She left school and came over there, wondering what in the world had happened. Lyndon had an eye doctor there, a famous expert on contact lenses. This was when contacts were first becoming well known, and Johnson had gotten them for all the members of his family who wore glasses. She had been nearsighted since she was 12 years old and wore glasses all the time. Without even telling me, he had Sally fitted for contacts by this expert. I found out about it later and appreciated it very much.

Johnson also offered to improve my appearance. He'd sent his wife and daughters, Mrs. Homer Thornberry (wife of the Congressman from his district) and several other women who were wives of his associates to New York, where they took lessons from Eddy Simms, who ran a famous beauty parlor up there. They all learned how to make up their faces and how to fix their hair. I heard Lady Bird say later that after that, it took her a full 40 minutes to make up her face. I think it would take me that long too. He was going to send me, but as a busy career woman, I guess I just didn't seem enthusiastic enough, turning up my nose about such things. So somehow we never got together on that trip.

LBJ liked to be helpful without having been asked. In fact he sounded a bit insulted when he found out from someone else that I was trying to find a summer job for one of my nephews. Lyndon came over to me in a hallway and demanded, "What's this I hear about you tryin' to get somebody to give a job to your nephew. Are you lookin' for a job for him?" I said yes. He said, "Well, why didn't you come to me?" I told him I didn't want to bother him: "I didn't want you to have to worry with it." "Well, I'll get him a job," he said, and with that, he did. Frank McClendon, Jr. had a job for that summer. He worked on Capitol Hill with the Johnson staff and grew to be great friends with quite a few of them.

The Johnson staff often had parties, organized by Walter Jenkins, LBJ's closest aide. Walter would plan lovely parties, and they had lots of fun together during their off hours. But they worked long and hard, so they deserved this. Lyndon drove his staff as hard as he drove himself. And once you were a Johnson employee, you were one for life: escape was impossible. LBJ expected absolute loyalty but rewarded it in many, often dramatic, ways.

A reporter who would give Lyndon that kind of loyalty could expect rewards, as well. Johnson had his great favorites among us. With a genuine sense for what was news, Lyndon would actually write the lead on the stories he handed out to his favored few. Phil Potter, of the *Baltimore Sun*, was one who could come by Johnson's office any day to be handed a scoop. Another great favorite was Nancy Hanchman. She was a broadcaster and was frequently in his presence. Marianne Means of the Hearst papers was still another.

According to one of my publishers, LBJ set it up for Marianne to write a column by asking all the publishers he knew best to run it. When they said, "Why should we take it? We don't know her, and she's just starting out," LBJ replied, "Well, I'm going to let her come by my office every day, and every day I'm going to give her a hot story for you all, and if you don't want to miss some real news, you'll take her column." She was a beautiful girl who genuinely liked Lyndon and always wrote nice things about him. To Lyndon, that was a winning combination, and he would do anything he could to help her.

John Kennedy assumed that I was also part of the charmed circle of reporters his Vice President favored. But because I was one of those who irked Lyndon, who never soft-soaped him or smoothed over his wrinkles in my stories, I was never part of that group. I was a friend, not a lapdog. Even so, Lyndon once told a group at a big Texas party that he "could not do his job without Sarah." I think he said that because I often kept him informed about births and deaths in Texas. I did so to get his reaction. He would follow through with messages of congratulations or sympathy, and the families were always very appreciative.

Johnson had a great way with reporters. After he had his first heart attack in 1955, he invited all of us to visit him in his hospital bed. As every reporter entered LBJ's room at Bethesda Naval hospital, he was given a portable transistor radio, which back then was something new. We were very glad to have it. I know I was delighted. Once he had us in a good mood, he used the occasion for a little bit of promotion. The doctors had apparently decreed that cantaloupe was a very good thing for him to eat after a heart attack, because there aren't a lot of calories there and they filled you up. They made you feel as though you'd had a lot to eat when you actually hadn't, and so they were good for losing weight. Well, he'd asked the people in Pecos, in west Texas, where they grew a lot of cantaloupes, to send him a lot of the melons. And he wanted to show the reporters how much weight he had lost. We were gathered around his bedside in his room. I was the only woman there, so Johnson said, "Sarah, if you'll go over in the corner and turn your back, I'll pull down my pants and show the boys how much weight I've lost." So, I did, and he did. He showed how healthy he was while pushing two Texas products—cantaloupes and himself—and giving us a story.

Lyndon Johnson was always a wonderful story teller. It was an honor, a treat and a temptation to listen to his detailed insider accounts enlarging upon familiar stories of the people we all knew. He gave us what happened after the door closed and the conversations that were too far away to hear. He had a marvelous memory for what had happened and I believe he could remember everything anyone ever said to him. I hung on every word of his behind-the-scenes stories of the Senate. I especially appreciated his tales about his mentor, Speaker Sam Rayburn, who was one of my heroes, too. Lyndon would tell us, hour by hour, of his own adventures as Majority Leader. He made me understand that he had a very important part to play in those chambers and that he was up to every moment of it.

I could tell the stories were accurate because I'd witnessed the key events of one of the best of them myself. Lyndon Johnson prided himself on being a person who got things done. He also admired this greatly in other people and would speak admiringly, at times, of someone as being "a can-do man." But I have rarely met anyone who could match Lyndon's own ability to turn "no" into "yes." I saw how he brought that to play in getting the Cordova Island Bridge open.

The Cordova Island Bridge was a structure spanning the Rio Grande River in El Paso, Texas that had been standing useless and unopened for years. Construction had stopped when it was almost finished because neither the U.S. nor Mexican government could agree on how to administer the bridge. It was much needed. The other facilities crossing the river were not adequate. So when it was brought to his attention, Lyndon was determined that he'd get this bridge open. He called together to his Majority Leader's office on the third floor of the Capitol, all at once, everybody in every bureau, department or agency who had anything to do with this bridge. And since I was reporting for the *El Paso Times*, Lyndon had asked me to be there, too.

Well, there was the State Department, the Commerce Department, the Transportation Department, the International Boundary Commission, the Border Patrol, and plenty of others. There was even the Defense Department, because there were military bases nearby. After this great assembly of people formed a wide circle in the room, Lyndon turned to them and said, "Gentlemen, we're here today to decide what we're going to do about this bridge." Then he put each one of them on the spot. He would call on one person who would say, "Well, I'm doing all I can, Mr. Leader, but I can't do it all by myself. I have to depend on what the people in the Agriculture Department think or what these people in the Army Engineers think." And Lyndon would reply, "Well, we'll get that done right now. Because sitting beside you is the man from Agriculture. You talk to him and get it straightened out right now. We don't have to have any letters. We don't have to have any waiting. And you, over there in Army Engineers, he says you're involved in this, too. Move over and talk to him—now."

Round Lyndon went, around the room. And there wasn't anything that the assembly could do but talk to each other and get it done right then. So they did. This was a fine example of Lyndon's "Can-Do-ism", which he quite justly prided himself on. And it would be hard for anyone hearing the story — especially those used to constantly hearing about bureaucrats passing the buck—not to be proud of him too.

LBJ liked the spotlight. And telling stories, whether during a press conference, at a party or while traveling was one way he used to stay in control and at the center of attention. He'd do the talking and everyone else would listen. I remember one lawn party in the D.C. suburb of Chevy Chase, Maryland. Lyndon was surrounded by a crowd as usual. It was nearly ten at night, and he was starting to really warm up. Suddenly he said, "Sarah, go get me a cup of Sanka," the only decaffeinated coffee you could get back then. Just as I would have done for one of my older brothers back in Tyler, I went inside to find a cup. I was shocked to find the hostess had no Sanka.

Everyone knew that Lyndon only drank decaf at night, and people all over the District kept a jar in the pantry in expectation of a visit from LBJ. Without his Sanka, he might just get up and leave.

I wound up going from door to door around the neighborhood until I found some to borrow. I brought it back, made him a cup and never said where I got it. As independent as I usually am, I never thought twice about doing just what Lyndon had demanded. The power of his stories, with all their incredible detail and insider's point-of-view, was so strong that you'd bend to his will just to keep them coming.

LBJ's best stories were often told on an airplane where the narrow aisle would make it hard to hear his low story-telling voice. Some 15 to 20 newsmen and myself would hang over the backs of seats, sit on arm rests or stand as long as we could, so we wouldn't miss a word. He'd munch on nuts and snacks and drink his Cutty Sark. He always ate when he drank. That's why, I guess, I never saw him intoxicated in the slightest bit.

Traveling with Lyndon was usually a treat. A treat that was sometimes used to keep reporters happy and writing the news the way he wanted them to. And by the time his attitude toward me soured, we'd traveled a great deal together. I had gotten to the point where if he'd call me and ask me to go join him, I'd just pack up and go. Lyndon got riled with me once because he'd gotten to the point where he assumed I'd always jump at the chance. I had been traveling with him quite a bit, but when he called up with another invitation, I told him that I couldn't go because my feet had swollen up from traveling so much on planes. The malady happens if you don't get enough circulation and you sit a lot with your legs dangling. So, a podiatrist had told me not to travel on any more planes for a while. Lyndon was furious. He thought that I was just using this as an excuse not to go because I didn't want to be with him or didn't want the trip. That, of course, wasn't true. I loved to travel with him all the time. He was a most interesting man — with an interesting temper, to be sure.

He never even liked to eat alone, so I'd often have to wait till he was hungry. I remember on one flight when Lyndon waited so long past midnight that I went to the back and told the steward to give me something to eat. So he did, and when Lyndon found out that I'd eaten already—by myself, without him—he was furious at me. But putting up with the temper was part of the price of being friends with, or even simply covering, this fascinating, larger-than-life Texan.

When he became Vice President, LBJ traveled even more, and I continued to enjoy traveling with him. In 1961, I was one of the lucky reporters who accompanied Vice President Johnson around the world. He always liked fellow Texans for company and enjoyed our reporting his adventures to the folks back home. Well, this time, I was able to do my part in making his adventures a little more notable.

When we arrived in Taiwan, it became clear that the government wasn't in a very welcoming mood. Relations between Nationalist China and the United States were touchy. Chiang Kai-shek and Madame Chiang, who ruled with him, were sure that JFK had sent the Vice President to lecture them and put restrictions on what they could do and what they couldn't do with any aid that the U.S. might, or might not, send them. So they decided that they would all but ignore Lyndon and Lady Bird.

Madame Chiang came to meet Lady Bird as planned. She was supposed to take her on a tour to some schools and the sort of other things wives usually see on diplomatic trips with their husbands. Though this wouldn't be very exciting, it turned out that it wasn't going to happen at all. Madame Chiang just stayed for a few minutes to greet Lady Bird rather coldly and then left, said she had some very important things to do for the government. We were shocked at this, kind of hurt and wondered what was going on.

Later on, as the reporters who were traveling with Lyndon were waiting for Chiang Kai-shek to have a press conference, we learned that Chiang was not going to see the American press at all. The situation was simply awful. So I decided that I was going to go and see about this. Without informing anyone why, I went to see the top official in the Taiwanese Press Office.

I didn't want Lyndon to know about this, because he had once followed my advice and regretted it. On an earlier trip to Paris, where the news establishment was very critical of him, I had told Lyndon that he ought to have a press conference: the press was treating him badly because they didn't know him. Well, he had the press conference and it didn't go too favorably for him, mostly due to a group of unfriendly American correspondents assigned to cover the European scene. So I guessed I owed Lyndon one.

I told the Taiwanese official that I covered Washington for many newspapers, including New Hampshire's *Manchester Union-Leader*, and my boss at that paper, the arch-conservative publisher William Loeb, was a great supporter of the Free Chinese government. I told him I was a friend of that state's Senator Styles Bridges, a respected Republican who was one of Taiwan's best friends in Washington and a very great enemy of the Red Chinese. I told him that William Loeb, Styles Bridges and all the others who supported Taiwan in the U.S. would be very concerned, very upset and very disappointed if the press who were traveling with my other good friend Vice President Johnson did not get to hear about the events going on in their country.

Despite their suspicions, the Taiwan government knew it needed all the support it could get and that the people in the United States needed to understand and know more about their country. Actually, Taiwan was doing pretty well in agriculture and exports. But, as I told the official, nobody would know about this unless the correspondents had a chance to meet with the head of the government.

I delivered my message and went on my way. About an hour later, I was called at my hotel. The Taiwanese Press Office said that not only would there be a press conference the next day, but it would be at the Chiangs' country estate, where LBJ and Lady Bird had suddenly been invited. When the press was bussed out to the residence the next day, we found that Horace Busby, who was the spokesman for Lyndon, was hurriedly drawing up a communiqué to be issued between LBJ and Chiang Kai-shek. Everybody, even Madame Chiang, was all smiles. They decided that they would have a picture taken of the entire group of reporters, with, of course, the officials in the foreground and the news people in the background. But just before the picture was taken, Lyndon sings out, "Sarah, why don't you come on up here and stand in the front row with us?" So I did. And something told me that maybe Lyndon had somehow heard just what I had done to arrange this meeting. But I know that his press people never knew a word about it, because I certainly didn't tell them.

Later in the trip, we went to South Vietnam. I was very impressed with Ngo Dinh Diem, the country's president. I knew that he was a devout Catholic who had mass said privately in his own chapel every day. I got the feeling he was a sincere man, dedicated to his country and determined in his fight against the Viet Cong rebels. His brother was helping him in the government, and, since Diem wasn't married, his sister-in-law functioned as a kind of first lady.

Well, I was quite interested to know what he and Lyndon would talk about. I sensed there was a story in the making. The two leaders had their conference late one evening, after all the other reporters had gone back to the hotel to sleep. Lyndon introduced me to Diem and we chatted a few minutes. Then I waited while they went off to talk alone. When the discussions were over, I went back to the hotel and woke up the other reporters to give them a pool report about the conference.

I thought that since I was the only reporter who'd stayed on duty, they would want to hear what happened. But the others felt that the little I was able to find out about what the two had said made for pretty dull news. Some of the reporters and LBJ's press man, George Reedy, made fun of me, saying it was ridiculous to wake up reporters to tell them nothing. But it was my job to do so and I did it, regardless of whether they thought it was exciting or not. They did not realize that by the end of the year we would have 15,000 U.S. military serving in the battle against the Viet Cong. It was only later that the press as a whole grasped what I sensed and realized that Vietnam was going to become the biggest on-going story of the decade.

The trip also took us to India, where we saw the great poverty of the people, groveling in the streets, groping for food, kneeling in the dust. But even among such horrible sights, we saw beautiful things, too. In Agra, we visited the magnificent Taj Mahal. While I was relaxing amidst this beauty, one of the Indian attendants came up, said "You need ice" and put some into my glass with his hands. I thought his hands might not be too clean, and I worried about getting sick. And so I did.

Most all of us had problems with contaminated food during the trip. And we had trouble with the doctor, who was one of Lyndon's buddies. He had come on the trip from the Mayo Clinic, I believe. But when we asked for some help for our maladies, he just said, "I'm through. The trip's nearly over, we're on our way home, my duties are done. I'm not going to attend you."

Not all of Johnson's staff had that kind of attitude. Bob Waldron, a nice man and good friend who we all liked very much, had been brought along to be the escort of Lyndon's secretary Mary Margaret, as well as to help handle the press corps. A Texan from near my home town of Tyler, he was a wonderful dancer and at night, he and Mary Margaret (who would later marry another of Lyndon's staff, Jack Valenti) would often go dancing together. Sometimes we reporters would join them.

One highlight of the trip for me was Pakistan. In Karachi, they assigned a wonderful newspaper woman to me as an aide. The reporters in Pakistan (and in Thailand as well) were very talented and capable. This woman went with me and told me interesting things about her country. We all saw that the people of Pakistan had a great thirst for information, but as good as their reporters were, the country lacked up-to-date communications, especially radio and television. Lyndon suggested that they put television, which was just then coming into the country, in the public squares and let everyone who wanted to gather around to watch and listen. The Vice President was shown a very interesting, very small form of shelter for individuals and families, which they had built as sort of a public housing project in downtown Karachi. And Lyndon said, "We could use some of these in Austin, Texas. We should have a lot of them in the United States for our homeless. It would help."

While we were in Pakistan, LBJ met a camel driver and invited him to come to the United States as his guest. The camel driver did, sometime later, come to Washington and visit Lyndon. He turned out to be very eloquent. Every time he spoke, Americans were astounded at his ability with words and what he had to say. Someone told me that more educated Pakistanis had written all his words for him before he left to visit our country, but I don't think that that was true. I tend to believe that the camel driver was really articulate, with that native eloquence you see in places from Africa to the Arctic.

Lyndon always stopped a day or two before he got home from a trip for his entourage to rest up and have a little vacation. On this trip, we stopped in Bermuda. I knew that, when traveling with Lyndon, I should always be ready to go, ready to move fast. For example, when I went with him and Lady Bird that time to Boston, there was no opportunity to see the wonderful history on display there. So I got up early in the morning and had a taxi drive me out to historic spots around the city. The buildings were closed at that early morning hour, but I went up to them and touched a door or a wall, thinking of the great events that had taken place there. It was the same way in Bermuda. I went out early in the morning to see the places where ships had landed, bringing settlers over from England to America. Off shore, I knew there was a graveyard of ships, some that had sunk back in the days when our country was new. People had died there, trying for a new life in our country. Bermuda was important to those who had wanted to come to the United States, and in the early morning mist, before I had to rush back home with Lyndon, it seemed like a holy place to me.

If there was a holy place for Lyndon Johnson, it was the LBJ Ranch in Texas. It was where he could most fully be all the many versions of himself: the rich Texan who'd clawed his way up from humble, insecure beginnings; the good provider giving the fruits of his efforts to his wife, daughters, brothers and sister; the indulgent sportsman who liked fast cars, boats and planes and good hunting; the generous, informal host who'd call you in to have breakfast sitting on his bed and who made the best steaks I've ever had; as well as the master politician, the great manipulator, the man in the spotlight and, eventually, the idealistic Father of the Great Society and victim of the Vietnam War.

The ranch was an amazing place, and when you were invited to it, there was always a reason: you'd either earned the invitation— or you were about to pay for it. I earned my first invitation by helping Lyndon get one up on Richard Nixon.

In the early 1950s both men were in the Senate. In no small part due to Lyndon Johnson's efforts, the Air Force's Aerospace Medical School was about to be constructed in San Antonio, Texas. I was covering Congress for the *San Antonio Light* when I found out that Senator Richard Nixon had made a deal with an Assistant Secretary of the Air Force to move the school from San Antonio to California. And it was going to be done quietly, and right away, so that no one would know anything about it until it had already happened.

I immediately called Johnson's office, late in the afternoon, and told him that he had better do something about this quick, or he was going to lose the installation. It might even be gone overnight. Well, he didn't believe this. He thought that it was solidly set for San Antonio and didn't think it was necessary to act quickly and look into it in a rush. I insisted. I said, "You've got to. If you don't, by tomorrow morning, you may not have this school." The *San Antonio Light*, very anxious for the economic boost it would provide, had me covering every phase of the site process.

I insisted to Johnson that my information on this was solid, that Nixon was about to get the school for California and that we'd better act quickly if we wanted to keep it in Texas. But Johnson was giving a big party that night at the Mayflower Hotel and had invited a whole bunch of prominent people. He didn't want to be bothered with working late that night. He needed to be at the party early and didn't think this was crucial.

Finally, I got him to agree that he would stay and work on it. I got to the party about 7:30 or 8:00 PM. Johnson finally arrived, later than that. He had made some telephone calls and realized I was right. And then he made some more. He had kept the school in San Antonio, kept Nixon from getting it. He was tired but very happy that he was able to keep it there.

Months later, when I was down in Texas for the dedication of this school, Johnson came over to me and said, "How about comin' out to the ranch for the weekend after the ceremony's over?" I smiled and said, "Well, all right, I'll do that." So I'd earned my first trip to the ranch. In those days, I didn't know Johnson too well. I didn't know whether or not to go, but I went and had a very enjoyable time. And the reason I was invited, I know, was because I had helped keep the Brooks Air Force Medical School in San Antonio, which the people there wanted and needed.

(Johnson and I fought side by side once again for another installation at San Antonio. We wanted and tried to get the new Air Force Academy built in Texas, at the place where many Air Force legends had started: Randolph Air Base. There's almost always heavy competition among Senators and Congressmen for these military bases, and this was one of the biggest. Though we worked very hard to get the Academy, we lost it to Colorado Springs. We were deeply disappointed. As the Alamo shows, Texans don't always win, but they go down fighting hard.)

Though Lyndon never drove in Washington, and was horrified that I dared to, on the ranch it was another thing entirely. Whether he was driving or being driven, every trip he made on the roads that crisscrossed the ranch and the nearby countryside seemed to be at twice the legal speed.

One time when LBJ was Vice President, I was in a following car trying to keep up with him as he sped along. We came over one of the ranch's many hills to find his big Lincoln Continental stopped dead. I still don't know how we managed to avoid crashing into him. There was a giant rattlesnake in the road, and Lyndon was standing over it with a huge rock. He hurled the rock at the snake, but that didn't kill it. So he ordered his bodyguard, Rufus Youngblood, to shoot it. And it took three shots until the snake was dead. To everyone's surprise, I asked if I could have the snake to take home and put on my wall. They hung the snake on the outside of a car but, after Lyndon took the wheel, it blew off and was lost. When we stopped, I shook my finger in Johnson's face and shouted, "You drove 95 miles per hour—so fast my snake fell off." It would have been some trophy. It isn't every Texas rattler that's been hit with a rock by the Vice President of the United States and then shot three times by a Secret Service agent!

If a visitor survived a drive with LBJ, a trip in his boat, kept on another lakeside ranch he owned, could be even more nerve-racking. In comparison, flying with him and Lady Bird in his small plane as he looked for deer in the late afternoon was a pleasure.

Everything on the LBJ Ranch had to be first class, but sometimes his love of good living got pretty strange. Lyndon once took me and a few others out into the forest. All of a sudden we came across a sort of a tower. I thought, "What in the world is this?" When we got out of the car to go into the tower, there was an elevator! We went up in the elevator to the top and there were comfortable chairs arranged looking out a window. There was a refrigerator up there filled with drinks and food, a stove and wall to wall carpeting. This was Lyndon's hunting blind for shooting wild turkey—or anything else that came along. And from up there it was pretty easy, I suppose, to bag one. He told me not to write about it, and I didn't for a long, long time. But it was both amazing and amusing to think of him, the fearless hunter, with a refrigerator handy and plenty to snack on, sitting back in a stuffed chair, looking out the window with a gun in his hand, just waiting for a gobbler to happen by.

I suppose Marianne Means, whose column got started with LBJ's help, summed up the spirit of the LBJ Ranch for most of

America. She had already been down there several times. Then one day when she and some other reporters were speeding along in a caravan of cars and Johnson was telling his stories, she looked over and said, "Mr. President...you're fun!" Well, this line got into all the columns and the magazines. And it was true—up to a point.

You see, the ranch wasn't only used for pleasure. Sometimes it became part of LBJ's political strategy. Once, for example, Lyndon invited the Washington reporters for the *Houston Post* and the *Dallas News* and myself to come down there for the weekend. And we wondered why we were there and what it was all about, because we didn't see much of Lyndon after we got there. We saw the Secret Service people, but they didn't give us much information. Though we didn't hear much from the Vice President, we noticed that he was on the phone almost constantly. We guessed that he was talking to Jack Kennedy in the White House, and we knew that we weren't getting the story. We were cut off from communication with the outside world, kept busy from hour to hour with trips LBJ had thought up for us to go on or things for us to see. Things that would take us away from the telephone and away from the house.

We were very curious about all his conversations with the President. We didn't learn until we returned to Washington early Monday morning that the telephone calls had been about the crisis that was arising over the attendance of James Meredith at the University of Mississippi. This had caused a lot of furor down there, because he was the first Black to be admitted. Johnson was talking to Kennedy about whether they should send troops from Fort Hood over to Mississippi. Fort Hood was just about 50 miles from where we were at the time, so we felt especially stupid for not knowing what was going on. They did send the troops in. They were there by Monday but we were in the dark about the news until after we arrived back in Washington about 2:00 AM. Although we all thought that we'd had a great weekend, when we picked up the morning paper, we found out that we'd been bamboozled out of a story, a big story with repercussions redefining the powers of the presidency. But since a Texas military base was involved, Johnson had wanted to keep the Texas papers from getting wind of the plans.

Everyone seemed to have more information than we did, and we were furious about it. This was supposed to have been an off-the-record trip, but Vernon Louviere of the *Houston Chronicle* was so mad that he decided to write up the whole story of the weekend. He did, and he got fired. Vernon was a fine man, a former President of the National Press Club, and a good reporter. But I don't think he ever got another full time job from that time until his death.

This was the way LBJ managed the press. Because Lyndon had a way of returning favors—and also anything he saw as an attack.

Once, Lyndon showed me a list that he had on his desk. It was the Beatitudes from the Bible. He said, "Sarah, if you're going to feud with somebody, make up to them before nightfall. Never carry a grudge over to the next day. Be sure that you straighten everything out." Well, this was the recommendation made in the Beatitudes, and it had great application to the way business was done in the Senate. There were many serious arguments on the Senate floor, in the offices and even in the corridors over bills and issues. And Lyndon always had his favorites for appointees. He didn't always win, but most of the time he did, because he would do almost anything to twist people's arms until they agreed with him.

One time later on, though, I went to look at his desk, and that list was no longer there. I don't know why. I do know that Lyndon admitted, privately to me, that he had investigated every man he ever had to deal with for a vote in the Senate. He had investigated their private life. He knew what was leading them on, what was motivating them. And this was a very important thing. He used this information often to win votes and to win conformance with his views. Sometimes it was a threat, sometimes not.

Arm twisting aside, LBJ was very fond of most of the Senators, except he did not like Ralph Yarborough of Texas. I happened to have written the very first story about Yarborough in my part of east Texas, back when he was running for Attorney General. Carl Estes, my editor at the *Tyler Morning Telegraph* and *Courier Times* expressed his unhappiness with me for writing too much about Yarborough. Nobody else would pay any attention to him, but I said, "This man is a candidate. I'm going to find out about who he is, what he's doing and I'm going to talk to him." Ralph never forgot that and was always grateful to me.

Some years later, Ralph realized that he had also known my father. As a delegate to the Democratic Convention of 1916, my father had been one of those who held out passionately and strongly for Woodrow Wilson to get the nomination. After the election, my father was named Postmaster for Tyler by President Wilson. Ralph said there was a certain country boy who was attending high school in Tyler who came in from Chandler, fifteen miles away, and sometimes needed to get his mail at odd times. The Postmaster was always nice and gave him special attention. Ralph Yarborough always appreciated the extras that my father, the Postmaster, gave to him as a young man.

Well, LBJ despised Yarborough. Ralph represented many things that Lyndon did not. Ralph was a liberal. Lyndon was much more conservative. Lyndon went along with the big corporations and wealthy friends he had in Texas. Ralph went along with the little people. He had been poor himself—and remembered what it was like to be poor. Ralph was a leader of the common man. It was sad that the two couldn't get along, but it was a question of different viewpoints, personalities and style. And despite what it said in the Beatitudes, Lyndon couldn't always forgive differences.

Lyndon set himself out to be sure that Ralph did not gain influence and power. As Majority Leader, Lyndon had a great deal to do with naming committee assignments. He was determined that he would keep Ralph off the important committees. But he didn't want to come right out and say, "I'm not going to let you have this," when Ralph would come to him in a kindly way for the assignments that he wanted. Lyndon, therefore, would sidestep Ralph. Once, to keep Yarborough from being appointed to an opening on the Senate Appropriations Committee, he steered Senator William Proxmire of Wisconsin, a newcomer who Johnson's cronies disliked as a maverick upstart, into the seat. Despite his colleagues' opinions, Lyndon gave Proxmire his start as a Senate power rather than let Ralph Yarborough get the committee spot.

On another occasion, a rumor was circulated that Yarborough had been paid by certain interests to run for the Senate. This story, which Yarborough swore was false, centered on one particular contributor, fellow Texan Billie Sol Estes, who had supposedly given the Senator $200,000, a large sum, not by today's standards, but quite sizable in the late 1950s. The unproved gossip hurt Yarborough's campaign in Texas and his standing in office and cost him a lot of supporters. Yarborough found out many years later, to his own great certainty, that the rumor was invented in Lyndon Johnson's office in Washington.

The whispers were, unfortunately, all too easy for most people to believe. In politics, relationships that strain ethical boundaries are very common. And at one time in Texas, they seemed to be the rule. There were loads of Texans who came to Washington, and it seemed like almost every one I met was here to ask a favor. Every time I would go into Speaker Sam Rayburn's office, there would be a congregation of visitors. I'd spot a big white hat on a man, sidle up to him and ask if he were from Texas. He would sheepishly admit it and say, "How did you know?" I seldom had to apologize for asking someone not from the Lone Star State. If the Texan told me he was in town "jes' visitin'," I felt sure he was here for something that involved high potential profits, so I checked back on him later and often got a good story.

I had never met this Billie Sol Estes. I only knew he was a lavish spender and frequent dinner host to whole groups of federal employees, especially from the Department of Agriculture. Since I had never been invited to one of these shindigs like a fellow Texan who wrote quite a bit about farming ought to be, my curiosity was aroused. I began inquiries and found out he had supposedly told one of his dinner crowds that he was avoiding crossing my path on purpose. Finally, Sally and I were going to a Texas function at the Shoreham Hotel during the 1961 Inaugural festivities. It was a command performance for Texans, and the elusive Mr. Estes would be there. But heavy snow on the ground got worse. Traffic on certain streets was tied up for hours, and it was impossible for us and many others to get to the event. I was sorry that I had missed Billie Sol once again. But later on, I was glad I never met him.

It came about that Billie Sol finally bought one dinner party too many. It included 43 of the top officials who headed key agencies in the Department of Agriculture, from the Secretary's office on down. When news of the lavish party got out, one departmental office-holder revealed that Billie Sol was allegedly trading favors to cover up some highly questionable business practices centered on an ambitious if improbable attempt to control the world's entire supply of grain. This incredible story resulted in nationwide publicity, further exposure, a hearing and a subsequent prison term. But not before two women who had helped bring Billie Sol down were practically destroyed themselves by widening circles of disaster surrounding his fall.

A Pecos Independent reporter, Marge Carpenter (no relation to Les and Liz), discovered that the local fertilizer tanks which Billie Sol had used for collateral on millions of dollars of credit did not, in fact, exist. When the Estes empire went under, the Pecos economy suffered greatly, she lost her job and her husband, a local banker, committed suicide. She felt forced to leave town with her three children.

Another good woman, who worked in the records office of the Department of Agriculture, was nearly sent by the federal government to a psychiatric institution, perhaps for life. When the Estes case broke, she and her male boss became concerned about the Billie Sol Estes file, which contained letters and records that might prove embarrassing to some departmental officials. When the boss was suddenly transferred to another position and she found a staff member trying to remove the file from the office, the clerk stood in the doorway. Suspecting that he and others were trying to remove their names from the file by destroying or altering the evidence, she refused to surrender the file. Eventually, she was dragged forcibly from the building by guards and, with no evidence but complaints from the employees involved, was sent to a psychiatric hospital for observation.

My friend and news source, the late Grace Johnson, a former Senate employee and constant Congress watcher, came to my home on a Saturday night to tell me that the clerk was going to be "railroaded" on Monday in a closed trial, without witnesses or audience, which would put her away in a mental institution. Grace had found the home number of the temporary "acting" health officer who would hear the case. She wanted me to call him and make it clear that the press would be watching what happened, ready to hold him accountable for his conduct. I told her it was unethical to use my position to threaten someone or exert power over events. By the time Grace's arguments had convinced me, it was nearly midnight. But when I called, the health officer sounded surprisingly polite and concerned. He promised he would take our information into consideration and act judiciously.

On Monday, Agriculture Secretary Orville Freemen called a press conference. As the conference was delayed again and again, word went around that we would get an announcement of the clerk's being committed. Instead, the Secretary finally appeared and said next to nothing. I rushed out to check on the hearing and found that the clerk—who I never had the chance to meet—had been released into the custody of her sister, to go home to North Carolina. I have since found that, from time to time, women clerks in other government departments have been subject to similar experiences. Not all were so lucky as to keep their freedom.

Though Billie Sol claimed that he was close to practically every influential Democrat in Washington, from President Kennedy to House Speaker John W. McCormack, no one, not even Ralph Yarborough, suffered from the scandal the way the two women had. Lyndon Johnson said he had never even heard of Billie Sol Estes until the man made front page news. In fact, sometime later, during a party at the house which had been turned over to the Vice President's use by Texas-born society grande dame Pearl Mesta ("The Hostess With the Mostest"), I heard Lyndon go on about this "Willie Joe" fella who'd gotten himself into so much trouble. For once, LBJ's perfect memory appeared to fail him.

Aside from the call I made at Grace Johnson's request, I had little involvement in the first government scandal of the 1960s. But a year later, I found myself investigating accusations about a man who both LBJ and I knew well. Even if I had known my story would bring about a serious break with Lyndon, I would still have written it. After all, I knew from the beginning that looking into the financial dealings of Lyndon's protégé, Bobby Baker, was like stirring up a hornet's nest.

When Shakespeare said, "Politics makes strange bedfellows," he could have been talking about Washington. But while most every politician has alliances that could be questioned by a partisan opponent, relatively few actually cross the ethical line. Lyndon, for example, had a certain understanding, which had existed since he had come to Congress, with a Texas engineering firm called Brown and Root. I knew that Johnson relied on them from time to time for money. I was told that he had a blank check with them; he could call on them for any amount if he were in a bind, and they would send it. They helped him greatly in financing his campaigns. And during a long relationship that saw Lyndon go from House to Senate to

White House, Brown and Root obtained a fair number of profitable contracts, especially overseas, and became a world-famous firm.

Lyndon Johnson's political experience made him a natural mentor for Bobby Baker to choose. Bobby had come up from South Carolina as a Senate page years before. From that job, he graduated up to bigger things. He made himself of great value to various and sundry Senators by running errands and doing chores for them. Eventually, he came to the attention of Lyndon Johnson, who always appreciated the right kind of ambition and drive. The Majority Leader taught him the ropes. With Johnson as one of his supporters, Bobby Baker finally became the Secretary to the Senate Majority Party, an influential position that had a lot to do with scheduling and keeping track of votes. People knew he was so close to Lyndon that he could do things in Lyndon's name.

I got to know Bobby Baker fairly well. He was a friendly source of information when I needed the Democratic Party's view of what was going on in the Senate. But one day a newspaper story about him made me wonder just how well I knew him. James McCartney, a reporter for the *Chicago Daily News*, had come across Baker talking to a group of tourists who were visiting the Capital. He listened in and was shocked by what Bobby was saying. Bobby seemed to be boasting that he had a large handful of Senators in his pocket, that he could count on their vote at any time and so have a great influence on legislation.

Now, counting votes is a legitimate part of politics about which a shrewd operator like Lyndon Johnson might naturally have given Bobby Baker tips. It was a valuable skill which Baker was known to have used to the advantage of some, especially Senator Bob Kerr of Oklahoma, and to the disadvantage of others, like Senator John Kennedy of Massachusetts. It was a matter of knowing exactly what the Senators were doing and thinking at all times, so the leadership knew when to take a vote and what to expect before the vote came through. But what McCartney overheard was something different: Baker was saying he could actually control these Senators' votes.

So I began to check around and came across a number of troubling reports. Tales of how Baker had built a private business empire spreading from Texas to Michigan and Puerto Rico to Hawaii right from his office on the second floor of the Capitol. Speculation about stacks of $100 bills seen lying on Bobby Baker's Senate office desk. Stories of rampant influence peddling on terms of legislation.

There were also stories about the resort hotel Baker ran over on the Eastern Shore of Maryland, at Ocean City. Called the Carousel, it was quite a large establishment. Bobby had a party inaugurating the hotel which was attended by Cabinet officers, leading Senators, corporate industrialists and the cream of the Washington social scene. The Johnsons, Perle Mesta and even the District Police Chief came over on a special chartered bus. The Carousel was soon a popular getaway among government officials. It was said there were some very interesting connections between Baker's running the Carousel and his running the Democratic side of the Senate.

There were more and more questions raised about Bobby Baker. Finally, a man named Ralph Hill sued Baker. And when he took this case into court, that meant that I, who had been watching the strange goings-on in Bobby Baker's office, could now write about them. Up until that time I didn't have enough documentation, enough proof. Now there would be something on the record.

I went to the court and read the briefs that Ralph Hill had filed against Baker. Then I went to see Ralph Hill himself. The first thing Hill said was, "Where are the other reporters? How come you're the only one here?" I said that I had enough background on this thing to know that there was something hot going on: "I want the whole story. I don't care where the other reporters are or what they know." So he gave me the whole story. He had tapes, he had documents, he had everything. He confirmed many of the whispers I had heard and alerted me to shocking new angles. I knew I had to get this story to the people.

It seems that Bobby had gotten Ralph Hill's vending machine business a contract with a large candy manufacturer which would allow him to sell the candy in a number of defense plants. But when Bobby said, "Now, I want a payback, a commission for getting you that contract," Ralph Hill became furious. He and Bobby had been friends, but he thought that this was the time to stop. So he took Baker to court over the kickback. But this, Hill said, was the small stuff. Ralph was prepared to allege in court that Baker was telling bidders he could get government defense contracts for them. I'd often heard it said that Bobby Baker could predict just which company would be awarded the next big contract. This put a whole new spin on that kind of speculation.

Using my conversation with Ralph Hill and information from his tapes, I wrote the story about Baker's outside business career and then tried to get it out. I wanted to get it to a syndicate or at least a bigger paper than I had. I also sent it to my papers in Texas, even though I was quite sure that most of those editors wouldn't print it. And sure enough, they wouldn't. Keeping to his arrangement, Harry Provence of the Waco paper sent the copy that I had sent to him back to Washington, for Lyndon Johnson to see what I'd written. As a result, Johnson had Walter Jenkins, his old Senate aide, call me back downtown to the Capitol. I had just gotten home. Seven miles from the Capitol, and they insisted that I come on back.

Jenkins asked me to drop the story. I was told that Johnson had said, "I know that Sarah's been trying to peddle this story all weekend. I've heard from one paper after another that she's been trying to sell it to." Well, I had been trying to do just that. I tried to put it with the *Chicago Tribune*, and they said no: "It must not be a story, or our man, Willard Edwards, would have had it." I took it to the *Des Moines Register* and *Tribune*, and they said no: "It must not be a story, or our man, Clark Mollenhoff, would have had it." The AP and UPI paid no attention to it and wouldn't for weeks.

When Walter Jenkins ordered me to hold back the story, I told him, "You can't stop it. It's too big. It's bigger than you are, and you don't know it." And since he was a Catholic, I told him about something else: there were allegations of abortions involved. Abortions given to young, beautiful girls working at the Senate who Bobby had sent to Democratic fund-raising parties. Abortions resulting from the girls' involvement with major Democratic donors at these parties. Abortions prearranged for at a house in Maryland. The donors paid $2,500 for each abortion, I had been told, but the girls only got $500 of it. The rest went into somebody's pockets.

I told Walter about the abortions because I knew it would shock him and maybe convince him that the story needed to be heard. But I hadn't put it in my story. My story stuck to the alleged sales of contracts and influence and to legislation supposedly being written the way Bobby Baker wanted it. What had particularly irked Lyndon about my story was that I had called Bobby Baker his "protégé."

Walter said that Johnson had barely even seen Baker since he was Vice President. So how could Baker be Lyndon's "protégé"? Well, that's exactly what Bobby Baker had been—for years. Johnson had tried to distance himself from Baker after he became Vice President, because he knew that the Kennedys despised Bobby Baker and didn't want any part of him. The President and Attorney General wanted to find out things about Baker so that they could get him out of his position at the Senate. Lyndon was afraid that if my story got out, saying that Bobby Baker was in trouble and reminding folks how close he'd once been to Lyndon Johnson, that President Kennedy would be furious with the Vice President and call him on the carpet. In fact, I think that's what happened!

Because, despite what they had said, my story did land on the front pages of the *Des Moines Register* and *Tribune* the next morning and South Carolina's *Charleston Courier* the morning after that. It was carried across the nation by the North American Newspaper Alliance (NANA), a small but powerful syndicate up in New York who I went to now and then when I had a story that was of interest to more than my regular local newspaper clients. The story was a good story, and I'm glad that it got out.

Even after I'd broken the story, it seemed like no other reporters would touch it. It was amazing to see their reactions. The *New York Herald-Tribune* Washington correspondent, Andy Glass, who is still covering Washington for other papers today, told me he wasn't going to write this story because Bobby Baker had given him so many leads. Though I'd learned about Ralph Hill's lawsuit from a little article in the *Washington Post*, that paper didn't follow up on it until much later. The *New York Times* waited six weeks before they started covering the story. Then they had to, because by then, it was in the news nearly every day.

When Republican Senator John Williams of Delaware got wind of my story, he went to Senator Mike Mansfield, the new Majority Leader since Johnson had become Vice President. Williams told Mansfield of the alleged maneuverings of Bobby Baker involving legislation and contracts. Williams said there would have to be a Senate investigation or else he'd tell everything that was being said to the public.

The Democrats had planned to pay no attention to this suit

that was filed against Baker. They had already overlooked what Baker was allegedly doing for years. But when Williams came to Mansfield, Mansfield knew he had to appoint a committee to hold hearings. Mansfield issued a statement saying that Baker had decided to leave his job, and that his resignation had been accepted with regrets. Then the Senate began an investigation on Baker that would go on for weeks. But since it was such an embarrassment to the Democrats, and they were the majority party, the hearings were very cautious and wound up sweeping almost everything under the rug. I am convinced that if the Democrats hadn't been able to get away with this, the Republicans involved in Watergate would never had tried the cover-up that led to Nixon's resignation.

It wasn't until Bobby Baker was called up on an income tax case that he finally went to court. He was indicted on the tax charge, convicted and sent to Allenwood, a "country-club" prison up in Pennsylvania, for a short while. He had several women who remained devoted to him through all this. One was his wife, Dotty, and there were others who'd worked in the Senate who helped him greatly when he was in power and continued to fight for his reputation. Bobby, who's had a very colorful life, still lives in Washington today. Ralph Hill, whose suit began it all, became my close friend.

It is ironic that once the hearings began, I had to let other reporters write the story. Though I had been covering it as best I could, I had so much else to do as a one-woman news bureau that I could not sit in on the hearings. I had other stories I had to write. I continued to turn in some exclusives to the North American Newspaper Alliance, including one about the federal grand jury investigating the alleged abortion ring. But other reporters, who sat in every day, covered the Baker hearings thoroughly. And although I had been the first with the story, I didn't get the credit. The others got acclaim for their coverage, even winning a journalism prize which NANA had nominated me for. The winners did a good job, but it still hurt to see them get the prestige. After all, I had initiated the story. It was my scoop.

What I did win, it turned out, was a real and abiding rift with Lyndon Johnson. He kept avoiding my questions at press conferences. When I forced him to take one by being persistent, he would dismiss it with a simple "Yes" or "No," as if the subject wasn't even worth his time. At one conference, he denounced me in front of all the other reporters: "McClendon, if you keep asking so many questions, we won't invite you back to these things"—and I was the one who had suggested he have the conference in the first place! Seth Kantor, who wrote for the Scripps-Howard chain, said, "We were horrified at the way he spoke to you," and later wrote about it several times. That was in October of 1963. One month later, he was President.

My insisting on calling Bobby Baker "Johnson's protégé" was apparently the "no" that broke the camel's back. Just days after becoming President, Lyndon, who had once told a party crowd that he couldn't do his job without me, began to say, "I can run the country or take questions from Sarah McClendon but not both." When I stopped him in the corridor of the Capitol to ask a question, he coldly told me that from now on I was to address him only as "Mr. President."

During one informal press conference in the Oval Office, where everyone present was asking several questions, the President cut me off by telling me to "stay after school." When all the other reporters had left and I was standing alone in front of him, he launched into me with a furious lecture: "Why do you keep tryin' to ask so many questions? You're takin' up time from the wire services and the other reporters! You're little compared to them!" I protested that I had just as much right to ask questions as anyone. I finally blurted out, "If that's the way you treat old friends..." and walked out of the Oval Office. There were tears in my eyes that I didn't want LBJ to see. I was taken off the list of those who were to have access to him at Texas parties.

President Johnson's reluctance to call on me at his press conferences became pretty obvious. At a reception at the American Newswomen's Club, a dear friend of mine, Representative Melvin Laird of Wisconsin, offered a tongue-in-cheek solution. He gave me a little flashlight with a whistle on one end. He said, "From now on, Sarah, all you need to do is blow this whistle at Lyndon's press conference, and I know he'll give you immediate recognition!" Everyone, including me, thought that was a wonderful joke. As a Republican, Mel knew how to get a dig in at a Democratic President. And don't think I wasn't ever tempted to use that whistle.

Lyndon would still sometimes listen if I sent him a memorandum, as I did about improving the awful housing conditions of black people living in slums of the District of Columbia. He'd let me know by stopping when he saw me and saying something like, "Your memo was on my reading table last night." But a lot of things stopped. I stopped being invited to social events at the White House or even parties at private homes that Lyndon was going to attend. Hosts were told it would be an affront to the President if I was there as a guest. Fortunately, my daughter continued to be in favor and was able to see her best friend, Lynda Bird, at parties in the Executive Mansion. But Sally, too, was to feel the effects of my "punishment," when, with no explanation, she was not invited to Lynda's White House wedding.

Lyndon started putting out stories that made me look silly. He said I jumped out from behind trees trying to get him to take my questions. And during a speech at the National Press Club, he changed the day at the hospital when he showed how much weight he had lost into the ridiculous story that I had made him, ten years later, show off his scar after an operation, which had become a famous photograph. Even though Liz Carpenter, who was still Lady Bird's secretary, admitted to me that she had simply made it up, people laughed and believed it. Some still do today.

Lyndon could banish me from the inner circle, but the Bobby Baker affair continued to haunt him. When Baker was finally facing his day in court, the common wisdom was that his case would eventually wind up in the U.S. Supreme Court. LBJ wanted someone he could trust to head up the Justice Department. He selected Ramsey Clark, from a Texas family he knew well, as his new Attorney General. This meant that Ramsey's father, Tom Clark, who was an associate justice of the Supreme Court and Lyndon's old friend, had to step down, giving President Johnson a space to fill. He and Thurgood Marshall had long been very friendly, and Johnson, it was said, wanted very much to have this particular close, personal friend on the high court. So he named Thurgood, who became the first Black man to ever serve as an associate Supreme Court justice. Most people thought that this appointment concerned largely race relations and Johnson's desire to have the kind of representation in the court that would help avoid racial strife— which Thurgood Marshall certainly did. But there was another thought behind the appointment. I knew that Johnson wanted very much to have this particular friend on the bench if and when the Bobby Baker case ever came before the highest court in the land.

I like to think that Lyndon missed me as a friend. He had always needed friends around him—and family, too. In Lady Bird, he had a devoted and loyal partner. His sister Josefa and his brother Sam adored him and wanted to help him in every way. They wanted to work with him in Washington. But Johnson, for some reason, hesitated to put them on his staff. They would have been a great help, had he done so. We never did quite understand why he didn't. But Josefa did a lot of clipping for him and Sam did a lot of planning of speeches and thinking of things for Johnson to do and say to enhance his image. Finally, Johnson did give Sam a job with the Senate Policy Committee, where he gave me and other reporters wonderful, well-thought-out stories about his brother, the President.

Sam had had his ups and downs, personally and otherwise. Finally, when Sam had gotten to the point where he was drinking a great deal, he fell and hurt himself quite badly. He never fully got over the broken bones. His disability added to his unhappiness. Lyndon brought him to stay at the White House and he virtually lived there, upstairs. A lot of people didn't even know he was there. But he stayed for a long, long period while Johnson was President. Lyndon may have felt that he had to keep him there to keep his eye on him and to keep him out of harm's way because every now and then Sam was still inclined to get into some trouble, as a result, mainly, of his continued drinking.

I suspect the way he hid his brother on the White House upper floors gives us an important clue about Lyndon. He was a man who wasn't above anything to get what he thought was right, but he was afraid of appearances. He was a man who changed society for the better by bringing "The Johnson Treatment"—that unwillingness to take "no" for an answer—to our country's serious problems with civil rights, education and sexual equality in the workplace. But that same "can-do" attitude, plus a typical Texas determination to seem strong, led him into an unpopular war. He got the office he had worked so hard to get—but got it in a way he never wanted to. He sometimes pushed the media—and the nation—to frustration, but he really just wanted to be loved.

In the summer of 1967, race riots took place in inner cities across the nation and hippies gathered in ever greater masses to protest the war. Even in my exile, I could sense Lyndon's deep worry over the country's woes. When he took a question from me at an August press conference, I used the opportunity to open a door for him to share the burden of Vietnam with his opponents in Congress, putting them in the position of approving the war or pulling out.

I asked, "Mr. President, the Constitution does not give you the right to carry on this war without permission from Congress. I am sure that you realize that more than anybody. In view of this misunderstanding that has occurred about the Gulf of Tonkin resolution, why don't you clear up this matter with your critics by calling for a new vote in Congress on this matter?"

His lengthy reply, which went on for several minutes, seemed defensive, defeated and deeply pessimistic. It could have applied to many aspects of his long, combative career. As he spoke of similar crises weathered by Truman and Eisenhower, I felt, in some way, he was trying to send a message to me about our shared past. His answer, in part, included these words:

> "Sarah, you don't always clear up your critics that easily. They will be with you before the vote, and they will be with you after the vote. That is the way it is in a democratic society...

> We stated then, and we repeat now, we did not think the resolution was necessary to do what we did and what we are doing. But we thought it was desirable. We thought if we were going to ask them to stay the whole route, and if we expected them to be there on the landing, we ought to ask them to be there on the takeoff...

> We think we are well within the rights of what the Congress said in its resolution. The remedy is there if we have acted unwisely or improperly. It is going to be tougher as it gets along. The longer the fighting lasts, the more sacrifice is required in men and materiel; the more dissent, the more difficult it is going to be."

Seven months later, Lyndon Baines Johnson would startle the nation by announcing that he would not run for re-election.

He was a man of accomplishment, and I was always sorry that we were denied all he might have done for us if he hadn't been driven from office by a feeling that he couldn't please the people. Despite how much we fought and the things he did to me, I miss him—and his wonderful stories. He was my friend. Almost like a brother.

CHICAGO, ILLINOIS, 1931;

TYLER, TEXAS, 1931-1939:

Respect is a precious thing. It makes you feel important, acknowledged, accepted. It not only gives you a reason to do your best but the strength to do it. In some ways, it is even more important than love.

Respect is a funny thing. It has little to do with how worthy you really are; it depends on what someone else thinks about you. What passes for it can be based on fear, envy, idolizing or simply believing a pack of lies. Many "respected" individuals aren't worth the air they breathe—and many who get little or no approval are better people than those who judge or ignore them. If your self-esteem is strong enough, it shouldn't matter how others feel. But it does. It certainly does.

Respect is a thing that is hard to get and hard to keep. I've fought for it practically every day of my life. My weapons are my intelligence, my writing skills, my ethics, and the way I persist at finding the truth and insisting on telling it. I feel respect when someone knows what I can do and trusts me to do it. I feel it when someone treats my facts as accurate and my opinions as worth considering. I feel it when someone really listens.

With the confidence born of youth and inexperience, I left the University of Missouri convinced I'd quickly earn respect as a reporter on some major newspaper. Instead of going home to Texas, I went north to Chicago with a girlfriend and her boyfriend to see a young man I had been dating. He had gotten out of school ahead of me and was working up there. It was supposed to be a lark, but, for me, it had another purpose: I was going to land a job on one of the "Second City"'s big dailies.

Socially and career-wise, the trip was a disaster. Completely intimidated by the noise, bustle and Depression-era squalor of the biggest city I'd ever seen—and by my young man's excuses that kept him from seeing me—I wound up spending almost the whole time in my hotel room. The more I thought about asking for a job, the more scared I became. This was very different from school. I was just a country girl; I wouldn't be able to adjust and they would fire me at once. I had a terrible inferiority complex. I wound up wiring my brother who sent me the money to get home. I returned to Tyler convinced I just didn't have the nerve to ever get a job in journalism.

After two miserable weeks of hiding my fear and despair, I ran off the tennis court in the midst of a Sunday afternoon game and made a "now-or-never" phone call to Carl Estes, the editor and publisher of my hometown's two papers, the Tyler Morning Telegraph and the Tyler Courier-Times. He told me to come in the next morning for a special assignment. I had a job—at $10 a week. It wasn't Chicago—or even Dallas—but I would be writing for not one but two newspapers. I would stay in Tyler eight more years.

My special assignment, it turned out, was to get a real hospital for Tyler. I had campaigned at college for higher milk standards in Columbia, Missouri; now I was to use those skills to help convince those who counted that Tyler needed more hospital beds to attract the commerce and economic growth that comes from a major health center. As it was, we had a little place with about a dozen beds for a city of forty or fifty thousand. And one of the world's great oil booms had just occurred within thirty miles of us. The fact we needed a hospital to care for all the workers injured in the oil fields and in the snarl of traffic going to and from them seemed, somehow, secondary, at least in Carl's strategy for getting the hospital built.

Carl Estes was a clever, hard-nosed, hard-working newspaper man who had come to town in a battered old Ford, gotten a job with the local papers and proceeded to marry their owner, Sarah Butler. He knew the way to get things done was to play to the interests of the influential upper crust of our once sleepy but now suddenly bustling, oil-rich town. And he knew that, as a native daughter, I knew the place—and its inhabitants—well enough to give him the ammunition he needed for his editorials.

I got fired the first week. As I began to find out what it would take to build a hospital, and who was for it and who was against it, I uncovered a story some local bigwig didn't want written. A complaint was made, and Sarah Butler had Carl fire me. Though he rehired me the next day, I had learned an important lesson: there are always forces at work to keep reporters from telling the whole truth. I never liked the fact that Carl sometimes killed stories if, for instance, a banker would call to ask him to. Or that Tyler had bankers who, because of their position and their friendships, felt they had a right to make that call. But even on big-city newspapers, this kind of pressure is ever-present.

I eventually learned that there are ways to get around the situation where an editor will not print a story—including the fact that a story doesn't always need to be printed to make a difference. Once I received a set of pictures showing how some prisoners in the Tyler jail were being tortured by a sadistic guard who was burning their hands and arms with cigarettes. The sheriff's office wanted the affair kept quiet, and newspapers would not run the pictures. So I bypassed all the locals and got the pictures to a visiting jail inspector for the U.S. Bureau of Prisons. The town's facilities depended on the money they got for holding federal prisoners before they could be transported to places like Alcatraz. So when the inspector refused to allow the local jail to hold federal prisoners until the torture was stopped, things got better fast.

Which is not to say that the Feds were always the good guys. During my time in Tyler, I reported how a man was convicted of bank robbery without being represented by counsel at his trial. He later used this to get himself out of Alcatraz. He studied law and hand printed up a brief which won himself another hearing. The U.S. District Attorney who was at fault for not getting the prisoner a lawyer would have to go to California and defend his actions. One of his friends, another lawyer, offered me a fur coat if I would write to the new judge and say I had made a mistake in my story. I said no deal, of course—and did not get a fur coat until years later when I bought my own.

There were many other lessons I learned in my years as a Tyler newspaper woman that have applied to almost every other editor or publisher I've worked for. One bitter truth was that just because I was a woman, I would always be expected to write a lot of society coverage and other drivel that editors called "women's stories." I never minded hard work or long hours, but to waste time on articles that must have been as boring to the readers as they were to me was infuriating. As The Association for Women Journalists pointed out in their clever invitation to a 1996 banquet in Dallas at which I was guest speaker, "When women invaded the news room, full battle dress included hats and gloves...(For) women who launched their careers at (that) time...the hats on their heads got more attention than the brains inside them."

My strategy against this discrimination was to work even harder at writing the kind of stories I would like to read. I slogged all night through the river bottoms with a photographer, Kenneth Gunn, looking for a rapist, who, perhaps luckily, we never did find. I attended a "men only" barbecue for 400, the first stag affair where I ever broke the line, but certainly not the last. I went undercover to visit two overall-wearing, reporter-hating farmers who had just become millionaires when oil was discovered on their land. I visited the notorious Ironhead Cafe near Arp, Texas in disguise to get to know its owner (and reputed "madam") "Ma" Daugherty. Things went all right until my cousin, Ma's attorney, showed up and said, "Hello, Sarah." I got out of there before they could use the iron chain from which the establishment got its name on the side of my head.

I risked my life more than once to get a story. Hoping to get an interview with a prisoner at the El Reno, Oklahoma federal prison, I asked to be deputized as the temporary U.S. Marshall needed to accompany a woman drug addict who was being sent there. I refused the offer of a revolver, since I didn't know how to shoot and perhaps the prisoner did. We rode up in the guards' section of a prison car filled with 125 men. Along the way, we made a stop for a doctor to come on board and give the addicts shots of drugs to keep them quiet for the night. When I looked into the doctor's eyes, I realized he was an addict, too. My prisoner had fallen into drugs as a teenaged gang member and had become a prostitute to feed her $600-a-day habit. When we stopped again to change engines, I walked outside with her. She had the shakes and needed another shot badly. When she moved toward a moving train engine, I got between her and the tracks, never realizing that she could have just as easily pushed me as thrown herself in front of the train. I got her to El Reno in one piece, but they wouldn't let me see the prisoner I had wanted to interview.

My fight for respect from Carl Estes was a never-ending battle. He was, like so many of the men in my life, a great joy, a great help and a great frustration. Carl called me "Mac" and relied on me, the one woman journalist on his staff, more than anyone except Floyd Aten, Jr., a fine reporter whom he considered his ace. I worked daily shifts on both papers to prove how efficient I could be. For my $10 a week, I would sometimes write most of the day's paper by myself. To earn a living wage, I also phoned in stories of national interest to the International News Service in Dallas and a few other papers. But no matter how good I got, there was always the society news to write and a certain patronizing tone to my relationship with Carl. Even after the day I saved his life.

An itinerant preacher had come to town and started a series of sermons on the courthouse lawn. When he began discussing some of our prominent citizens by name, it created quite a stir. Those being mentioned pressured Carl into writing an editorial criticizing the preacher profoundly. The preacher vowed to "see" the editor about this and marched with flailing fists into the newspaper office. All the men in the office fled, leaving me alone with the two fighters. The preacher had Carl pinned to the floor and was dragging his head toward a pipe that had been uncovered when a desk was overturned. I thought Carl's head was going to be bashed in, so I grabbed the only thing I could, a desk telephone, and brought it down hard on the preacher's head. I knocked him cold and stopped the fight. Carl was very grateful—but still the same old Carl. As for me, I shied away from mentioning it for some time because I felt that the folk in Tyler would think my actions had been "unladylike."

The day I think I finally realized that it didn't matter how much Carl Estes respected me as long as I respected myself was March 17, 1937. Feeling a sense of accomplishment because the new Mother Frances Hospital that I had fought so long and hard to have built was finally ready, I decided to slip away for an afternoon visit to the beauty parlor to look good for the next day's opening ceremonies. But when I returned to the office, it was clear that something was terribly wrong.

Everyone was just standing there, stunned. A public school at New London, near Arp, eighteen miles away, had blown up. It had happened five minutes before the end of the school day.

I grabbed my photographer (and, since I did not yet drive, chauffeur), Kenneth Gunn, and we raced to the scene. Somehow, we were the first reporters on the scene. It was like a vision from the end of the world. Most of the school had, literally, vanished, leaving a rubble-littered crater to show where it had been. I found one man walking, dazed, among hundreds of bodies, mostly children, covering the ground. He managed to tell me that he was the Assistant Superintendent and what little else he could. I called my office in Tyler and the International News Service in Dallas just before the telephones went out. No one could phone in or out for hours. It was my first big scoop—but as painful a story as I have ever covered. It turned out that 282 children and 14 teachers had been killed. In only one classroom did every child survive, though all 22 of them were injured. In almost every other classroom, no one made it through the blast alive.

After telephoning out my story, I simply pitched in. I rode into town with some of the injured, sitting on the floor of the back of a truck, taking them to the new hospital. Luckily, the Catholic nuns who had agreed to run the hospital were prepared to open it a day early. When I returned to New London, the town had begun to fill with helpful citizens, doctors and nurses, and newsmen from Dallas and Houston. One was a man I was seeing, Bill Gardner, a reporter for the Houston Post I had first met when he worked in Tyler. Volunteers were digging through the rubble and tearing down the ruins of the surviving wing to get to the basement, where there might be more survivors.

All through the night, more people arrived to help, including any available federal agents from the regional offices. Among them was J.W. Milam, with whom I'd had a secretive affair for almost a year. But there was no awkwardness in having two of my boyfriends on the scene. Finding the remains of a 12-year-old with her bones stripped as clean of flesh as if she had been boiled in water made everything else seem petty. We did not stop to eat. A swig of whisky which someone offered was all I needed to settle my stomach and keep up my energy.

My saddest memory of that long night in Hell is of the parents who did not know if their children were dead or alive. Unable to find their sons and daughters, they couldn't know if they were among the unidentifiable bodies or had been picked up, dead or alive, by one of the many ambulances that had arrived from other cities and taken victims to hospitals and funeral homes throughout the area. They wandered like lost souls, asking questions no one could answer.

In a very real way, that story marked my coming of age as a reporter. I had my first major news scoop. I even learned that newspapers in London, England had telephoned for information about the disaster in their Texas namesake town and that my editors had pictured the horrifying scene in my words. And I was about to see how coverage that makes the news matter to the readers—the kind of stories I've always tried to write—can also help bring about positive action, not just at a local but a national level.

For I was to cover the hearings held to try to explain how this could happen. Ironically, the explosion was a horrible byproduct of New London's civic pride and the spirit of cooperation the town had gotten from the neighboring oil businesses. New London, which had been dirt poor before oil had been discovered, had not had adequate school facilities to accommodate the large numbers of people who had suddenly moved into the area. So the oil companies had not only put up money for fine new brick buildings but had tapped into the gas pipelines to provide them with free heat. The wrong combination of air and gas had led to the explosion. The one good thing that came out of this disaster was the campaign initiated by the National Junior Chambers of Commerce which led to putting an odorant into gas so that leaks can be smelled. Thousands of lives have been saved because escaping gas is now easily detectable. I know I am especially alert to that warning aroma whether in my home or in public places. And I like to think my stories helped put it there.

Eventually, Carl Estes and Sarah Butler were divorced and Carl moved on to another paper in another town. My new editor succumbed to pressure from some groups that didn't like my reporting and fired me. Both the bankers and the illegal oil producers took credit, I understand. Rather than face the agony of job hunting (Chicago all over again, even though I was seven years older and now knew just how well I wrote), I started my first one-woman news service. After eighteen months covering east Texas for papers throughout the state (and even an Atlanta trade journal concerned with, of all things, the shoe business), I was offered a staff position on the Beaumont Enterprise. I took it. I love it when they come to me.

It feels like respect.

LARGE IN MY MEMORIES Built around 1876, the McClendon House in Tyler, Texas, is where I was born and raised. It's now a historic monument. *I'm* still a work in progress.

Collection of Sarah McClendon

FAMILY VALUES (Top) My parents with my oldest brother, Whitaker. (Below) Sister Patience lives up to her name, tending, left to right, younger brothers Frank and Robert and the baby of the family—me. (The rest of my large, lively family, not pictured, includes brothers Charles and Sidney and sisters Annie Bonner and Martha.)

LITERARY LESSONS (Left) As Touchstone in a Tyler Junior College production of *As You Like It*, I learned that "The little foolery that wise men have makes a great show."

Collection of Sarah McClendon

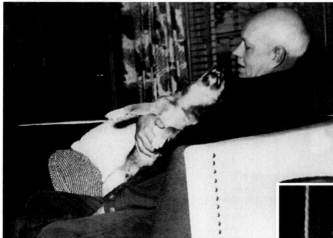

THREE EARLY INFLUENCES (Top) These columns at the University of Missouri symbolize age, strength and continued knowledge for students at the Journalism School, in the distance, which I attended 1929-1931.

(Center) Carl Estes, my first newspaper boss, taught me to crusade in the 1930s—at $10 a week.

(Right) I watched two brothers go off to World War I and gained a lifelong respect for the military. My favorite, Charles, was a transportation officer in Europe.

Collection of Sarah McClendon

DISASTER IN NEW LONDON
When the New London School was demolished in a natural gas explosion in March 1937, I was the only reporter who got the story out before the phone lines went down. My first nation-wide scoop was not a happy one: 296 died, almost all of them children.

Courtesy of *The Tyler Courier-Times*

The Tyler Courier-Times

COMBINED DAILY CIRCULATION 13,500 · East Texas' Greatest Newspaper · Leading in Advertising Circulation · For 19 Years The Courier-Times Has Set the Pace for East Texas Journalism · SIXTIETH YEAR ★ ASSOCIATED PRESS ★ TYLER, TEXAS, FRIDAY, MARCH 19, 1937 ★ UNITED PRESS ★ NEA ★ CENTRAL PRESS

425 BODIES TAKEN FROM LONDON BLAST DEBRIS

Workmen Dig Away in Debris Hunting for Bodies as Rain Drenches Scene of Explosion

41,300 BARREL INCREASE SEEN IN OIL DEMAND

April Needs Placed At 1,297,900 Barrels, Slightly Above Figures For Present Month

Austin, March 19 (AP).—The state railroad commission reported to-day, at its monthly hearing the federal bureau of mines estimated market demand for Texas crude oil in April at 1,297,900 barrels daily.

The estimate was 41,300 barrels more than that for March but about 100,000 barrels less than the state allowable at the start of the current month, which was 1,398,514.

C. V. Terrell, commission chairman, said the allowable today and 1,430,969 barrels, having increased normally since March 1 due to new completions and adjustments.

Several days ago Terrell said national production and storage figures indicated that Texas allowable apparently was about 80,000 barrels too high, and some operators took the statement as, fore-casting a probable reduction in an order to be issued soon.

Terrell also reported that in the past 18 days a total of 532 wells had been completed.

BOY TELLS OF SCHOOL BLAST

Calvin Corrie, 14, De-scribes Detonation

Helpers At First-Aid Stations Are Dead Tired As They Round Up 20 Hours on Duty

By SARAH McCLENDON

Workmen, an average of 250 in a six-hour shift, finished wrecking the main wing of the New London High school by this morning. The job of digging into the basement had begun, bringing with it the tasks of unearthing bodies.

As the weary workmen finished their shifts, they were replaced by other crews, sent here from oil companies in near-by fields or towns as well as all sections of the East Texas field. The Ohio Oil company sent over 120 men to help this morning. The Sun company was sending a large number. Virtually all operations in the field were halted today, with all attention turned to the giant relief work at hand. Ever present in the minds of the workmen is the ghastly dread that there might be some still left living beneath that tangled mass of steel, concrete and tile. Although weary of using their man-power like that of elephants at pulling the steel cables attached to motors on trucks, the men keep on hour after hour.

Aid Recognized

Lieut.-Col. C. E. Parker, one of the commanding officers of the nat-ional guard, said, had the catastro-phe happened in any other section of the state, it would have required weeks to remove the debris and get to the bodies. "But here in the oil field, with the companies co-op-erating so wonderfully by bringing in their trucks, which is the exact equipment needed, the entire build-ing in the explosive zone should be wrecked by Friday afternoon."

Major Gaston S. Howard, assist-ant adjutant-general, arrived this morning, sent here by Governor James V. Allred to take charge.

See WORKMEN DIG, Page 2

MILITARY MANEUVERS (Top) As a public affairs officer at Ft. Oglethorpe, GA, I had the mess staff produce a four-foot cake to celebrate the birthday of the WACs. They had to take the door off of the mess hall to get the cake outside. It wound up in the newsreels and was seen worldwide.

(Right) An East Texas rose in her old WAC fatigue cap, on the prowl for news of our fighting men and women.

(Bottom) In 1949 I interviewed the crew aboard the carrier, *U.S.S. Franklin D. Roosevelt.* I stayed overnight, my cabin guarded by a Marine. I've never figured out whether he was protecting me or the sailors.

(Top) Official Photograph of U.S. Army, (Right) Collection of Sarah McClendon, (Bottom) Official Photograph of U.S. Navy

BRINGING UP BABY (Top and right) Motherhood proved to be a joy. Although being a single working mother needed day and night planning, I gave Sally as normal an upbringing as I could.

(Bottom) Along the way, I learned—before Hillary Clinton was even born—that "It takes a village to raise a child."

Collection of Sarah McClendon

THE PRESS CLUB BATTLE BEGINS (Top and left) My first office in the National Press Building, with the *Philadelphia Daily News* masthead on my door. But since the National Press Club was male only, I had to share my office with a man—and the Club upstairs was off limits.

(Bottom) Sally had to watch the children of male reporters go upstairs to see Santa at the National Press Club Christmas party. Here, age 4, she makes due with a department store version.

(Top left) Courtesy of the *El Paso Times*, (Top right) Courtesy of the *Philadelphia Daily News*, (Bottom) Collection of Sally MacDonald

THE IMPERIAL TOUCH (Top) Franklin Delano Roosevelt didn't so much "meet the press" as allow us to come to him. His cars were specially equipped because of his paralyzed legs.

(Bottom) This *New Yorker* cartoon got FDR's press conferences just right: we stood jam-packed in the Oval Office, hanging on every word, taking notes on each other's backs.

(Top) Courtesy of the Roosevelt Library, (Bottom) Cartoon by Gluyas Williams, courtesy of *The New Yorker*

THE MAN FROM MISSOURI (Top) Harry Truman moved his press conferences to the Indian Treaty Room of the Old State Department Building and let us have a seat.

(Right) I admired Truman's willingness to stand by his decisions...and to never give up the fight (below).

Courtesy of the Truman Library

COMING INTO MY OWN (Top) A growing reputation got me invited to Finland with a select group of newswomen.

(Left) When not stalking the halls of Congress and the White House, I was always on the phone.

(Bottom) I said Ike should spend more time on public works and less time playing golf, then realized he needed exercise to recover from his stroke. My apology brought this same-day reply, which I still treasure.

Collection of Sarah McClendon

THE WHITE HOUSE

WASHINGTON

April 21, 1958.

PERSONAL

Dear Mrs. McClendon:

It was kind of you to write as you did concerning the press conference of last Wednesday.
I appreciate your thoughtfulness. Actually
no apology was needed because I am quite
sure that you had a special interest in the
matter of community public works.

I am grateful also for your comment on the
usefulness of the Presidential press conferences.

With best wishes,

Sincerely,

Dwight Eisenhower

Mrs. Sarah McClendon,
807 National Press Building,
Washington 4, D.C.

PERSONAL

President's Angriest Moment

U.S. Delegation Factions Fight At Latin Parley

President Kennedy at his news conference yesterday.

Associated Press wirephoto

Puts Sharp End To Question On Security 'Risks'

By Robert J. Donovan
Chief Washington Correspondent

WASHINGTON.

President Kennedy was infuriated at his press conference yesterday when a reporter, Mrs. Sarah McClendon, characterized two State Department officials as "well-known security risks."

With the most chilling anger he has displayed at any of his twenty-one Presidential press conferences, Mr. Kennedy challenged Mrs. McClendon to name the men. From her third-row, center-aisle seat she fired back these names:

William Arthur Wieland
J. Clayton Miller.

She had said in her original question that these men "have recently been put on a task force in the State Department to help reorganize the Office of Security."

This was categorically denied by State Department officials later. The two are assigned to the department's management affairs.

In low tones with icicles clinging to them, the President told Mrs. McClendon:

"I would say the term you have used to describe them is a very strong term, which I would think that you should be prepared to substantiate. I am familiar with Mr. Miller's record because I happened to look at it the other day. He has been cleared by the State Department. In my opinion, the duties which he is now carry-

Sarah McClendon

Associated Press

White House Backs 'Gag' Under Fire

FACE-SAVING?
By The Associated Press

PUNTA DEL ESTE, Uruguay. America's most powerful nations—proposed yesterday that the Western Hemisphere co-exist with Cuba but condemn Fidel Castro for embracing communism.

The United States, which came to the Inter-American Foreign Ministers conference hoping for a collective ban on trade and diplomatic ties to counter Castro's communism, rejected the co-existence idea but accepted other parts of the proposal as a basis for negotiating united action against Cuba.

[At Washington, President Kennedy expressed confidence that the Punta del Este conference would make "very clear" hemispheric opposition to the intrusion of communism, as represented by the Castro regime, into "our OAS (Organization of American States) family."]

In addition to denouncing the Castro regime as a threat to the hemisphere's way of life, the Argentine-Brazilian proposal would formally exclude Cuba from the Inter-American Defense Board (from which, in fact, it has long been excluded), and promote a collective ban on arms trade between Cuba and

... AND FEUDING
By Dom Bonafede
Special Correspondent

PUNTA DEL ESTE, Uruguay. Two factions, one composed of professional liberals and the other of practical politicians, are grappling for control of United States policy here.

Thus far there has been no open breach within the United States delegation, but as the conference gets down to hard cases a rift appears inevitable.

On one side is the formidable Kennedy administration braintrust of Arthur Schlesinger jr. and Walt W. Rostow, professional White House advisers, and Richard Goodwin, Deputy Assistant Secretary of State for Inter-American Affairs.

As one member of the United States delegation remarked, "They favor working within a framework of reality. They know they must reach a settlement satisfactory to both the anti-Castro forces and the big powers of the pro-Castro bloc, namely Mexico, Brazil and Argentina, or wreck the Inter-American system."

But standing firm for the application of extreme sanctions against the Castro regime is the United States Congressional team: Sen. Wayne Morse, D-Ore., chairman of the Senate Inter-American Affairs Committee; Sen. Bourke Hicken-

The President's 'Goal'

40-Hour Week, Not 25 Hours

By James E. Warner
A Staff Correspondent

WASHINGTON.

President Kennedy spoke out yesterday against the twenty-five-hour work week that New York City construction

---

MOMENTS WITH KENNEDY (Top) JFK reacted sharply at a press conference when I dared to name names. But my colleagues were even rougher on me.

(Bottom) I think Kennedy sensed how little time he had. But even a young man in a hurry sometimes stops to laugh.

FUNNING AND FUSS-
ING WITH LBJ (Top) In
a Women's National
Press Club skit, I play
(and spoof) my old
friend Senator Lyndon
Johnson.

(Right) Vice President
Johnson poses with a
pair of lively teens,
who happen to be
best of friends—his
daughter, Lynda Bird,
(right) and mine, Sally.

(Bottom) Though it simply wasn't true, Lyndon got back at me by telling everyone I was the one who made him show his gall bladder scar.

(Top) Collection of Sarah McClendon, (Right) Courtesy of *The Diplomat*, (Bottom) AP/WORLD
WIDE PHOTOS

FACING THE TRUTH (Top) After Lyndon became President, my visits to the Oval Office became few and far between. I'm not too pleased about this particular one.

(Sequence) George Bush said "Watch my lips"—I say "Watch my face." My expressions in these four photos from one press conference can tell you a lot about LBJ and me.

CIVILITY AND CIVIL DISOBEDIENCE (Top) Having fun in the "civility days," the late 1950s, with three of four top congressional leaders: minority and majority leaders Senator Everett Dirkson (R-Ill.) and Senator Lyndon Johnson (D-Tex.), and House Speaker Sam Rayburn (D-Tex.). No gridlock here.

(Bottom) Rep. Melvin Laird (R- Wisc.) suggests that in order to be called on at President Johnson's press conferences, I become a "whistle blower"!

(Top) AP/WORLD WIDE PHOTOS, (Bottom), Courtesy of the National Archives

GETTING NIXON TO LISTEN
(Top) When Richard Nixon came into office, I didn't need Mel Laird's whistle to grab his attention...

(Left)...nor a gimmick like my neighbor's sign. Just a little judicious leaning to catch the President's notice...

(Bottom)...and we make contact. And that's what it took to shake the Veterans Administration to its roots.

Courtesy of the National Archives

THE GOOD FIGHT (Top) In 1969, I enlarged my News Service to include broadcasting. Here I tape an interview at an Army infantry base with a soldier headed to Vietnam.

(Right) The weapons in *my* ongoing battle: my phone, my typewriter, my pen. I think they're *all* mightier than the sword.

(Bottom) Dressed as a suffragette for a another skit—but this time, the subject is serious. (The tiny word between the bottom two lines on the sign is "discrimination.") We would finally break the sexual barrier at the National Press Club in 1971.

Collection of Sarah McClendon

Chapter 6

RICHARD NIXON: HE LISTENED

I felt Richard Nixon respected me. And to him, respect was all-important. His life was a continuous search for it. His downfall came out of a misguided attempt to protect it. Has any President-to-be ever shown as naked a need for approval (and as open a pain at the lack of it) as he did, when, after his defeat in the 1962 California Gubernatorial Election, he called reporters together for a "last press conference" to tell them they "wouldn't have Dick Nixon to kick around any more"? I will always honor the esteem in which Richard Nixon seemed to hold me—because esteem meant so very much to him.

By the time Nixon became President, a little kindness from the occupant of the Oval Office was a refreshing and needed change. His predecessor, Lyndon Johnson, had, over his five years in office, largely ignored and, more than once, publicly humiliated me. Expulsion from Lyndon's circle of friends once he became President had been his way of punishing what he considered a grievous sin: despite our long history, I had refused to toe the line and write only what LBJ wanted me to write about him. Johnson prided himself as a master of press control, yet he couldn't silence one of his oldest and closest Washington cronies, the little lady with the loud voice.

Richard Nixon, on the other hand, seemed to expect the press to be antagonistic and, at times, treated us in a way that would almost insure it. He regarded us as the enemy and tried to make the people feel that we were out to get him. With Nixon's apparent approval, his first Vice President, Spiro Agnew, carried on open warfare with the "netting nabobs" of the press (as Agnew once called us), trying to whip up public indignation against our "elitist" attitudes.

Nixon seemed to resent the press for what he felt were slights in the past, as well as any real or imagined current unfriendliness. After all, hadn't we always made a bigger fuss about his failures (his being pelted with eggs in Venezuela while on a vice-presidential tour in 1958; his uninspiring performance in the 1960 Presidential candidate debates) than we had about his successes (his 1959 Moscow "kitchen debate" with Krushchev; his astounding comebacks like the 1952 "Checkers" speech and his political rebirth at the 1968 Republican Convention)? He seemed puzzled and perhaps a little jealous about our continuing infatuation with John Fitzgerald Kennedy. Why were we presenting Nixon as a "hawk" when he was merely trying to end the unpopular war which Kennedy got us into? How could we have let JFK get away with all his marital infidelities without reporting them? Wasn't THAT a bigger story than this Watergate nonsense?

I can understand why Richard Nixon believed he received worse treatment from the press than any President before him had. In a way, he did. The turbulence of the 1960s had given anti-authoritarianism a certain legitimacy; the country would, it seemed, never again take things at face value in the way it once had. (This idea, of course, failed to take into account how the enormous personal magnetism of a man like Ronald Reagan would make us, as a nation, quite willingly retreat into blissful ignorance.) The press got under Nixon's skin because reporters were getting better at their jobs. They were better educated, more knowledgeable about how government really works and they had more nerve, though not often about the things that really count.

I witnessed time and again, especially during the Watergate era, just how ill at ease reporters made this President. Once, after a nationwide broadcast, he ducked out of the Oval Office and unexpectedly entered the press center through a side entrance. I was among the few people who happened to be in there. I saw that he was heading to the rostrum and realized that he was going to say something. So I dashed over to connect my tape recorder. At the microphone, Nixon mumbled a few sentences that eerily echoed the notorious 1962 California "retirement" speech, then concluded by saying, "I just hope that some day you people will trust me." By the time I could get my tape recorder working, he was gone.

Did the press unfairly batter Richard Nixon? As one who has taken pride in taking Presidents to task, but who had a surprisingly amicable relationship with this one, I have to say that, as a whole, we did not. We were merely as suspicious of his motives as he was of ours. For example, he would often bypass the press and take his announcements directly to the people in televised speeches. What had worked for him back in 1952, when he kept the vice-presidential nomination with the help of his wife Pat's "Republican cloth coat" and his little girls' cocker spaniel, would, he was sure, work for him again and again. The networks would, from time to time, threaten not to broadcast one of Nixon's ever-more-frequent announcements, but they usually gave in to the power of the office and gave him televised exposure even when it wasn't justified.

Nixon was the man who invented the "photo opportunity," those occasions when news people are permitted to take photos and video but ask no questions. It has become a practice among all the Presidents since. Except for photographers, all we can do, if we choose to attend, is listen, hoping to pick up clues for a story. Some among us thought Nixon came up with the photo op as a cynical way of teaching us "our place."

There were, of course, a few newspaper people who received the Nixon administration's blessing. One was, oddly enough, a reporter for the *Washington Post*, the President's Watergate nemesis. Ken Clawson got a lot of inside information, especially from John Mitchell, Nixon's Attorney General. The Post was probably happy to have the balance of one pro-administration voice on its pages.

To my astonishment, I seem to have been another reporter whom Richard Nixon did not regard as an enemy. Despite the fact that most of the press had a rough time with him, Nixon was, as President, considerate of me and concerned with my questions. This surprised me because, compared to my friendship with LBJ and frequent brushing of elbows with Jack Kennedy during their years in Congress, I had had relatively few encounters with Richard Nixon since he had first come to Washington from California in 1946—and those few we did have hardly gave him any reason to consider me a friendly pen.

I knew, of course, about Richard Nixon's work with the House Un-American Activities Committee and his success in discrediting Alger Hiss. I knew a little about the mud-slinging Senatorial campaign he had run against Congresswoman Helen Gahagan Douglas—and had considered one of the techniques he'd used to win that race, his constant repeating of the phrase, "It's awfully hard on a woman, this campaigning," smug and anti-female.

Nixon was working hard to become recognized as an up-and-coming young Republican, but, despite five years of hard work, he was still barely recognized outside of California and Washington D.C. His congressional years would later become widely known as part of the Nixon saga, but in the early 1950s, to most of America, he was still "Richard who?" So, I was startled when his name suddenly popped up as the solution to a mystery every political reporter in the country had been trying to solve.

Though their 1952 National Convention was well underway, the Republican Party had not been able to come up with a vice-presidential candidate to team with Ike. The kingmakers had come to a stalemate; they simply couldn't decide on who to pick. I was prowling the corridor outside the main floor of the International Amphitheatre in Chicago, where Eisenhower had just been selected to be the presidential nominee.

Suddenly a familiar face came down that corridor, John Knight, the editor and owner of the *Detroit Free Press* and former president of the American Society of Newspaper Editors. I knew he was well-connected to the circle of top Republicans and, therefore, probably in the know. So I pressed him for an answer: "Who is going to be the vice-presidential nominee?" He told me that it was going to be Senator Richard Nixon. "They chose Nixon on the advice of Helen Sioussat," who was the Executive Vice President of CBS, the first woman, I was told, to hold that high a title in the broadcasting field. She had produced the television coverage of the HUAC hearings in which Nixon had first shown his potential, and she thought that he would prove to be an asset to her party because of his leading role in such activities.

It was a choice that surprised the nation as much as it did the press, and one that almost proved to be not the asset Sioussat predicted but a liability. Though Nixon's candidacy survived its finances coming under question—the widely viewed "Checkers" speech actually led to an increased positive public image for him—the Eisenhower administration seemed to keep the new Vice President at a distance. Even Nixon's press conferences were private affairs, held in his office for a small group of invited reporters. I tried to get on the list of those he asked but never could. So I saw even less of Richard Nixon than some of my colleagues did. In fact, until he became

President, my most memorable association with him had been the fact that I was the one who had asked Eisenhower what decisions his Vice President had participated in, to which Ike had replied he couldn't think of any—an admission which the Democrats lost no opportunity in exploiting. But if Nixon held that particular public embarrassment against me, I never saw any evidence of it. He could have hated me for it, but instead he chose to listen.

Richard Nixon treated my questions with a degree of attention and follow-up I have seldom experienced. I got results from asking him questions. In fact, my questions provoked more action from his staff than they did from the men and women working under any other President. In press conferences, Nixon would respond to my questions, often asking questions back, trying to see the problem. And once he saw it, he would really do something about it. For example, when I told the President about a terrible drought in Texas, he immediately sent Secretary of Agriculture Clifford Hardin to survey the conditions, telling him to "be sure and take Sarah along." After Hardin said the plane was too small to bring a reporter, Nixon told him to take a larger one. That way, other journalists got to go, too, and the problem received wider exposure.

Despite Nixon's on-going, often self-imposed war with the press, his administration added a researcher whose job was finding answers to those questions which couldn't be easily handled at press conferences. I was told I was at least partly responsible for this innovation: I asked so many questions that required follow-ups that the new staff position became a necessity. John Carlson proved to be excellent at it, digging out facts and keeping everyone involved, including himself, calm. He stayed on to do the same job after Jerry Ford became President.

I did, on occasion, receive my share of the hostility some of the Nixon staff directed toward reporters. When Senator Bill Brock of Tennessee, a Nixon Republican, told me that remedial training centers for retarded children were being closed, I brought the problem to the White House's attention. Brock had received three thousand letters about how mentally disadvantaged children were being sent home to face bare walls and to rock back and forth, but the Department of Health, Education and Welfare denied the problem existed. As I persisted in trying to get an answer, bringing it up at press conference after press conference, the other reporters grew restless, and John Ehrlichman, the President's top aide for domestic affairs, grew rude. Shaking his head at my question, he said, "Now, if you were to ask me if you had been to the beauty parlor lately, I would say no..."

Eventually I came up with a taped interview with parents of these unfortunate children, and Deputy Press Secretary Gerald Warren arranged for me to play it for a HEW official. After hearing it, the official said, "Oh, they're talking about day-care centers!" as though it was simply a matter of the wrong words. Changes to alleviate the situation got underway.

I don't know if the President ever heard about his aide's personal comment to me, but a few hours after he made it, Ehrlichman left a conversation with Secretary of State Henry Kissinger to come over, kiss my cheek and apologize. I brushed him off, saying "I'm on my way to the beauty parlor right now."

On the whole, though, I received fewer insults and more apologies from this President and his men than most other administrations. Spiro Agnew once made up a stupid joke about how Hubert Humphrey, former Minnesota Senator, LBJ's Vice President, and the first Democratic Presidential candidate to lose to Nixon, had taken on a new job as an airline steward. Though he liked the work, Agnew said, Humphrey was shocked when Sarah McClendon pinched him on the bottom. When I heard about the story, I was furious. Agnew eventually said he was sorry for using my name, but I was the only female reporter he could think of that everybody knew. In a way, it was worth it to be the only reporter that Spiro Agnew ever apologized to in his life, I'm sure.

Even I wound up apologizing on occasion. I have always been opposed to the cliques of long-term careerists within the government working behind the scenes to protect themselves—and their accumulation of power and influence—against changes of administration. Their lack of responsibility to the Executive, Legislative or Judicial Branches make them a government unto itself, with no checks and balances and no oversight from the public. It was my disdain for these well-entrenched parasites that led me to embarrass John Kennedy back in 1962 with my question about Weiland and Miller. In 1969, in an effort to expose a boondoggle involving career bureaucrats in the Pentagon who thrived by assigning government contracts, I managed to embarrass not only Richard Nixon, but my dear friend Melvin Laird, myself and a rather sweet man named Barry J. Shillito.

The bureaucrats, headed by a Democrat, Edward "Big Ed" Sheridan, had been running the procurement system out there in the Pentagon for so many years that they thought they owned the place. They liked to pick the appointees who, as administration officials, would be their so-called bosses. So they had a meeting with the major defense contractors, down in Puerto Rico, before Mr. Nixon took office, and at this meeting they decided who some of the officials supervising in the Pentagon should be. One man they picked was Barry Shillito as Assistant Secretary of Defense for Logistics, or supply. They thought that, having been a logistics contractor himself, Shillito would understand the way they did business. They lobbied hard for him, and he got the position.

When I learned of this arrangement, I thought Shillito's past made his appointment an obvious conflict of interest. It seemed a perfect chance to show up the clique at the Pentagon for what they were. So at a September 1969 press conference, I asked Richard Nixon the following question:

> "Mr. President, would you please tell us when you are going to make some real, honest-to-goodness changes in personnel in these bureaucrats who have been in power through many generations, who are still wasting the taxpayers' money and making errors on the war and policy and promoting their friends, who are unqualified, to high jobs? I refer particularly to the office in the Pentagon of Assistant Secretary of Defense, Barry J. Shillito."

President Nixon's response was an awkward and confused "I don't know the gentleman, but after that question, I am going to find out who he is." *The New York Times* wrote up the exchange under the headline "President Forgets About an Appointee He Named" and the Washington *Evening Star* put it under the banner "Mr. President... Then Came Sarah With the Shillito Stiletto." Because it had a certain resonance, asking "Who is Barry Shillito?" soon became a byword across the nation. I'm sure Mr. Shillito heard it himself hundreds and hundreds of times.

Within a few hours after my question, the White House put

out a statement that the President and Defense Secretary Melvin Laird did indeed know Mr. Shillito and fully supported him. The Defense Department issued pages of Shillito's biography showing he was clearly qualified for the job, with a thorough knowledge of military procurement and management. He had served in the military as a pilot and had even been a prisoner of war. I realized that in my pursuit of a pack of scoundrels, I had completely misread and unwittingly humiliated a decent human being.

Under the previous administration, a mistake like that might have gotten me barred from the press center. As it was, I found President Nixon to be understanding and forgiving. And he was not the only one. A few months later, at the annual White House reception given for the military by the President, a number of Shillito's coworkers noticed that their boss and I were both there. When they saw us speaking, they came up and suggested we dance. So, in the front lobby of the White House, to the music of the Marine Corps Band, Barry J. Shillito and I shared a waltz. As we did, his friends formed a circle around us, and when we finished, they all applauded. I have lost track of whatever happened to Barry Shillito, but wherever he is, I wish him well. He has already caught enough hell from me.

In many other ways besides his attention to my questions, Nixon went out of his way to be kind to me. He saw that I got certain information ahead of others, like an announcement that he was going to Texas or some other place I had a connection to. He would say, "Sarah would be interested in that," and tell John Ehrlichman or his Chief of Staff Bob Haldeman to see that I got the news first.

He invited me to one of his famous Sunday church services at the White House, which I had previously attended as a reporter but never as a guest. These services were always filled with an unusual mix of people. At this one, I met and talked with Billy Graham, Nixon's aunt, heavyweight boxer Joe Frazier and race car driver Cale Yarborough.

He even took me with him on his trip to Austin, Texas for the dedication of the Lyndon Johnson Library. When Lyndon seemed a bit surprised to see me, I told him, with more than a little satisfaction, "You see how I got here? The *President* brought me."

Though many thought of Richard Nixon as a cold man, uncomfortable with emotions, I found him eager to offer his own brand of friendship. Almost every time I appeared in the Oval Office, he would smile at me and say something personal. A White House photographer once told me, "The President must like you. He mentions you by name more than any other reporter."

I will always regret that I missed hearing one of the nicest things Mr. Nixon ever said about me. Once, as he spoke at a Women's National Press Club banquet, he announced that "Sarah McClendon asks questions that no man would dare ask." And where was I at the time? In the Ladies Room, I'm sorry to say. When I came back to my seat everyone was grinning and looking at me. Just as I was beginning to think, "Well, what's wrong?" a friend told me what the President had said.

I think Richard Nixon enjoyed teasing me. One morning, because it was cold, I went out wearing pants, a purple pantsuit, which I'd never worn before and never would again. I intended to change before going to a reception for the Chinese Ping-Pong team in the State Dining Room of the White House, but I ran late and had to show up at the event looking a little like a grape with legs. When the President left the podium, he led Mrs. Nixon through the crowd directly to me. In the middle of the room, with everyone standing around, he kept looking at me, up and down and up and down. I began to wish I could just disappear. Finally he said, "Sarah, you have on pants." He turned to Pat and said, "I thought she was a traditionalist." A lot of women were wearing pants to the White House by then, but I never had. Thinking quickly, I pointed toward the Chinese, who, both the men and women, were wearing Mao jackets and trousers. "Since all your guests are wearing pants today," I replied, "I wanted to make them feel at home." He got quite a grin out of that.

As I grew more comfortable with the President, I began to tease him back. Eventually, Richard Nixon and I usually had some comment or other to make to each other. Once, after a press conference as he walked by me on his way out, I said, "Oh, Mr. President, you're getting gray!" He stopped, thought a while and replied, "That's not gray—that's streaking." Everyone howled with laughter, surprised that Nixon was even familiar with what streaking was.

I even learned how to find the silver lining in the silence of President Nixon's widely disliked photo opportunities. I once got an excellent story by listening as some black leaders thanked him for giving federal aid to research on sickle cell anemia for the first time. None of the other reporters picked up on it. Not knowing much about the disease, I called a black man on Nixon's staff and found out that he knew even less than I did. When we both found out how large a segment of our population is threatened by sickle cell disease, we were both ashamed. I wrote a story I was proud of about Nixon's foresight in funding the research.

At another photo op, the President found a way to use me as a convenient prop. In the midst of an intense Oval Office conversation with King Faisal and Ambassador Ibrahim Al-Sowayel of Saudi Arabia, a discussion also involving Melvin Laird and Henry Kissinger, Nixon turned away to engage me in some rather idle chatter about travel. As our talk went on and on and the President showed no inclination to return to his guests, I grew uneasy, especially since the ambassador knew me well. My daughter had served as a member of his embassy staff. Later, I learned that the Saudis had been pressing for an agreement which Nixon had wanted only his two Cabinet Officers to discuss at that time, so as not to compromise his relationship with Israel. I had become a rest stop in the midst of the tightrope balancing act of international relations.

Even as all this was occurring, I had to wonder about my own delicately balanced relations with Richard Nixon. How had I, a lifelong Democrat, developed such a degree of mutual cordiality with this man who was anathema to most of my fellow liberals? Why did I find so many of his ideas progressive and his initiatives admirable, even as I sensed the potential for the wrongheaded thoughts and actions that would make him hated and cut short his presidency? Perhaps it was the disappointment I had lived through with the President before him. Perhaps it was his shyness and physical awkwardness, which I could identify with. Perhaps it was the eagerness with which he seemed to seek out my approval—and gave me his.

At any rate, Nixon's push to make me feel a part of his team began as soon as he became President. At the first White House reception he and the First Lady held, he sought me out among a bunch of "society" writers, all women. When he took me off to one side and told me, "I will always take your questions," I was too dumbfounded to speak. He asked, "Well, isn't that what you want?" "Yes, suh, Mr. President," I blurted out.

I never found out what led to his giving me this assurance. Once, later, he said, "Well, I have to call on you—yours is the loudest voice." And of course he was right about that. But his apparent trust that I would be friendly, or at the very least fair and accurate, came from something other than how loud I had to make my voice to be heard among my mostly male colleagues.

Perhaps it had something to do with my whole-hearted support of our men and women who were fighting in Vietnam. Even though I had very mixed feelings about our involvement there, I was becoming a spokesperson of sorts for the veterans. I appeared on the Merv Griffin Show in Los Angeles with Jane Fonda and got into an informal debate with her. She brought the sister of one of our soldiers, a brave man named Alvarez, who had been captured and was being held as a prisoner of war. Having met Mr. Alvarez before his capture, I said he would have been ashamed to see his sister demonstrating against the war.

Though we kept things civil on camera, during the commercial breaks, Jane turned to me and told me how ignorant I was. I realized she was trying to make me blow my cool and say something idiotic, which made me even more determined to hold my temper. When the show was over and we were in the elevator, the argument heated up some. A little fellow was standing there as we got off. He said, "I heard you arguing all the way down." I was a bit embarrassed. When we got out on the street, two or three young girls came up to me and told me they had never realized the other side of the question and had been very impressed by what I said. That made me feel better.

Perhaps Nixon's trust came from knowing I had an unusually friendly relationship with his Secretary of Defense. As a Republican Congressman from Wisconsin, Melvin Laird had served with distinction on the House Defense Appropriations Committee, which I covered with some regularity. Because I had a Wisconsin paper at that time, Mel and I got to know each other well. Despite my frequent questions on the status of women in the Armed Forces, or maybe because of them, Mel always seemed to look forward to my coming around. We were as close to being buddies as a politician and a reporter could be.

After he became Nixon's Secretary of Defense, I lobbied him to appoint our first women Generals and Admirals—and like his boss often did, Mel listened. He refused to approve any more lists of promotions to the rank of flag officer unless there was at least one woman on it. The Navy held out, and he had to send their lists back several times. They tried appointing a woman to Commodore, but Mel said that wasn't good enough. Finally, after fourteen months of having no new Admirals appointed, they gave in. During his time as head of the Defense Department, Melvin Laird made eleven women into flag officers, the first females ever in the top rank of our Armed Services. It was amazing that he had the courage to do this while we were in the midst of fighting a war. He, quite graciously, gives me full credit, saying he did it because he knew he would catch hell from me if he didn't. And even though I love him, Mel might have been right about me giving him hell.

So there were several reasons Richard Nixon may have assumed that I was supporting the war. But, in fact, it was our soldiers I was supporting. As time went by and the war drew closer to its end, I began to realize more and more how unnecessary and stupid it was. I have now come to believe that behind our elected officials' backs, some in the CIA and the Defense Intelligence Agency were actually using the war to cover activities like political assassinations and buying narcotics.

I see our involvement in the Vietnam War as a tragic waste of our country's financial, emotional and human resources. I believe that Kennedy was led into it unwillingly, assured it would be a short-term commitment of troops. Johnson inherited it, and, with all good intentions, attempted to win it. Nixon tried—but did not know how—to get us out of there, if not by winning, at least with honor. Many fine and dedicated public servants in those three administrations got drawn into this no-win situation, just as many soldiers lost their lives or their health in what they believed was serving our country. Like most Americans, I was disillusioned by what went on over in Southeast Asia. Unlike many of them, I never lost faith in our military men and women. But once we ended our participation in the war, it seemed that even some in the government were ready to put not only our mistakes behind us but the veterans who had suffered for those mistakes, as well.

Perhaps the proudest moment I shared with Richard Nixon came from our shared desire to see that our veterans should get everything they deserve. Late in a Presidency that was soon to be cut short, I discovered a grave injustice and asked the President a question. He listened—and his response eventually caused a shake-up throughout the entire Veterans Administration.

In the fall of 1973, a woman who worked for a Democratic Congressman from Texas called me up. "You'd better come up here and read some mail we're getting. There's something happening to the veterans who are entitled to go to school under the GI Bill of Rights." When I got to the office, she showed me a stack of letters from veterans complaining that the checks for their tuition, books and living expenses while they were attending high school, vocational school or college were arriving weeks, sometimes months, late— and sometimes not at all.

I checked with other congressional offices and found that a lot of veterans were not getting the checks that they were entitled to receive. Some arrived late and others were simply never showing up. This was causing great problems. Since the government was no longer paying tuition directly, as it had after World War II, some of the schools were kicking the students out. Many veterans were having trouble paying their bills. Some were facing eviction from their homes and apartments.

What made this worse was that the Nixon administration kept issuing statements about how much they were doing for the veterans. My repeated inquiries to the White House were getting an odd response; oh, I was told, there had been a problem, but that's been solved. I eventually found out that one college administrator who knew Nixon personally had called him at the "Western White House" in San Clemente over Christmas and told him about problems at his school. VA Director Donald Johnson held a press conference to say that he had personally gone out to California to clear things up. "But what about Pennsylvania, New York, Maryland, Texas?" I asked. He said I didn't know what I was talking about. The problem was local and under control.

I was in New York City, covering a labor story for the *El Paso Times*, when I heard that Nixon was finally going to have a press conference. I hurried back to Washington. Once there, I prepared my question like I always do. I checked with the VA one more time and found out that since the VA did not read all their mail, only sampled it, they were still unaware of how big a problem this had become. The third largest agency in government, which deals directly or indirectly with almost half the population—and they were completely out of touch on a serious issue that was beginning to ruin lives. When I went to Mr. Nixon's press conference, I was determined that he would hear the news that had been kept from him directly from me.

I waved my arm and shouted out "Mr. President! Mr. President!!" After he had acknowledged me, I told him, in part, "Sir...I am sure it is not your fault, but maybe the people that you have appointed to office aren't giving you the right information... Many a young man in this country is being disillusioned totally by his government these days because of the hardships being put upon him."

When Nixon replied that Donald Johnson had told him the late checks were a minor problem which was already being taken care of, I pointed my ball-point pen at him and said, "He is the very man I am talking about who is not giving you the correct information. He stood up there at the White House the other day and gave us false information. He has no real system for getting at the statistics on this problem." (A Secret Service man later told me never to point any objects at the President, as it made the agents very nervous.)

As often happens when I put a direct accusation before a President, Richard Nixon chose to end the exchange with a sarcastic poke at my style: "Well, if he isn't listening to this program, I will report to him just what you said. He may have heard even though he wasn't listening to this program."

But as all too seldom happens in these confrontations, he followed up on my question within minutes. Though it was after 9:30 at night, he told an aide to get Donald Johnson on the phone. I had forced the President to look into a can of worms —all the errors, injustices, delays, insensitivity, rigidity, and take-it-or-leave-it decisions that made up the Veteran's Administration. To his credit, Nixon decided to do something about it.

As always, many of my colleagues were ready to say I had "done it again." The *New York Times* wrote an unfavorable editorial about me. Eric Sevareid said on the air that I had "given rudeness a new dimension." But I knew that what I had done was right, and the veterans knew it, too. Hundreds of calls and truckloads of letters came in from men and women who'd fought in every one of this century's wars, saying they didn't think anyone knew or cared about their problems. A WAC told me she had gotten up at her isolated post in Louisiana and "danced around the room with joy." For months and months, veterans' groups from across the country sent me awards and asked me to come and speak to their chapters.

But what mattered most was that, as troubled as he was by his mounting Watergate woes, Richard Nixon took action. He found out that the unemployment rate among veterans was nineteen percent, that many who had received "bad" discharges could not get work and were on welfare or had turned to crime. He found out that very few veterans knew that the GI Bill could help them finish high school as well as college. He found out what a shambles the medical program was, with thousand-bed hospitals lacking a chief of medicine or surgery and wards completely unstaffed over weekends.

Nixon immediately brought on a new Chief of Medical Services, and Donald Johnson was banished into a position in the Commerce Department. In a March 12, 1974 radio address, the President mentioned me by name as a "spirited reporter...(who) had rightfully called this to the attention of the nation." I was told Nixon's advisors debated at some length about how to describe me before finally agreeing on "spirited." Whatever the words, I felt honored that Nixon had seen fit to give me credit. Very few Presidents would have admitted that they had needed a White House reporter to alert them to a problem in one of their agencies.

Years later, when I was out in Colorado making a speech, a woman came up to me and said, "I work for the VA, and the reason I have my job is because of you." She told me that the Nixon administration had fired so many people after I had asked my question that there were hundreds of job openings. I had not realized that the housecleaning had gone beyond a few top people.

Our war for the veterans was to be the last time when I felt Richard Nixon and I were working in the same direction, or, as I believe he liked to see it, that I was on his team. The country was already deeply immersed in the agony of Watergate and what had happened to cause the problems with the Veterans Administration only served to point out the Nixon presidency's fatal flaw. Time and again during his six years as President, the White House did not really know what its own people were doing.

It was clear to me that Mr. Nixon sensed the worrisome nature of this long before things began to fall apart. He always seemed unhappy with the State Department and his Secretary of State, Henry Kissinger. He thought that they tried to take on too many of the duties that really belonged to the White House—and then tried to keep things too secret. He wasn't happy about that at all.

I think that during his long retirement, Richard Nixon eventually realized just how many secrets were being kept from him when he was in office. But I think he set the tone for that to happen, because he was by nature a secretive person himself. Secrecy was the real "cancer on the presidency." During Nixon's campaign for re-election, this became painfully apparent. When you walked through the office where his staff people were working on his campaign, each one of them would turn over the papers on his or her desk. As though you must not see what they contained. As though you would try to read them upside down. I found that insulting—and a little frightening.

I think that he felt insecure, as haunted by the memory of Jack Kennedy as Lyndon Johnson had been, afraid that he would never measure up to that ghost in the eyes of his countrymen and women, the people he wanted to admire and love him. Like LBJ, Nixon had been born poor and had grown up feeling financially insecure. I think Bill Clinton feels this, too. He had a somewhat similar boyhood, but instead of seeking power, he seeks reforms.

President Nixon was too scared to let the American people know what he was doing. He was afraid that if we knew more about his actions, we might not approve of them—or him. I always thought that if Nixon had come out straightforwardly and admitted to America the mistakes that had been made in the name of secrecy, the country would have forgiven him as they had back in 1952. He might even have overcome the distrust of his enemies. But once you begin keeping secrets and telling lies, it is just too hard to stop. Like he had with Vietnam, Nixon kept waiting for "a light at the end of the tunnel" that never came. He thought stonewalling equaled courage and would preserve whatever esteem the nation still felt for him, when simply telling the truth might well have been the only way to save himself.

I took no joy in seeing Nixon's downfall. At Special Prosecutor Archibald Cox's press conference after he had been fired in the so-called "Saturday Night Massacre," I think my despair showed as I asked, "What made you think they would ever let you do your job?" I was now feeling the efforts of the Nixon administration to whip up ever more public opinion against the press. I would not have been surprised to see a reporter tarred and feathered by Nixon supporters. I was among a group of reporters who covered a luncheon in the final few weeks of the Nixon presidency. Rabbi Baruch Korff, the self-appointed defender of the President, was the main speaker. During his speech, we journalists were surrounded by angry Nixon loyalists who denounced us for not copying down the Rabbi's every word. There was so much hostility that I felt in personal danger, as though I were covering a war from the front lines.

During those last weeks, I kept thinking of how Pat Nixon, that dear woman who entertained more visitors at the White House than any other hostess, had told me she could tell what mood her husband was in when he came back from the office by what he'd play on the piano. If it was something Wagnerian, she'd know that he was in a bad mood or that something was going very wrong. I knew what he must be playing now. And I kept remembering how, when I had attended that Sunday church service as a guest and was finally able to sit up front near the Nixon family, I had looked across at Julie Nixon and seen an expression of abject pain and deep sorrow. That had been back in April. The President would be out of office by the end of August.

Near the end, I met Senator Barry Goldwater of Arizona coming out of the White House. I had known Goldwater for years and, even when he was unsuccessfully running against Lyndon Johnson for President, had admired his truthfulness and candor. So I was not surprised when he told me he had just suggested to Richard Nixon that he resign. I asked, of course, why Barry had done that. "Because he has lost all respect," Goldwater said. Congress would never cooperate with him again.

After his resignation, Nixon weathered years of exile at San Clemente, but he eventually pulled off one final comeback and became a well-regarded elder statesman. I saw him in that role when he was speaking to the American Society of Newspaper Editors. When I walked up to try to get in a question, he said, "Well, I see that you're still in good voice!" But when the ex-President would come back to Washington, hire a hotel room and asked certain people to come talk with him, he never invited me. We were back to square one, the non-relationship we had had when he was Vice President.

Nixon was at heart a traditionalist. I think he got just the type of state funeral he wanted. I suspect he must have chosen that hymn, "Amazing Grace." It served as a reminder that Richard Nixon had done much to take down the last formal signs of segregation and had been the one to make affirmative action a key point in the nation's civil rights efforts. It reminded us that Nixon was surprisingly progressive in many ways—and may well have been the last Republican President to be so.

Next to the cut-off Kennedy years, I feel the Nixon administration was one of the saddest of our Presidencies. I think the newly established Nixon Center for Peace and Freedom, which California's huge Nixon Library has set up here in Washington, means that Mr. Nixon's thoughts are going to have some influence on the future in this country. I think that in a way, Mr. Nixon's voice will still be with us. I know he would have liked that.

I have one memory of Richard Nixon that sums up the contradictions that he represented to me. It comes from that trip we made to Texas together, when he so kindly invited me to fly with him to the dedication of the Lyndon Johnson Library. As we traveled halfway across the country, the President gave me an exclusive interview in his private cabin on *Air Force One*. We talked so intensely that neither one of us broke in when it came time to land. We didn't put our seat belts on, merely continued talking, eye to eye. I was more than a little worried about the President's safety (not to mention my own), but I felt it would be rude to interrupt. He just simply never seemed to notice. I think he was happy to have the full attention of a reporter who wasn't sniping at him. With an audience of one hanging on his every word, he ignored something simple that could have been the difference between life and death. I think to Richard Nixon, a crash was less to be feared than a loss of control or respect.

WASHINGTON, DC, 1944–1996:

It's 10 o'clock. Do you know where your congressman is tonight? Is he studying that procurement reform bill coming up for a vote tomorrow before his committee? Is she on the phone with your mayor, discussing the impact of illegal immigration on the local economy? Or is he, over after-dinner port and a good cigar, accepting a generous "campaign donation" from a lobbyist for the tobacco industry or the N.R.A.? Or attending an expense-paid seminar at some plush resort where a group of CEOs is attempting to convince him to ease taxes on corporations and create loopholes for the rich—while denying federal money to "welfare mothers" and their hungry children?

I have always considered covering Congress as important a part of my job as the more high-profile task of taking Presidents to task. Early in my Washington career, I thought Congress would be the focus of my reporting—until I realized that to keep my one-woman news service in business, I would have to offer some "glamour" in the form of presidential coverage. But I still try to let the voters back home know how, or even if, their representatives in Congress are voting—whether she's managed to get federal money to build a storage dam which can prevent a repeat of last year's flooding or he's been able to keep the Army base open or improve conditions at the veterans hospital.

Congress is where federal government meets local needs, where those you've sent to Washington should know—and care—about the crop-destroying pest that's threatening your farm or that new industrial park which is bringing jobs to the 'hood. But the appropriating and law-making in which we should all take an interest is made hard to understand by a confusing system of committee assignments and procedural rules which unfairly favor the party in the majority—as well as a constant tangle of trade-offs, patronage, hidden agendas and partisan in-fighting.

To remedy this, the two thousand or so reporters who are accredited to cover the Senate and House (and use the free press galleries as convenient headquarters) owe both the elected officials and the public which elects them an accurate, accessible, daily account of what happens on the Hill. This means reporting the hard work and devotion to duty—as well as any scandals, political or economic malfeasance or even just plain laziness and stupidity.

I've generally had excellent relations with the Senators and Representatives I have covered. I have, at times, been as hard on some of them as I've been on the residents of the White House, but that doesn't often make for headlines—nor would I want it to. What I'm trying to do is to simply give my readers in the congressmen's home states or districts all the information they need to understand the men and women they have elected to guard their interests. That means not merely accepting the members' press handouts or talking to their aides, but getting to know them personally, evaluating their judgment and their values as well as their record. Often staffs will try to insulate their boss from reporters. When I get tired of receptionists asking the nature of my telephone calls, I have, on occasion, gotten the congressman to the phone by saying, "Just tell him his old girlfriend is calling." With a woman, my line goes, "Tell her that her boyfriend's wife wishes to speak to her."

I once went on a "Scandals Tour" of Washington, run by a bright fellow named Rick London. He gave everyone a whistle and told us that if we knew of a scandal that took place at any site we passed, we should blow it and then share our gossip with the group. I thought the script needed a little enhancement, so I kept right on being a whistle-blower, even interrupting the actors who were portraying Nixon and Reagan. As we passed the Capitol, I blew so hard I nearly got a headache. When the tour was over, two schoolteachers from California came from the back of the bus and told Rick that they thoroughly enjoyed his show—especially that actress who impersonated Sarah McClendon.

I can joke about that kind of scandal because, for the most part, it doesn't worry me nearly as much as a violation of the public trust through arrogance, prejudice or greed. That's the kind of immorality that angers me. I am also put off by incompetence or by an unwillingness to learn, something I see all too often in members of Congress. When they first arrive, the "freshman class" usually displays such a shocking lack of knowledge of the way government runs that they should be required to take a civics class. The first-termers in the Republican majority that swept both houses in 1994, largely under the aegis of Newt Gingrich of Georgia's "Contract With America" (sometimes known as the "Contract On America"), seemed particularly at a loss. I think most of them showed up in Washington not knowing much more than where the Washington Monument is.

Even for those who've been in the Congress for years, learning should be an ongoing process. Just as I think a regional reporter should study the industries and resources in the states and districts of the congressmen they cover, I think the Senators and Representatives should leave off the taxpayer-paid trips home each weekend to stay in Washington and actually read some of those long health and tax bills. They, as well as the President and his staff, need regular briefings on rapidly changing subjects like the environment and hazardous wastes, the cost of medical care and the state of medical research, and advances in telecommunications and energy sources. These reports should come from not only the manufacturers or providers but from public interest and watchdog groups, as well.

One frustrating example of how out of touch—or simply wrong-headed—some congressmen can be involved the former manager of all the restaurants in the House of Representatives, Ann Walker. Over a 12-year period, Ann had not only balanced the yearly budget of the House's food services but turned a steady profit. She accomplished this even though she had to subsidize the low prices at the members' dining room and absorb much of the cost of catering one to two dozen private receptions held by Representatives every night. Though the food for these parties was usually paid for by a constituent or trade organization, the preparation and service were also provided at subsidized rates.

Despite serving hundreds of thousands of meals annually at below-market prices while keeping the only balanced budget among any congressional service, Ann Walker was fired. Representative Ed Jones, a Democrat from Tennessee who chaired the House restaurant committee, said Ann's $45,000-a-year salary was "too much for a woman." She had witnesses to that remark and sued him and Congress for millions. The case was settled out of court for $50,000. Anne went on to run a catering business used by anyone in Congress wanting higher-quality (if a little higher-priced) food at functions. And no Congressional service has had a balanced budget since.

I guess the air on Capitol Hill gets a little rarefied from time to time. One way I've brought a few selected congressmen down to earth is by asking them to be my date for one of those occasions when a single reporter is expected to be squired by a familiar face. At the annual dinners of the White House Correspondents Association or the Radio and Television Correspondents, you're often judged by the news source on your arm.

I had known Republican Senator John Warner of Virginia since covering him in the Defense Department, where he had held several positions, including Secretary of the Navy. When I brought John to one of these affairs, there were more than a few raised eyebrows. He had just been divorced, you see, from Elizabeth Taylor, who had helped him so greatly in his Senate campaign. As he explained when I introduced him around, "This is my first date since Liz. I told my ex-wife about it and she approved." Liz may have taught John the Hollywood way to "mix and mingle," but I taught him the Washington way.

Among my other dates over the years have been Senators Alan Cranston and George Murphy of California and Strom Thurmond of South Carolina. Talk about a spectrum from liberal to conservative! Alan brought me home but seemed more interested in my cat than in me. George seemed so devoted to his late wife's memory that I was surprised when he eventually married again. Strom startled me by parking in a no-parking zone. "You can't park here," I told him. "I'm a U.S. Senator," he said, "and I can park wherever I want to."

Strom and I are personal friends. Covering him for radio stations in Charleston and Greenville, I, with my daughter beside me, sat through much of his famous Senate filibuster, which went on all night and into the next morning. It was the longest ever up to that time. Only his first wife and the late Clarence Mitchell, a highly regarded black lobbyist, remained in the gallery throughout. When Thurmond found out that I almost "went the distance," we became close. He helped me on several stories and took a shine to Sally. I still admire his long record of service, staying in the Senate into his nineties, and I get peeved when folks confuse his gentlemanly Southern conservatism with the ideas of someone like North Carolina's Jesse Helms.[1]

The two members of Congress with whom I shared a bit more than friendship were both named Cooper: Representative Jere Cooper of Tennessee and Senator John Sherman Cooper of Kentucky.

Jere Cooper and I went together for some time in a rather secretive fashion, closely watched by his office secretary. As chairman of the powerful House Ways and Means Committee, which had the responsibility for naming all the other Democrats to committees in the House, Jere wielded considerable power in the party. He taught me a lot about hardball politics. I still smile to think of him slipping out of his presiding officer's chair during hearings and coming to the back of the hall, where the press had been relegated. He'd sit beside me and we'd hold hands under the press table. I wonder where the relationship might have gone if he hadn't suddenly died.

I was set up with John Sherman Cooper by Governor Allen Shivers of Texas, who had known him in World War II. Four war buddies had decided they would all go into politics after getting home, and they all did. The other two became a senator from Washington state and a congressman from Colorado. I liked John from the start, but I found an article about him that said he was married, so I declined his offers. I eventually found out he had married a nurse while a hospital patient, and they no longer considered themselves a couple. But by the time they divorced, the attractive Senator Cooper was being grabbed up at parties.

---

[1] My most telling memory of Helms is when he introduced a Constitutional Amendment declaring that the fetus, from inception on, should have the full rights of citizenship. My friend, the outspoken Reagan White House staffer Barbara Honegger, called his office to point out the hypocrisy involved in his stance. Since he was adamantly against the Equal Rights Amendment, she asked, "What if the fetus turns out to be female?" I like to think her comment had something to do with Helms' amendment going nowhere.

Cooper ran for unexpired terms in his state, so he was often in Washington for short periods. Then he was defeated, and he came back here to practice law. He looked me up and told me he thought the time was right for us to get together. I was delighted. However, we figured this without the matchmaking talents of Eisenhower's Secretary of State, John Foster Dulles. Dulles said he wanted to appoint Cooper Ambassador to India but told Cooper he needed to be married for the job. He put John together with Lorraine Shevlin, an heiress to an oil fortune who "just happened" to be studying the Indian language, Hindi, and had expressed an interest in funding the refurbishment of the tired old U.S. Embassy in New Delhi.

They were, as far as I could tell, a happy couple, even though Lorraine always did glare at me a bit whenever I'd come to one of the parties they gave when they returned to the U.S. After she passed away, John would invite me out to the expensive home she'd left him, but things weren't the same. I still had feelings for him, but it was too late. Eventually his health failed, and he died. Considering all my years with first J.W. Milam and then John, I guess I'd have to admit that Kentucky Republicans are my weakness.

But even when emotions have been stirred, my reporter's instincts and ethics have kept my journalistic approach to those in Congress on a strictly professional level. These men and (all too rarely) women are, after all, the subjects and sources of my stories. If, from time to time, some of them became friends or mentors, it's because I've found in them the qualities I deeply admire. In the Executive Branch, the ultimate power resides in one; in the Legislative branch it is split over five hundred ways. So it is only natural that for every instance of a true public servant I've seen in the White House, I've seen a dozen at the other end of Pennsylvania Avenue. Those from my home state alone, past and present, could fill a few baker's boxes.

Take the late Senator Tom Connally of Texas, for example. He was everything a people's representative ought to be. During the Depression, he worked constantly to get more jobs and money for his state. I'm convinced that the United Nations would never have been founded without his hard work as chairman of the powerful Senate Foreign Relations Committee. But as busy as he was, he never failed to read his mail from the folks back home.

Then there is former Democratic Speaker of the House Jim Wright, who represented his party, his house of Congress and his home state ably and at length. He recently reminded me of the sense of mutual purpose that existed between Congress and the press back when he first came to office in the 1950s. Though my friend Lyndon was always an exception, Jim and most of the other Texas law-makers trusted me, my fellow Missouri graduate and long-time pal Tex Easley, Les and Liz

Carpenter and the other reporters from the Lone Star State to present their accomplishments in a straight and fair manner. Jim says some of his colleagues from other parts of the country simply couldn't believe how open we all were with one another.

Another Texan whose career I've covered with admiration is former Senator Lloyd Bentsen, who, by pushing legislation insuring pre-natal care for poor women, has saved our government millions in what we would have to spend on damaged lives that could have been whole. The financial expertise that made him a strong Secretary of the Treasury for Bill Clinton showed its human side in Lloyd's reforms in retirement savings and his attempts to provide good health for all at reasonable cost.

Since his district includes Tyler, Democratic Congressman Ralph Hall considers me his "constituent." I've certainly kept my eye on him as though I was. He is a wonderful argument against term limits, proving that the experience gained in long service can lead to the best service. He is often responsive on a one-on-one level with those he represents. How can I not admire a man who says that on those rare occasions when he and I disagree, he's probably the one who's wrong?

And then, of course, there are all the non-Texans I've come to know and, in many cases, admire to the point of affection. Longtime Senator Robert C. Byrd of West Virginia, who, quoting Woodrow Wilson's "I would not give the snap of my finger for any man who is not surrounded by a bevy of admiring females," counted me and his wife as his bevy. Louisiana Senator Bennett Johnson, who swears I called him "Cousin Bennett" the very first time we met. Mississippi Representative Gillespie V. Montgomery, who tells me to go on "riding him" about our veterans hospitals, knowing darn well I will. Representative Pat Schroeder of Colorado, whose unflagging support for women will be sorely missed. Ted Kennedy of Massachusetts, who is now senior keeper of the Kennedy flame.

It's a source of amazement to some people how well I get along with certain deeply conservative souls. The simple answer is that it's simply a matter of mutual respect. I admired, for example, Barry Goldwater's independence and willingness to speak his mind. So I went along with the joke when, during the Reagan administration, Senator Goldwater asked if I'd been behaving myself and then swatted me, "paddling my behind" with his cane right there in front of the Capitol. I was a little embarrassed, however, that he did it in front of a few other Senators. I suspect my old friend Barry knows he's safer now that he's retired to Arizona.

In a way, his replacement in my affections has been the sharp and witty Republican Senator Alan Simpson of Wyoming, with whom I frequently exchange friendly verbal firepower. If Alan tells me he's accomplished something, I'll say, "Show me." If he gives me generalities,

I'll say, "Put it in writing." And if, as he once did, he says, "By gad, I'm going to put it in writing, and by gad, I'm going to hand deliver it to you, and by gad, it's going to be right, and by gad, it's going to please you!" I'll answer, "I'll decide that!" Whenever he sees me, Alan always gives me a kiss on the cheek. They seem to like my cheeks, those Republicans.

Whether liberal or conservative, my favorite members of Congress all have two things in common: a sense of humor and a sense of dedication. They may not take themselves too seriously, but they are serious about their work. None of them sees their job as a stepping stone to a lucrative job in the private sector or a lifetime berth in the government bureaucracy. And though they realize that the path to the White House usually leads across Capitol Hill, they do not treat Congress as though it were only a stop on the way to the Presidency.

It is a fact, however, that seven of the eleven Presidents I've covered got most of their political experience, knowledge and clout from being in the House or Senate, as did an even higher percentage of their Vice Presidents. Most of the serious candidates for those two offices have served on the Hill, as well. For better or worse, even some of my closest congressional friends have been bitten by the presidential fever bug.

It's 10 o'clock. And if you don't know where your congressman is tonight—check in the direction of the White House.

Chapter 7

JERRY FORD:
STILL THE PRESIDENT

During my fifty years in the White House press corps, I've seen three Vice Presidents thrust, overnight, into the hot seat behind the desk in the Oval Office. Two of the three went from Congress to the Vice Presidency to being President in a matter of months, not years. Like Harry S Truman, Gerald R. Ford became our President before, it seemed to me, he'd ever really considered whether he even wanted the job. Unlike Harry Truman, it took Jerry Ford most of his presidency to decide that, yes, he did. Perhaps that indecision came from the fact that of all the Vice Presidents in American history that have become the Chief Executive, only Gerald Rudolph Ford did it while the man he replaced was still alive.

Harry Truman became President less than four months after becoming the President's standby, in the midst of the greatest war we've ever fought on foreign soil. Lyndon Johnson became President because of an assassination which shattered our image of ourselves as a nation and ushered in the most turbulent decade of domestic dissent since the Civil War. Jerry Ford became President in the wake of eleven troubled years marked by war, assassination and racial strife. In his inaugural comments on August 9, 1974, Ford referred to Watergate as "our long national nightmare." He could have just as accurately been referring to everything we'd been through since November 1963. His assignment, he knew, was to put an end to all the turmoil.

And make no mistake about it, if any President ever came into office with an assignment, it was Jerry Ford. The very reason he was around to assume the Presidential mantle was because Richard Nixon needed him, in two different ways and for two different reasons. When, in the midst of the Watergate mess, Spiro Agnew was accused of financial improprieties, it became clear to Nixon that he could not protect both himself and his Vice President. Agnew was on his way out, and what Richard Nixon now needed most was a replacement for Agnew who could help stem increasing congressional doubts about the President's ability to run the country. To control the widening gap between the White House and the Capitol, Nixon needed a man those on the Hill could trust, someone who was not only a familiar face to Congress but a well-liked one.

Gerald Ford had been Representative from the Fifth District of Michigan for twenty-five years. For the past eight years, he had been House Minority Leader, a job in which he had demonstrated an ability to negotiate and compromise. Ford seemed to be the right mix of experience, integrity, amiability and, just as important, loyalty—to his country, his party and his President.

Just as Lyndon Johnson had wanted his friend Thurgood Marshall on the Supreme Court bench if and when the Bobby Baker matter ever came before them, Richard Nixon wanted a high-ranking, respected Republican in the right spot if and when it became clear that Watergate would lead to impeachment proceedings. When Jerry Ford agreed to become Nixon's new Vice President, he undoubtedly knew that he was expected to mend fences with Congress. He may also have known, far better than Nixon could, how unrepairable those fences were. Just what else Jerry Ford knew is a question I'd love to get an answer to but probably never will. Did he know that he might wind up replacing not just Agnew, but Agnew's boss? Did he know how swiftly that could happen? And did he know, as many suspect, that there would be another huge expectation placed upon him should that occur?

Before the 25th Amendment to the Constitution had been ratified in 1967, Jerry Ford would not have become Vice President— or certainly not in the way he did. The Amendment finally gave the government a way to fill the office of Vice President if it becomes vacant, something that had already happened sixteen times in U.S. history: eight times because of the death of a President, seven because a Vice President had died and once when a Vice President resigned. The last time the office had been unfilled was while Lyndon Johnson finished Jack Kennedy's term, leaving us with no Vice President until Hubert Humphrey was elected on Lyndon's ticket in 1964. Once the Amendment was part of the Constitution, any President facing a vacancy was required to nominate a Vice President and seek Congressional approval.

On October 10, 1973, Spiro Agnew resigned; on October 12, Nixon announced his nominee to replace Agnew. I had been at the House of Representatives earlier that day and had heard rumors that it would be Jerry Ford. I didn't believe them. I expected it would be, and was pulling for, former Secretary of Defense Melvin Laird. I had known and liked Jerry Ford for years, but I never thought he would leave the Congress. After a quarter century in the House, "Good Ol' Jerry" was an institution, the Republicans' hard-working—and occasionally frustrated—deal-maker.

Like those who had been Minority Leader before him, Gerald Ford knew that his party was often powerless against the Democratic majority and its strong-willed Speakers like Sam Rayburn and his successor, Representative Carl Albert of Oklahoma. Back then, there seemed little hope that the Republicans would ever control the House. So Gerald Ford's job often came down to merely currying favor and seeking compromise with the powers that be. There might be a big show of being partisan out on the floor, but behind the scenes, it was mostly log-rolling between the party leaders, with the minority Republicans often taking the short end of the stick.

Most of the press looked at Gerald Ford as far more inclined toward calming the waters than making waves, anyway. He was thought of as good-natured, unassuming and seldom given to grandstanding. Some of the more cynical reporters called him the ultimate product of the congressional career system, a man who'd risen to prominence in the House simply because he'd been there for what seemed like forever. Jerry Ford, some joked, was what you get when the folks back home rubber-stamp their ballots every two years, sending the same man back to Congress again and again and again. But both the press and Capitol Hill would see a different side of Jerry Ford soon after he became President.

On December 6, 1973, following a quiet six-week investigation by his congressional colleagues, Nixon's nomination of Gerald Ford was confirmed.[2] (On August 9, 1974, after nine more months of Watergate cries and whispers, Gerald Ford became our 38th

---

[2] The only other time a President has appointed a Vice President was when Ford himself, shortly after taking office, nominated Nelson Rockefeller.

President. Thirty days after that, he granted Richard Nixon "a full, free and absolute pardon"—and the shouting really started.

Across the country, there was immediate outrage. Was this what Gerald Ford had meant when he promised us an end to our "national nightmare"? Had a deal been cut, and if so, when? Though Ford defended the pardon as a way to show compassion and start the healing, many just saw it as one more layer of conspiracy and cover-up. Even some in the Ford administration were angry. Ford's new press secretary, Jerald F. terHorst, a wonderful reporter for the Detroit News who the press all saw as a welcome addition to the White House staff, quit in protest because he'd been used without his knowledge to feed the media inaccurate information.

But the pardon was an irrevocable fact, and eventually, the roars of protest began to fade. Just as Nixon's resignation had saved him from impeachment, the pardon insulated him from the cover-up trial which was shortly to begin. As Gerald Ford had hoped, the pardon had defanged Watergate, reducing it from an ongoing obsession to just a bitter taste in our mouths.

I couldn't get as riled up over what Jerry Ford had done as people expected me to be. Though I deplored the secrecy under which the pardon was arranged, I had liked Richard Nixon and admired his often liberal tendencies. I had no need—or desire—to see him further punished. While it's certainly tempting to think that there had been a deal in the works since Day One, I also think that Jerry Ford sincerely believed that he was doing the right thing. His years on the Hill had taught him how to give and take, and, trying to spare both Nixon and the nation an ordeal, the new President had, without our advice or consent, arranged what he felt was a compromise.

In a compromise, everyone gives up something. Most agree that what Gerald Ford lost through this one, barely a month into his administration, was any hope of ever being elected President in his own right. As if to underscore that prediction, the Democratic landslide in that November's congressional elections strengthened their control over Congress. The party leaders rubbed their hands, waiting for 1976 and what they expected would be an easy recovery of the White House. But there, too, Jerry Ford would give the country a few surprises.

But that was two years off. There were far more pressing matters for now. Though he'd been known for keeping the Congressional waters calm, Ford had as President almost immediately stirred up a whirlpool. Had he destroyed his chance to lead us out of the bitterness and polarization left by the Johnson and Nixon years? Could he use the abilities for which he had been summoned off the Hill to somehow change the divisive and partisan nation we had been steadily becoming? Could this "accidental" President, who had never been elected to public office by anyone but the voters of his home district in Michigan, become a President for us all?

I thought back to the two other Vice Presidents I'd seen dropped into perhaps even worse messes. Both Truman and Johnson had made their mark in Congress. Truman had spent ten years in the Senate and Johnson, twenty-four years split between two houses.

I feel sure that Harry Truman never expected to be President. He would have been content, I imagine, to have seen almost any point in his political career as the high point, whether it was being presiding judge of the County Court in Jackson Country, Missouri or Vice President of the United States. But what he learned as a judge served him well as a Senator, and what he learned in the Senate helped him to be an outstanding, courageous President.

Lyndon Johnson, on the other hand, was not only prepared for the Presidency, but had always wanted it. From almost the minute I met him, I knew his eyes were on the prize. But that didn't keep him from being a consummate Congressman. Few knew the nuts and bolts of getting legislation passed better than Senate Majority Leader Johnson. When he became President, he used that knowledge to get an amazing number of his proposals through a not-always cooperative Congress. His time on the Hill made him perhaps our most effective President ever at turning his platform into reality.

It's clear that Jerry Ford remembered these two who had gone through a transition much like his own. In fact, though he'd worked for Tom Dewey's campaign back in 1948, Ford now seemed to identify quite strongly with Harry Truman. He even had Truman's portrait put up in the Cabinet Room. But did Jerry Ford really stack up to either of these two men?

Though he turned out to be a better President than some I've known, and was more knowledgeable about government than Eisenhower, Carter and Reagan (none of whom were ever in Congress), I never thought Gerald Ford was really cut from

Presidential cloth. He was a dedicated, excellent legislator who, if he'd remained in Congress, was in line to become the next Republican Speaker of the House. He probably could have been one of the best. I think that, until quite some time after he actually became President, he would rather have been Speaker than anything else. He had served in the House long and well, with discretion and restraint, and he had clearly earned the right to preside over it and set its tone. But after years of building toward that goal, Jerry Ford was suddenly pulled in a different direction. Out of loyalty and patriotism, he left Congress and gave up his dream of being Speaker of the House.

I think that was a shame, because I feel Jerry Ford could have made a greater contribution to our country if he'd remained on Capitol Hill. Many other outstanding congressmen have chosen to stay there rather than run for President. Sam Rayburn, Senator Richard Russell and Representative Carl Vinson of Georgia, Representative George Mahon of Texas and a lot of others have realized that Congress also needs its leaders and its loyalists.

The Presidency can bring out the best in a person, but it can take the best out of him, too. Its unique pressures and temptations can wind up dampening—or even destroying—the very qualities that made him an attractive candidate in the first place. A look at three great Senators who gave in to the siren call of a presidential run may illustrate what I mean.

Senator Hubert Humphrey was my idea of a perfect member of Congress, always operating on a human level, with no fancy protocol to separate him from those who elected him. He loved people and fought for them, whether writing legislation, speaking on the floor or negotiating behind the scenes. He is the only Senator I ever saw picking out graduation gifts to give to high school seniors among his constituency. He was far more comfortable in the Senate than he was as a Vice President, defending LBJ's war with passionate words he clearly never felt. I admired Hubert greatly and mourned his death but feel he lived his life best as the extraordinary congressman he clearly was.

In a similar way, my good friend, former Democratic Senator Eugene McCarthy of Minnesota, is quite possibly too great an intellectual to have ever been President. He was a phenomenon of his time; his principled opposition to the war in Vietnam caught the hearts and minds of a vocal segment of the American people.

Though his 1968 campaign had great impact on Lyndon Johnson's decision to step aside, the majority of Americans never sensed Gene's internal strength, hidden as it is behind the soul of a gifted poet. He was an impressive candidate who would have brought unique qualities to the Presidency—but I can't help thinking that a heart that caring and a mind that brilliant would have suffered under the tensions of that great and terrible job.

To be a bit more current, let me tell you how I feel about Robert Dole. I have long been an admirer of this Republican from Kansas who first campaigned for Congress back in 1960. His sharp wit is a fine-honed tool which he uses in the service—and occasionally the disservice—of an impressive knowledge of politics and government. His four years of recuperation from his World War II wounds gave him both understanding and an understated kindness. Though he was Ford's running mate in 1976, Dole's edge has given him an up-and-down relationship with the Republican National Committee and, I feel, delayed his getting the Presidential nomination until 1996, when suddenly (and quite unfairly), his age became a factor. I feel those twenty years with one eye on the White House distracted Bob from his true calling as an outstanding leader of Congress. Giving up his Senate seat was a sacrifice he should not have had to make. He is another instance, I think, of a remarkable man best appreciated within the setting of his congressional service.

I'm glad I first got to know Jerry Ford during his long years in the House. Like Hubert, Gene and Bob, he seemed at his best in those days before the White House invaded his attention. In a gentle, quietly humorous way, he showed himself to be a man of true compassion for the people around him. He was a very human being. Stories circulated about Jerry Ford, told by folks he'd been sweet to, and then retold by others. Stories that, if he happened to hear them, might turn his ears a little red.

Stories like what happened one cold, snowy night when he left the Capitol and found he couldn't start his car. When help arrived from a nearby garage, Ford noticed the man was working in the bitter cold without gloves. With no hesitation, the Congressman pulled off his own gloves and handed them to the mechanic, saying, "Here, take these. You'll need them more than I will. When you get me started, I'm just heading home." The man was astounded but

PRESIDENTIAL ACCESS TO "GOOD 'OL JERRY" (Top) President Ford invited me to an intimate Oval Office conference for a select few members of the press...

(Bottom)...and earned my sincere thanks.

Courtesy of the Ford Library

INSIDE WITH OUTSIDER (Top) Their questions already answered by Jimmy Carter, Helen Thomas and Sam Donaldson sit writing in the front row. You can tell I'm anxious to get *my* question in.

(Bottom) When my son-in-law, David MacDonald, was snubbed by the CIA because he wrote for the Canadian press, Jimmy and Rosalynn Carter understood all too well.

(Top) Courtesy of the Jimmy Carter Library, (Bottom) Courtesy of the White House

In some ways, I'm still that East Texas rose growing in the sunlight of a Tyler summer afternoon.

Collection of Sarah McClendon

WOMEN MOVING FORWARD (Top) Why do some Americans still insist on mistrusting strong and intelligent women? Hillary is a dear.

(Bottom) On Earth Day 1996, dressed in dungarees and my Habitat for Humanity cap, I walk up the White House driveway toward yet another press conference.

(Top) Courtesy of the White House, (Bottom) Christy Bowe

took the gloves with great appreciation.

Or stories like the charming exchange that I heard about from my friend Celia Martin. She ran the office for the southernmost congressional district of Texas with such efficiency that each new congressman kept her on. She was there practically from sunrise to sundown. Jerry Ford also arrived every morning about 7:00 AM. He began to notice that this Celia was often the only other one around at that time of day. Finally he spoke to her, asking, "Does your boss require you to show up this early?" "No," she said, "he doesn't. It's just that we've always got so much to do that we're always trying to get caught up. I feel I can get more done if I come in early." Not recognizing Jerry as a Congressman, she asked, "What about you? Does your boss make you come in this early?" "Yep," Jerry answered with a straight face. "If I'm not here by seven, he comes down hard on me. He's a terrible boss." That was like Ford in those days.

I had seen men change when they became President, for the better or for the worse. Given the demands of the office, it would be amazing if they didn't. I've seen men we elect grow while in the office, and I've seen them merely age, ten or fifteen years in a four-year term. It would be a great challenge to stay the same, and these men have other challenges to face.

I was encouraged by the first formal press conference he gave as President to think that perhaps Gerald Ford wouldn't change. He got off to a great start with the press. He was relaxed and natural, without the television make-up Nixon had worn. It quickly became apparent that he had a firm grasp of government and could explain its workings in a clear way that the average citizen could understand. His answers seemed to come from the chest, maybe even from the heart. There also appeared to be a new freedom and openness to the proceedings. Instead of the usual "two questions from the wire services, three from the networks and the rest of you can fight for what you get," the new President seemed to call on questioners at random. I counted seven questions from women, which was a record. He picked out a quiet black reporter who I couldn't remember having ever had the chance to ask a question through the entire Nixon administration. For one memorable half hour, it looked as though he intended to remain the same Good Ol' Jerry I had known in the House. I found myself thinking that the odd chain of events that had brought him to the podium before us couldn't have happened to a nicer guy.

He did change, of course. Though I could quite easily see evidence of the "nice guy" in this President, there were many who had a harder time, especially in the Capitol. Though Gerald Ford remained the decent human being I had known and respected on the Hill, he became combative and confrontational toward the Democratic-controlled Congress with which he had to work, pushing disagreements into deadlock after deadlock. Perhaps he felt his old congressional image lacked presidential dignity. Perhaps he had weathered too many compromises when he was Minority Leader, too much giving in. Perhaps when he gave Nixon the pardon, he received in return the "us against them" mentality that had characterized the Nixon White House.

The press, too, was to have its disappointments. Instead of the open access I had hoped for, the Ford administration continued to keep its staff hard to get to, channeling most requests through Ron Nesson, just as had been done under Nixon. I was never able to get such a seemingly simple item as a staff list. Some names were not given out at all. When I called the White House switchboard to check on someone's title, I was told, "We don't give out titles."

The tight security and the feeling that the White House had become an armed camp continued unchanged from how it had been under the previous occupant. So little changed, in fact, that I can't even remember whether it was under Nixon or Ford that I witnessed a prominent member of the President's own party being, for all intents and purposes, chased off the White House grounds. I caught up with Senator Howard Baker of Tennessee once when he was leaving the West Wing. With two Tennessee radio stations among my clients, I had gotten to know Howard and reported on his activities. As I began to talk with him, a guard came up and told us, in no uncertain terms, that we'd have to move on. "You can't talk here," he snarled.

I was outraged. "This man is a United States Senator," I said, "and he can talk to anybody any place he chooses!" But the guard stood firm.

"Sarah," Baker said, "Let's get into my car. We can talk while the chauffeur drives us back to the Capitol." As I got my story on the ride, I could tell the Senator was as infuriated as I was.

I was, frankly, a bit shocked at how stormy President Jerry

Ford had seemed to become toward Congress. From being the individual who perhaps best symbolized life on the Hill, he became a critic and tormentor. It was as though he were waging a war. I could understand that stance once he had decided to run for election in 1976. Many campaigns I'd seen, from Truman in 1948 on, had gained first sympathy, then votes by picturing the candidate as one courageous man working against the ungainly, even ungodly, system Congress so often seems to be. I don't think that until 1976 drew near, Jerry Ford saw himself as more than a caretaker of the Presidential office, someone there to fill the years left by the resignation and to repair the damage left by the scandal. He was there to restore order and sweet normalcy. But, although working closely with Congress seemed, to most of us, to be the best way to accomplish those caretaking goals, Ford seemed to draw a line in the sand and take them on from the start.

Ford's weapons included aggressive contact men, who would breathe down the legislature's neck, and the veto, which he constantly threatened to use—and wound up using more often than any President had before him. He tore down budgets and trashed bill after bill. In the name of economic restraint, he cut off or cut back federal programs, even some of Nixon's, in a way that seemed to lack compassion for those the programs helped. That certainly wasn't the Jerry Ford I had known. He also voiced his complaints loudly and at length before the American public, downgrading Congress in a way that occasionally made me cringe. And many Americans listened. Public opinion of both houses began to plunge, reflecting what I felt was an unwarranted, unrealistic loss of confidence.

At the same time he was deriding and derailing the work of Congress, President Ford was strangely indecisive about many of his own policies. He took so long to announce a critical energy program that by the time it reached Capitol Hill, the winter was almost over and a new approach was needed. He seemed to be waiting for too much input from others before he'd make a decision. Instead of fighting for his vision of what was best for America, he seemed to be relying on decision by committee.

Some in the press said Ford was acting this way because he had never been elected to an executive post, that he was waiting until, should he choose to run and manage to win, he could feel like his own man as President. He would take on the really controversial problems, all the tough stuff, then. But I had seen the White House practice government by committee before and would again. It seems a common enough political strategy, especially among Republicans, though it is, in my opinion, a rather ineffective one if progress is your goal. While hesitation is natural and seeking others' advice and approval is not only tempting but often wise, doing too much of either is not in the definition of "pres'i·den·tial" you'll find in McClendon's Dictionary.

If I was disappointed that the Ford White House mirrored the Nixon White House in some ways, there were other ways it did in which I delighted. Like his predecessor had, Jerry Ford often went out of his way to be kind to me. Many charming aspects of his personality had not been affected by the move into the White House. He was still easygoing, considerate, friendly and honest on a personal level. It was clear that he deeply loved his wife, Betty, and was an excellent father to his children. He was fun to watch on the dance floor or the golf course. Despite the rough job he had undertaken, and the rough way in which he was sometimes doing it, he had retained his personal integrity.

I will always especially appreciate one experience in which Jerry Ford saw fit to include me. All the Presidents gave interviews to which they would invite a few selected reporters on an exclusive basis. Usually these were people from television or the large papers in key cities around the country. I had rarely had this kind of official time alone, or in a small group, with a President.

Sure, I had spent hours and hours with Lyndon, JFK and a few of the others before they assumed the office. And I had spent that long flight to Texas with Richard Nixon in an exclusive solo interview. But I had shied away from asking to be included in these chats the Presidents' staffs would periodically arrange. For one, I felt the President always had his own agenda for them; he'd be talking about what he was for and how he intended to accomplish it. And I already knew what he was for. What I wanted out of my "up-close-and-personal" chances with a President were more of an analysis of his character and his performance in office. Another reason I didn't ask is because I knew most Presidents thought the regional papers for which I worked didn't have a large enough circulation to warrant special attention. But when it comes to the grass roots, most Presidents need a better gardener—and the smarter ones knew that I had a green thumb. Anyone who bothered to total up the circulations of all my newspapers would realize I reached a very large readership indeed.

Jerry Ford did invite me, with a few others, into his office for an interview—and made sure I had the chair beside him. It was quite a surprise, and I found the interview far more useful than I had imagined it would be.

Another thing that President Ford did that surprised me was to bring one of my old WAAC buddies on to his staff, Jeanne Holm, who had been in my class at Officer Candidate School. By now, she was Major General Jeanne Holm, the first woman in the military to achieve that rank, and former director of women in the Air Force. In that assignment, she had been the one to persuade the high brass to send women to Vietnam. Knowing all the duties women personnel could take on, the commanders there had asked for them, but the Pentagon blocked it. Jeanne kept after them in a poised but firm way until she brought them around.

Now Jeanne was brought on to President Ford's staff as his assistant specializing on women's issues. Under her guidance, Ford had authorized a study of all the departments and agencies of government to see what policies, procedures, laws and regulations discriminated against women. This was the study that, a decade later, I fought with Ronald Reagan to have released. Though it is seldom referred to publicly, it remains the bible for the government's attempts to clean its own house of sexism. Jerry Ford's foresight and concern in commissioning it stands high compared to Reagan's attempts to bury it.

As he grew used to the office, Ford apparently decided that he liked being President. The action he took in May of 1975 when Cambodia seized an American merchant marine vessel showed a new desire to appear presidentially strong and decisive. The Mayaguez Incident, as it became known, did boost Ford's popularity, but represented, in my opinion, one time when he should have taken the time to get more opinions.

In response to the seizure, U.S. pilots sank three Cambodian gunboats and a hundred Marines were landed on Tang Island, the closest solid ground to where the Mayaguez had been captured. By the time of the landing, however, the boat and its crew had already been released. Forty-one American and uncounted Cambodian lives were lost in all the related actions.

I wrote strong words about the incident at the time, pointing out that if Congress had been consulted before hostilities began, we might well have avoided many of the casualties and certainly the ones arising from the pointless landing after we had already obtained the release. Ford, his Secretaries of State and Defense and the military hierarchy had acted before informing (as opposed to "consulting," which is what the War Powers Act mandates) selected Congressional leaders. I have always objected to Presidents usurping the war-making power clearly given to Congress by both the Constitution and later law. Presidents Eisenhower, Johnson, Reagan and Bush, as well as Jerry Ford, have faced my questions and heard my objections on this subject. I felt that in this case the administration's actions had blown the incident out of proportion and cost American lives. It was not diplomacy but the kind of grandstanding that I had always thought Jerry Ford was above. "Strike first and ask later" seems to be one unfortunate presidential tradition that he picked up without any hesitation.

As the election year of 1976 drew ever closer, Gerald Ford became more and more conscious of public relations and publicity. The administration began to hold an increasing number of interviews and briefings with the sole purpose of spreading the word about Ford's activities and accomplishments. The rather shy man of quiet accomplishment he had once been seemed hidden beneath the media-savvy, image-conscious politician he was becoming. He became expert at heading off problems by bringing in dissident groups for personal meetings, listening and promising that his staff would do a study. Not many of the studies led to action.

This practice of face-to-face meetings to neutralize potential problems did, however, lead to another, excellent White House innovation. The Office of Public Liaison was created to help Jerry Ford mix with groups of people from many walks of life. And though it generally excluded the press, it proved to be a uniquely effective and original idea that served the American people as well as it did the President.

By the time the election drew near, Jerry Ford had transformed himself into an effective political machine. The stupid old jokes about his supposed clumsiness or old football injuries just didn't seem to apply anymore. For better or worse, he had achieved a thoroughly presidential mien. It was clear Ford was here to fight, and fight hard, to keep his job—this time with the public's ballot-box approval.

Ford gave his opponent, Jimmy Carter, a run for his money. If one or two big industrial states had gone the other way, or if the South had not held solid (with the exception of Virginia) for Georgia's favorite son, the election could have had a different outcome. Perhaps no one could have overcome the onus Jerry Ford took on when he, as he felt he must, gave Nixon a pardon, but the new, "improved" Ford came amazingly close.

After 1976, Gerald Ford returned to private life, retiring to southern California. Perhaps he should have considered returning, as President John Quincy Adams had, to Congress. Despite the tensions that had surfaced during his White House years, an encore performance by "Good Ol' Jerry" would probably have been welcomed. He might even have made it to that Speaker of the House position he had once aspired to.

In actuality, however, Gerald Ford has hardly "retired." The spirit of the Office of Public Liaison still burns brightly within him. Jerry Ford is, among all the ex-Presidents I have known, the most dedicated to meeting the Americans he once served. With a generous spirit and enormous good will, Jerry and Betty always seem to be on the road, making themselves available on a "people-to-people" basis that usually ignores the fancy trappings and statehouse formality associated with the appearances of other former Presidents. Like Harry Truman, who would answer the questions of visitors to the Truman Library, Jerry Ford wants the people to have the experience of actually meeting a President. Unlike Truman, Ford goes to where the people live, work, study or play to help give them that experience.

He may never have been elected to the job, but to millions of people around the country who have met him face-to-face, Jerry Ford is still the President.

TYLER, TEXAS, 1910-1940;
COLUMBIA, MISSOURI, 1929-1931;
EUROPE, 1937-1938;
WASHINGTON, DC, 1943-1996:

There are times when Washington can seem like a cruel and godless place. Compassion and piety are all too easily lost amidst the bureaucracy and constant pressure to tighten budgets. It is easier to simply pass problems along to other people, who, in turn, pass them along—and so on and so on. "Render unto Caesar..." becomes more important than "Love thy neighbor..." The heart and soul are sacrificed in the name of the brain and pocketbook.

While I allow myself a bit of pride for having kept not only my wits but my hearth and home together for 86 years, I feel my life would not have meant nearly so much without the help I've been able to give to others and the faith I've been able to give to God. If life is a climb toward being the best we can be, I believe we ascend fastest when we stop to help others up.

I learned kindness from my parents. Before they married, they agreed that they would spend their efforts helping the sick and the old, the underprivileged and the down-and-out. And they made good on that promise.

My mother was an early version of today's feminist. She taught me that this country will never fulfill its own promise until women walked alongside, not behind, men in the march toward a better tomorrow. My father always championed the underdog, and I am clearly his daughter in that. He befriended the Jews, Greeks, Syrians (as the Lebanese in Texas were called back then), Asians, blacks and the poor. He taught me to listen to issues not only for their impact on "us" but their impact on "them" as well, because, when all was said and done, they were "us" as well. And he taught me that listening was just the start—action had to follow. He would take surplus vegetables out of our large garden, tomatoes, beans, corn, and drop off a package to some widow almost daily in the growing season. During the years my father was the Postmaster, the Tyler Post Office was a place you could always bring a problem.

My values were shaped by family stories like that of Willis McClendon, my grandfather's eldest son, who once saw a white woman startled as a black man quite innocently appeared from a side street. She screamed, the black man ran, and bystanders, who assumed he had assaulted her, began to talk about a lynching. Uncle Willie knew the black man hadn't done a thing. He got out his shotgun and drew a line in the dirt between the mob and the man. "You'all are my friends and neighbors," he said, "but the first one of you comes across the line, I'm gonna shoot you dead." That stopped the mob.

My father's family, which had once owned slaves, had come to Texas from Louisiana to avoid the deprivations of the Yankees during Reconstruction. My mother's family, the Bonners, had also been slaveholders in Texas before the Civil War. I am grateful for the lifetime friendship of a descendant of two of their slaves, a wonderful woman and day care worker named Effie Morgan Caldwell. The Morgans were our friends back in Tyler. Effie's father, Sugarlou Morgan, was a fine pianist. He composed, at the piano in our home, the song "There'll Be Some Changes Made." He sold it for $5 when down on his luck and the buyers turned it into a popular song which is still sung today. Effie and I love each other and often talk. I help her where I can. I've been happy to fight a few battles against the government to make her life a little easier. When Martin Luther King's widow, Coretta Scott King, heard about my relationship with Effie, she said I should write a story about this friendship between black and white families that has lasted since slavery.

Just as having a social conscience was a given in our family, so was an active belief in God. My forebears had long been noted for some strenuous activities in the field of religion. My mother's line stretched back to a Bishop Bonner who'd been very active in merry old England at saving souls by putting people to death. Among my other ancestors were some noted characters in colonial New England named Mather. They made their mark by persecuting women who'd been accused of witchcraft.

Well, at least they had religion.

My mother took us to church every time the church door opened. She was born a Methodist, the great-granddaughter of a circuit-riding preacher who'd roamed east Texas and married three times. That was seen as rather shocking, but one or two of them had died. Mother, who had become an Episcopalian when she married my father, would, impassioned as only a convert can be, lead the youngest McClendons like ducklings the mile or so to the Episcopal church downtown. But her religious beliefs never tempered the fire which burned in her eyes whenever she witnessed an injustice. One of my most vivid memories of her was when a team of runaway horses wound up, breathless, in our front yard. They had panicked because their driver, a drunken farmer, had whipped them brutally. As he raised his whip to punish them again, Mother stomped her foot on the porch and screamed, "Stop that at once." He could have turned his whip on her, but her fearlessness simply froze him.

Another religious influence was to come into my life. While I was at college, I was visited by Mrs. Julester Shrady Post, a lovely socialite from New York who had come to Columbia, Missouri to work as a counselor at Christian College, which was near the University. An Episcopalian herself, she had been left by her husband with two children to raise, and she needed help. If I would tutor them, I could have a room at her home and one main meal a day. I jumped at the offer. That was before I knew there would be no heat in my room. I wound up not only tutoring her children, but helping Mrs. Post counsel some of her younger college students. I learned a lot about coaxing the truth out of people by revealing the truth about yourself. It's a technique that's been useful in my journalism—and in my life, as well.

When Mrs. Post rather suddenly announced she was going to leave the Episcopal church and become a Catholic, everyone was shocked. Even I tried to talk her out of it. With a college student's rebelliousness, I had been flirting with agnosticism and thought that religion was nothing more than a big show. Then, one Sunday as I walked in a park, I realized I was seeing God all around me—in the flowers, the river, the brightness of the sun—and that when you celebrate that astonishing a fact, the more show the better. I would become a Catholic, too.

My parents took the news with a surprising amount of understanding. I think they were just glad that I had religion of some kind. Others in the family didn't take it nearly as well. Though I was there for a Christmas visit, my eldest sister, Annie Bonner, said she wouldn't stay in the same house with me and moved out for the holidays. My boyfriend, a devout Baptist, heard the news and just stood there, rattling my Christmas present in his pocket. He never did give it to me.

Back then, people had quite a prejudice against the Catholic Church, which they associated with immigrants and the poor. The church in Tyler had Mexicans, a few Irish families who worked for the railroad and lots and lots of "Syrians," all of whom were, despite the bias of the time, good people, devoted to their families and their God.

When I returned to Tyler to work on the newspapers, I found support and companionship with three devoted Catholic women: Maude Hewett, descended from an Irish family which had actually been brought to Texas by my grandfather; Margaret Brogan, from another old Irish Catholic family; and Pauline Glasco, the wife of an Oklahoma oil operator and part Indian. We "Four Musketeers" proselytized for the Church (without great success), then decided to join the Third Order of St. Dominic, a group of lay women who help the nuns with missionary work and service to the church community. We received saint's names and the right to be buried in a habit, if we wish. The priest, amused to have four women so eager to join, gave us the names of the strangest, least-known saints he could. I'll bet most of my friends have never known that I am Sister Albergo.

While my work on the paper kept me politically conscious and active on a worldly level, I always found time to let Sister Albergo get in a little good work, too. In the one-hour break I had each afternoon between my shifts on the two newspapers, I would go to the church down the block and teach catechism. That's how I met Father Ambrose Smith, a saintly Dominican priest with whom I became warm friends. He also became my confessor—and encouraged me to fulfill my destiny as a nun.

Lord knows I tried. Though I'd always been social and liked the boys very much, I gave up dating for two years. But I had my doubts, like on the hot summer day over in Houston when I first saw the long underwear nuns wore. "Oh, oh," I thought, "I couldn't take that." And of course my family was having fits over the idea. Finally, on the day Governor Huey Long was assassinated over in Louisiana, something helped me make up my mind. I worked long hours on the story with a new young man at the paper named Bill Gardner. It was dark when we finished, so Bill offered me a ride home...which led to a talk in the car...which led to a kiss...which led to me giving up all my ideas of becoming a nun.

My first trip out of the country had its inspiration in my continuing fascination with religion. By the late 1930s, my former employer, Julester Shrady Post, whose conversion to Catholicism had inspired mine, was living in Ireland. She suggested I come over to visit. In 1937, I took a leave of absence from the Tyler papers, borrowed on my insurance policy and headed overseas. On my way to Europe, I briefly visited Washington DC for the first time. I thought it was pretty but not nearly as interesting as where I was headed. Little did I know that, in the larger scheme of things, Washington was exactly where I was headed.

Mrs. Post was living in a centuries-old cottage which she had modernized. I wound up staying in Ireland for six months. I wrote from there for the Tyler papers and the Houston Post. I made contact with an Irish newspaper, the Irish Independent, which later named me their Washington correspondent. I visited many Catholic churches in Ireland, Scotland and England and then, thirsting for the real thing, went first to Paris and finally Rome. At the time, with war in the air and fascisti in the streets, it was a somewhat risky adventure. But my attention was on the heavenly and the Lord saw me through: I climbed the 39 steps of the Holy Stairs on my knees and visited the Vatican, the catacombs and sites where martyrs and Crusaders had died. I returned from Europe in 1938 on a ship filled with Jews fleeing from Hitler's Germany. I interviewed several of them and was shocked by their stories.

My travels since then have tended to be more work and less pilgrimage. In fact, I appear to have become the focus of more than a few pilgrimages myself. Sometimes I think my various homes in Washington have all had written, somewhere on the doorstep where I couldn't see it but everyone else could, those words by Emma Lazarus they put up on the Statue of Liberty: "Give me your tired, your poor, your huddled masses..." Sometimes it seems like everyone with a problem comes to Sarah McClendon.

Not that I don't appreciate the trust that so many people seem to put in me. My daily mail is filled with requests for advice and help. The White House has gotten so used to receiving letters from folks who don't know my office address, that they now just messenger them over, sending parcels of envelopes addressed to "Sarah at the White House" or even to "That Loud Red-Haired Reporter." As I get older, my days seem to get fuller and fuller, but I am still a pushover for 11:30 PM calls from people in distress, especially fellow veterans. I have helped many a woman to get a job and helped to train others. I have helped others find a caring place to stay in what seems to them like an increasingly uncaring world. But requests from those in need of work or shelter are only the tip of the iceberg.

A man who has had his home unfairly seized and sold by the Internal Revenue Service asks if I can get his letters of protest to sympathetic eyes. A woman asks me to find her husband, a Marine Corps officer who she thinks the government has sent out on a secret mission. A lawyer wants advice on how he can expose the way the government is losing money on insurance for casualties in combat. A man from Vermont wants to know if I think he should expose the persons who had abused and molested him as a child. A New York corporation tells me that their software system was taken from them at gunpoint by federal agents and is now being used by their competitors for federal contracts. A retired social worker with arthritis asks where she can get the walker she saw me using at a press conference. A member of the Michigan Militia asks how, in the wake of the Oklahoma City bombing, he can tell people he's a concerned citizen, not a dangerous radical.

I have taken a few of those who have come to me for help into my life and even into my home, meeting them personally or giving them some temporary work or shelter. I slowed down a bit in this regard in the mid-1980s, after my daughter objected. She had, by this time, married a gifted and charming newspaper correspondent named David MacDonald and had given me, by a first marriage, a beautiful and brilliant granddaughter named Allison. After living a number of years in London, England, they now reside in Winnipeg, capital of the province of Manitoba, Canada.

When Sally came to visit my home on 28th Street, she noticed a bowl of keys in the front hall and asked what they were. I told her that with so many people in and out of the house all day, I let people who were expected on a regular basis have a key so I wouldn't have to interrupt my work to answer the front door. She was horrified. "Do you have any idea how many people all over town have keys to your house?" she asked. Needless to say, the bowl of keys did not become a permanent fixture. A few years later, Sally, David and Allison moved down to Washington, and since going up and down stairs was getting rough for me, I moved into my present single-level apartment and office, letting them have the house. Sure enough, Sally immediately had the locks, and later even the doors, replaced.

Which is not to say that Sally hasn't inherited her full share of the McClendon conscience. I can remember her sitting at the dining room table of the 28th Street house proofreading for Ralph Nader. When he first came to Washington, Ralph had few friends and contacts and needed help with his output of press releases, articles and testimony before Congress. He was living in a small room and his office phone was in a telephone booth across the hall. Sally was among the first to help him during this critical time. Over the years, Allison, too, has worked for him.

So three generations of McClendon women are friends and fans of this people's lobbyist, who has in many ways set the standards for activism in the public interest. I was extremely pleased that he spoke at a 1990 fund-raising event at which my friends honored me by setting up a McClendon Scholarship at the University of Missouri School of Journalism to help needy students study how to cover Washington. I am proud to know this true history-maker who has been called everything from Muckraker to Consumer Crusader.

I admire almost any activism, no matter what the cause, as long as it is non-violent and in the name of compassion, progress or freedom. The urge to help our fellow humans can cross political lines and create unlikely allies. I recall Susan Baker, wife of Reagan Chief of Staff and Bush Secretary of State James A. Baker III, telephoning her husband and President Reagan as they returned from California aboard Air Force One and asking them to respond to a hunger strike in which the controversial Mitch Snyder was engaged. Snyder, an ex-Wall Streeter who gave up his financial work to become a full-time advocate for the homeless, was trying to get the federal government to let an empty government warehouse become the first homeless shelter in the nation's capital. Mrs. Baker's quiet persistence eventually got the shelter up and running. She not only helped the late Mr. Snyder on many occasions but continues his tradition of fighting for food and shelter for those in need.

Advocacy crosses generational lines, as well. The scores of activists with whom I've shared a cause or a stage have ranged from the young comedian Paula Poundstone, who somehow, between her comedy concerts and being foster mother to a brood of racially diverse and handicapped children, writes a column for Mother Jones magazine, to the late great Maggie Kuhn, founder of the Gray Panthers, at whose 89th birthday gala I was privileged to speak. I shared a special interest in two of Maggie's causes—that there should not be any forced mandated retirement and that older people should practice and enjoy sex. When Brian Lamb, in a C-Span interview, later quizzed me on this topic, I replied, "I think it's great!" That comment went around the world, I heard.

I am grateful that the federal government is about to proceed on three projects which I can take some credit for having helped instigate. The first is, of course, the National World War II Memorial, which I am determined will be built while there are still veterans of the conflict alive to see it.

The second involves the Veterans Administration. The officials in charge of checking on the problem of homelessness among our former fighting men and women have gone to Congress for funds to build the first homeless shelter specifically for homeless women veterans. Since I have pushed this idea for years as both a journalist and Commander of the National Press Club American Legion Post No. 20, the VA recently telephoned me and asked if I "would mind if the shelter is named The Sarah McClendon House." I told them I would be delighted! When a colleague said, "Haven't you ever had anything named for you before?" I could only smile and answer, "I think someone named a calf for me once at the East Texas Fair."

The third item on the planning board is disabled access to the White House. Though the President and Congress have mandated handicapped entrances and bathroom facilities for all kinds of public and private buildings, neither the White House nor the Capitol meet those standards. Finally, after years of reminding Presidents of this fact, I have been questioned by construction officials about my ideas for making both the East and West Wings of the Executive Mansion accessible to visitors and the press in wheelchairs.

Knowing the way government usually moves, I realize all three of these projects will take time. It may be a while before they get off the ground...but it's good to know that at least they're on the runway. I am enough of a realist to know that change is usually slow, but enough of an optimist to think that it is inevitable. And no change that promises real progress frightens me. Just as I am the kind of Democrat who doesn't get nervous when Jesse Jackson appears on the convention floor, I am the kind of Catholic who supports a woman's right to choose. I feel there is a place even in my Church for change.

One man who helped me realize this was Joseph Huttlinger, a journalist I met in Washington shortly after I left the Timmons bureau and started out on my own. Like me, he had his own one-person bureau in the Press Building, specializing in oil much as I specialized in politics. And like me, he was a devout Catholic. He had one continuing worry I did not, however: he and his wife kept having one child after another, until they had at least six. About that time he wrote a letter to the Pope, asking His Holiness if there wasn't some way the church could address the problem of families becoming too large. In a time that most Catholics would not have even whispered the phrase, "birth control," Joe wrote about it directly to the Pope. I never did get to see the reply he got from the Vatican, but I have always appreciated the fact that Joe had the nerve to write that letter, that he felt strongly enough about it to do something. When he finally died, I feel he had literally worked himself to death, trying as hard as he could to make ends meet for the large family he loved.

I have discussed this issue with my dear friend Monsignor William F. O'Donnell. I met Father O'Donnell when I realized that, despite having been Catholic most of my long life, I still didn't know enough about the liturgy to find my way around all the ritual. When I told Monsignor McMann, pastor of St. Thomas the Apostle Church, that I felt I needed counseling, but didn't want to go to a class, he said, "I'll turn you over to Monsignor O'Donnell. He's lived in Washington all his life, so he speaks your language." Monsignor O'Donnell and I do indeed have many bonds. While a soldier in World War II, he took Christmas Eve Mass during the Battle of the Bulge in a barn. "As we sang Christmas carols," he remembers, "it suddenly dawned on us that we, too, were in a stable." He eventually left a career in government service to become a priest. Monsignor O'Donnell is not only my friend but my spiritual guide, advising me in my public as well as church life.

I have come to realize that most of the people in my life for whom I have held the highest regard are those who have found a balance in their own lives which includes service to others and respect for some higher power or idea. All the Presidents I have known have been, to some degree, both charitable and religious—though some have made a bigger show of either than I think they truly felt. For many, the display of good will and good faith was like a campaign promise, honest, perhaps, and well intentioned—but designed to impress.

One ex-President has impressed me in a very different way. Far from the spotlight of the Oval Office, he has quietly continued to rise to new levels of spirit and service. Few of us realized when he was in Washington how much he would achieve once he'd left the White House behind. In Jimmy Carter's continuing climb toward grace, it turns out the Presidency was just a foothill.

Chapter 8

◦•◦•◦

JIMMY CARTER: THE OUTSIDER

I liked Jimmy Carter the moment I first met him. I not only like him but deeply admire him today. In between, however, we had our ups and downs. In my mind, he is one of the most humane human beings who has ever resided in the White House. He was not, however, a particularly successful President. He was idealistic, compassionate, and, when circumstances allowed him to be, surprisingly effective. But he simply had too much going against him. His many enemies, his friends, and even some elements of his own fine personality combined to rob his presidency of its potential for greatness.

I first met the newly elected Governor of Georgia in 1970, at a National Governors Conference seminar for those freshmen newly elected to head their states that year. When my friend Malvina Stephenson suggested we go to Pinehurst, North Carolina and meet the new crop, I enthusiastically agreed. My father had taught me, after all, never to pass up making contacts. Among the more interesting material I came away with were a pair of taped radio interviews with Jimmy and Rosalynn Carter. He was impressively bright and filled with good but untested ideas. She was gracious, serious and so soft-spoken that I privately doubted if she would succeed in the ambitious mental health program which she intended to bring to Georgia.

The next time I spoke to Jimmy Carter was five years later, after his formal announcement at the National Press Club in Washington that he was running for President. The leadership potential I had seen in him had flowered, and this time I took him seriously indeed, though I suspect I was one of the few in the room who did. I was so impressed by his words, by his ideas on public service, and by his experience as a naval officer and engineer, a farmer, and now a governor, that I declared aloud, "This man is going to be elected President." He had tested his ideas for governmental reform in Georgia, working hard to reorganize the state agencies and create a system of zero-based budgeting. My colleagues, who thought I was amusing, convinced me that Carter had no chance.

I continued to follow his campaign, though. And in speech after speech, he showed that he was one of those independent southerners who, because they don't know when to quit, sometimes win against long odds. He was a populist if I'd ever seen one, and I had always been a bit of a populist myself, sharing their desire for individual rights, better government, and a higher standard of living for everyone. His populism began to strike a chord with the voters, too. He was not just sincere; he had the common touch, an understanding of the people back home in the small towns and villages like Plains, Georgia, where he had come from. He was not just forthright; he told the truth and did it in their language. He was not just James Earl Carter; he was Jimmy, a good ol' boy like them.

As it began to seem that Carter might actually become the Democratic candidate, I began talking about him as the real alternative to Jerry Ford. Though I liked President Ford, I was upset with the increasingly harsh campaign he was waging against Congress. As I spoke my mind on one radio interview after another, I apparently seemed such a Carter fan that listeners in Detroit complained and a staff person in Chicago told me, "Please say something on the other side."

At the Democratic National Convention in Madison Square Garden in New York, I had a rude awakening. Carter's campaign had emphasized that he was an outsider and would bring new ideas to Washington. I didn't realize that his anti-Washington bias would include me. The Carter camp was firmly closed to the Washington press. Only regional reporters, in particular those from Georgia, had free access. One Washington newsman, Eugene Methvin of *Reader's Digest*, reverted to his native Georgia accent and got in right away. Security guards were checking for Georgia driver's licenses. I asked if they would give me a blood test; after all, some of my ancestors came from Georgia.

At one point Jimmy Carter spotted me in the crowd, came over and shook hands. But he went inside without me. When, at a press conference for Rosalynn Carter, two Carter guards questioned my press credentials, I knew I had to do something about it.

I went to the Carter press office and inquired whether I could get a special badge that would admit me more easily to Carter functions. While I waited, I sat down in a chair at the head of a flight of stairs. I heard later that a guard had been sitting there watching who was going in and out of the Carter press office, but he had left. So I happened to be the lucky one in the seat when it decided to tumble its occupant down the flight of six steps. I was taken by ambulance to an emergency room but, as I had no broken bones, was released. When I went to my hotel room to change my bloody clothes, Carter was on the television making his acceptance speech.

My convention experiences were my first taste of the legendary "Georgia Mafia" which surrounded Jimmy Carter and, in the name of protecting him, managed to isolate him from the realities of Washington. This inner circle had already selected the reporters who would, throughout Carter's term, have the best access to the President and his staff. I still believed in him and his promises to reorganize government. But I had expected something different than the tight control over the press which I had learned to expect from other administrations.

As soon as Carter was elected President, he began working like a prairie fire. When he broke convention by walking part of the way to the White House on Inauguration Day, it seemed as if, indeed, a new spirit had arrived in Washington. He spent his first hundred days coming up with solutions that had been swept under the rug by Presidents as far back as JFK.

The first thing he did was deal with the problems left over from the Vietnam War. Since Ford had pardoned Nixon, Carter felt it was morally correct to grant a full pardon to all Vietnam era draft evaders who had not engaged in violence. Even more importantly, in my eyes, he began to straighten out the dishonorable discharges of many a young man who had gone to fight but had run into a problem which sent him home early from the war. These veterans, who in many cases had made just a simple mistake, had been branded for life by their bad discharges. Carter figured out a system in the Pentagon where they could be brought in for further hearings and have their discharges adjusted. Though some, like my old friend Barry Goldwater, thought Carter's kind treatment of draft evaders and those with dishonorable discharges was disgraceful, I considered Carter's actions those of a patriot.

One has to realize that a disproportionate number of the people drafted were black, inner-city youth who couldn't sit on an educational deferment or flee to Canada. These were young men who had been sent home for fighting in the barracks, doing drugs, or being simply unable to adjust to military life. So I thought correcting those bad discharges was even more important than letting those who had fled the draft return. One reporter from the *Chicago Tribune* criticized me when I said this in print. I told him I was a veteran myself, and that I understood the problems these young men had encountered. I suggested he go back to Chicago where he would find thousands of young men on the streets who badly needed this help.

Veterans were delighted when Carter named Max Cleland, a triple amputee from the Vietnam conflict, to head the Veteran's Administration. He then moved on energy and government reorganization. He made each Cabinet member autonomous, able to run his or her department with far less guidance—or interference—from the White House. Carter showed, at least at first, an impressive sense of purpose and organization. However, Betty Anderson, a woman whom Carter appointed to a high Treasury position, gave me another picture of the President when, after he had lost his battle for re-election, I asked her why. "He was an engineer," she said without hesitation. When I asked, "What does that mean, Betty?" she replied, "It means that he simply could not delegate to other people what had to be done. He had to be in on all of these things himself." Ironically enough, I felt both his impressive sense of organization and the feeling that he had to do everything himself could well have come from his Naval training.

I was impressed by his background at Annapolis and the fact that as a young officer he had been hand-picked by Admiral Hyman Rickover to navigate a nuclear submarine. Submariners are the Navy's elite and the nuclear fleet was Rickover's special concern. Few men stood up to his high standards. However, that same Naval training may have been at least partially responsible for Carter's inability to connect with the Washington establishment. The U.S. military teaches its officers to stay clear of politics. It infuses in them a disdain for those in Washington, especially the Congress. This, alongside Carter's independence, made it difficult for him to communicate with the old boy network of even his own party. In a capital city dominated by professional Democrats, professional Republicans and an old-line residential aristocracy, Carter was more of an outsider than even he knew.

President Carter's problems were not long in starting. When, four years later, he lost the Presidency to Ronald Reagan, hardly anyone within the Beltway felt the least surprised. We had all seen five things at work that took many of Carter's best intentions and turned them to dust. The first was his ineptness in dealing with Congress. The second was the Carter staff, who earned the nickname "Georgia Mafia" by their clannishness—which made many others, including myself, feel unnecessarily ignored. The other three factors came into play as the election drew near, but were there in spirit from the get-go: opposition from not only the Republicans but the leaders and rank and file of his own party, the theft of his inner office papers and secrets by at least one "mole" within the White House staff, and the dirty tricks played on him in connection with the Iranian hostages.

The problems with Congress were by no means all Carter's fault. The old-line political pros in Washington don't like to see any newcomer, especially someone from the South. There's still a great deal of bias, you know, from the Civil War. Carter's outsider status played into that prejudice. He had developed good relations at the state level when he was Governor, but he had no really close ties with the Democratic Party leaders at a national level. Once he became President, he tried to establish better relations, but by then it was too late. The course of his previous political life had not led him into the power brokers' orbit. He had no network of permanent friends in Washington whom he could count on to come to his defense.

I feel one reason Carter did not get along well with politicians was he was perhaps too much like the average American voter. The average man does not think in strategical terms or see the overall picture.

It's true that Carter did not show proper respect for members of Congress. He was insensitive to their cherished positions, their protocol, their power and their experience. Dale Hennington of Texas, an aide to Representative W.R. Poage, told me of a number of these incidents.

Once, President Carter was preparing to fly *Air Force One* to Mississippi to view damage from one of the worst hurricanes in history. That state's junior Senator, Thad Corcoran, wanted to go, but when he asked the White House, he was told there was no room on the plane. Mississippi's senior Senator, John Stennis, Democratic Chairman of the Armed Services Committee, arranged to get a military plane to view the havoc. He invited his fellow Senator to accompany him. As they prepared to board their plane, the presidential plane was nearby. Frank Moore, Carter's staff man for Congressional Relations, suddenly realized his office had goofed. He approached the Senators and asked if they would like to ride on *Air Force One.* He was thanked but told if there was no room for one Senator on *Air Force One,* there was certainly no room for two.

As if this were not enough damage to White House/Senatorial relations, after Carter had surveyed the disaster zone, he granted more relief to Mississippi, when in fact the storm had hit worst at Mobile, Alabama. Donald Stewart, a freshman Democratic Senator from Alabama, was outraged.

Representative Kiki de la Garza, Democrat of Texas, was first vice chairman, then chairman of the House Agricultural Committee. He learned that President Carter planned to send a delegation to Mexico to discuss agricultural problems. Though de la Garza was the only Mexican-American on the Committee, Carter named others to go. It was only when one Carter selectee dropped out that de la Garza went along—as a second choice.

Representative de la Garza received another affront from the Carter White House. He had long been requesting early consideration from the Department of Agriculture for farmers in his south Texas district since they have to plant their crops ahead of others. One day he discovered the DOA publicly announcing special terms for south Texas farmers, but they had not notified him. Presidential courtesy has always required that any announcement affecting a Congressman's district should be given first to the Congressman so that he could make the announcement, especially if he's the one who made the request in the first place.

Incredibly, Hamilton Jordan, White House Chief of Staff, did not even meet with the Senate Majority Leader, Senator Robert Byrd of West Virginia, or the Speaker of the House, Massachusetts Representative Tip O'Neill, until very late in the Carter term. O'Neill was so peeved with the Carter White House's failure to keep him informed of Presidential planning that, at times, he would not let Frank Moore in his office. To make it worse, as though in self-defense, the administration would have Press Secretary Jody Powell make charges of self-interest against Congress when relations got strained.

As bad as they were, relations with Congress looked good beside the administration's relationship with the bureaucracy. This closed community rejects change and resists outsiders like no other force in Washington. During Carter's administration, my family witnessed this personally. While he was still writing for the *Winnipeg Free Press*, my son-in-law David attended an exclusive seminar on America in the 1980s. Part of the program was a short, unclassified briefing at CIA headquarters in Langley. But because he was representing the Canadian press, David was excluded from this briefing, treated as though he were from somewhere behind the Iron Curtain. When he later mentioned this to me, I raised hell. I tried to call CIA director Stansfield Turner, but the security man who answered Turner's phone hung up on me.

The next night I related this to President Carter, the First Lady, and Attorney General Benjamin Siviletti at a White House function which David and I were attending. I said, "Canada loves the United States, and half the time we treat it like a dog." Having experienced the same sort of resistance from the intelligence establishment, Carter not only seemed sympathetic, but insisted that at least David and I take a picture with him and Rosalynn.

Carter's problems with the career military and intelligence communities were not the kind that could be solved by a kind word and a souvenir picture. Their hostility to the Carter administration went so far, I believe, that some among them actively worked against Carter when he ran for re-election against Ronald Reagan.

But even Carter's allies added to his dilemma. Unfortunately, most of his extremely loyal staff reflected his inexperience in Washington. They were not well informed about Congress, its practices or its powers. To many in Congress, they seemed ignorant—and arrogant about their ignorance. They were aggressively informal, working in jeans and putting their feet on tables while they talked, and to some, it looked like the White House had been taken over by the hired hands. They were intensely loyal to the President, however. And when, part way through the term, he asked them to shape up and establish a better image, they started coming in wearing ties and being more careful about the wisecracks. They still remained pretty much a closed family group, tending not to mix with townfolk, partly because of long hours and the fact they got more telephone calls and requests for White House tours than anyone up to that time. Country music stars came frequently to the White House, and they seemed more welcome in the Oval Office than the politicians.

The man on the Carter staff with whom I had the most contact was Jody Powell. I thought Jody was a good press secretary but his idea of the press secretary's job did not always agree with mine. He often felt that enhancing Carter's image was more important than giving us information about the country. A former military man himself, he also seemed to have a negative attitude about Congress. I offered to take him down there and introduce him to some of its leaders. He said, "I might just take you up on that," but never seemed to find the time.

Carter's press relations started out surprisingly good. Unlike during the campaign, we were given access to the White House staff and could put our questions to them directly. During the Nixon and Ford years, those same questions would have had to go though Zeigler and Nessen—and often got "lost" on the way. One day during Carter's first month in office, I called four staff people and left a message for each of them to call back. They all did, and each of them helped me with a story.

At first, Carter did a great job with his regular and frequent press conferences. He seemed very much in control of himself and the room. As Ford had during his early press conferences, Carter took questions from all over the room—but he, too, later reverted to taking "two from the wire services, three from the networks, two from the Washington papers," and then, after one from Judy Woodruff (an NBC correspondent from Georgia), let the rest of us scramble for attention. During the Carter administration, I got in my share of questions, but I also got slapped on the wrist from time to time. At his very first press conference, I asked Carter about a possible conflict of interest within the Federal Energy Administration, and though Carter said he would look into it (and, in fact, did have some of the people involved request back-up material from me), I never got a real answer. Instead, for quite a while, I found myself waving my hand without being recognized.

Unlike the president, Jody Powell seemed to enjoy fencing

with me. We had, at times, an almost playful relationship, though it always kept its edge. In the administration's early days of enforced informality, he seemed to think it amusing to slip in a four-letter word now and again. One day I told him he ought to have his mouth washed out with soap. He got back at me a bit later when I dared to say something negative about the First Lady. I still have the note he sent me which reads, in toto:

"Sarah,
You can kick my bird dog, step on my blue suede shoes, and say anything you wish about the President; but cheap shots at the First Lady are out of bounds.
You ought to be ashamed of yourself.

Jody."

Perhaps he was right, because, in fact, of all those helping at the Carter White House, Rosalynn was probably not only the most helpful but the one least deserving of criticism. In many ways, I saw her as reviving the tradition begun by Eleanor Roosevelt, acting as her husband's staff advisor, special emissary to the people and his confidential messenger.

The others in Carter's family were unusually visible as well during his time at the White House and much was made of his background as a peanut farmer in the little town of Plains. His sweet mother, Miss Lillian, was an asset, but reviews on the others were mixed. They ranged from sister Ruth, a gospel preacher who could hold audiences of 20,000 spellbound as she performed healings, through his other sister Gloria, who rode a motorcycle back before it was considered a fashionable thing for women to do, down to brother Billy, who was colorful, to say the least. Besides urinating in public and lending his name to a brand of beer, he embarrassed the President when the Justice Department was forced to investigate a possibly inappropriate financial relationship involving Libya. And then, there was cousin Hugh, who wrote a book about the family fights.

With all the turmoil, Carter still managed to build a record of achievement. He signed both the Nuclear Non-proliferation Act and a comprehensive government ethics law and, in his second year, helped bring about the first major break in the Middle East crisis with the signing of the Camp David Accords. I like to remember Carter standing there in a group handshake with Egyptian President

Anwar el-Sadat and Israel's Prime Minister, Menachem Begin. But problems in defining his energy policies led to a crisis of confidence which was compounded when, in November of 1979, Iranians in Teheran seized the U.S. Embassy and took 90 Americans hostage. Some were released, mainly women and blacks, but eventually, 52 remained captive.

Problems with the economy, which varied between high inflation and high unemployment, had caused the administration's popularity to fall. The hostage issue would seal its doom. Jody Powell once told me that Carter's re-election hopes "began to go downhill from false reports issuing here and in Iran about the Carter dealings to free the hostages." Though Powell has been careful not to link those reports to the Reagan election campaign, there are many others who have.

At least two men on the Reagan campaign staff had worked in the CIA, or its predecessor, the OSS. They would have known how to get in touch with sources in Iran and how to use that intelligence to hurt Carter. William Casey, Carter's campaign director, had extensive experience with the OSS and would later be named by Reagan to head the CIA. George Bush, who was to become Reagan's vice presidential running mate, had been head of the CIA and is reported to have maintained close connections there for many years.

Jody Powell remembers a day in April 1980 as "one of the blackest days" the Carter administration ever experienced. A false report came out of Iran saying that Carter had written to the Iranian leader, Khomeini, "virtually apologizing for US activities in the past and admitting doing wrong...That letter was a total fabrication," but the beginning of the downward spiral. "We had sent a letter, but it was the exact opposite of what was reported. Our letter was an ultimatum pointing out that the Iranians had promised to transfer the hostages by a specific date. If the Iranians did not transfer the hostages...we were going to have to take some action, and we reserved the right to reveal that the Iranians had made this commitment in secret, yet did not keep it." Around this time top officials in Iran did, in fact, announce that Iran would transfer the hostages. Eventually—and rather mysteriously—the negotiations broke down.

Barbara Honegger, who served on both Reagan's campaign and White House staffs and eventually became my close friend, tells me that the people around Reagan had astonishing access to papers, documents, memos and ideas that were floating around the Carter White House. She said the Reagan campaign directors would look at the information received and gloat, "Look at what we have now. You won't believe it! Boy oh boy, do we have the good stuff now!" Just who made the deliveries, Honegger never said. I know she suspected one or both of two secretaries who had worked in the Carter White House and were kept on to work for Reagan. It is widely accepted that Carter briefing books were used to prepare Reagan for his televised debates with Carter. But what other uses that and other leaked material was put to remains open to speculation.

I have heard undocumented rumors from people in the military that when Carter tried a strategic air and ground operation to rescue the hostages, his efforts were sabotaged. Even more persuasive, though unproven, is the persistent speculation that an agreement was made in Reagan's name to derail progress on the hostage negotiations until after the election.

This so-called "October Surprise" allegedly came at a time when Carter appeared to have a real hope of bringing the hostages home. If he had been able to do so, it would have greatly increased his chances in the 1976 election. Though I have heard from two people who say they have first-hand knowledge that this did indeed occur (one a pilot who said he flew certain parties to the meeting in Paris at which the "Surprise" was arranged), both Carter and Jody Powell have said they do not believe it happened. I wish I were as sure as they are. There have been several interesting books written on the subject.

Whether or not Ronald Reagan had anything to do with the timing of the hostages' release, they left Teheran on the same day Jimmy Carter left Washington: January 21, 1981. Since then, Jimmy Carter has, if anything, gone on to greater respect as a private citizen than he did as President. He has devoted himself to writing and to teaching at Emory University, where he has also established the Carter Center for research and advocacy. He is also closely identified with a wonderful organization called Habitat for Humanity. This activist group, which values action over words, puts up brand new, completely furnished houses within a day for poor people who have never had a home in their lives. I have participated in these events, which have the feeling of an old fashioned barn raising, doing my part by raking leaves in a yard where they had just finished the house.

In a way, in fact, though he was a one-term president, Jimmy Carter now could be considered "President of the World." His continuing interest in foreign affairs has led him to monitor elections in developing nations, to mediate the civil war in the Sudan and to support international relief organizations in places like Somalia.

As President Clinton's unofficial emissary, Carter has traveled to both North Korea to help defuse a crisis over their development of nuclear weapons, and to Haiti, where he urged the *junta* to leave. Always the outsider, Jimmy Carter is still showing how much good an outsider can do.

TYLER, TEXAS, 1910-29;

WASHINGTON, DC, 1944-1996:

It's funny to see how people react when I tell them that I am by nature quite a shy person: "Sarah McClendon? The woman who's made life miserable for a half-century's worth of Presidents? The one who asks THOSE questions? Shy?"

But the truth is that every time I wave my hand in the air shouting "Mr. President! Mr. President!!" I am forcing myself to be something I am not—loud, aggressive and pushy. I do it because I usually feel it is the only way to make myself heard. I do it because I am short, female, Southern and, for the past few years at least, elderly, all things that work against your being noticed in our society. I do it so I can confront our leaders with the important questions that, as one of them, Richard Nixon, noted, sometimes only I have "the nerve to ask."

One reason I have been able for all these years to push myself into doing something that does not come naturally is that a decided streak of drama runs through the McClendon family. My father, who had been very poor as a child, was given the Bible and Shakespeare's plays instead of toys to keep him busy. He would memorize long passages of both and spent many weekend afternoons alone in the woods, reciting them. This early practice led him to become one of the finest orators in east Texas, much in demand for speeches and orations, especially at Masonic funerals.

My mother was both literary and musical, with a strong interest in forming literary clubs and attending opera. At Hollins College, she had appeared in several plays. As prominent citizens of Tyler, Texas, both she and my father continued to patronize community theater, encouraging their children to appear in local performances. Every year while I was in grade school and high school, the Chatauqua Society would come by for a week of lectures. On the last day of the week, the children would put on a show they had been practicing. A McClendon or two was usually in the cast. At other times, a traveling director would come into town and organize the locals in a show.

A few of my sisters and brothers showed a talent for dramatics. My oldest sister, Annie Bonner, taught me to speak by having me give recitations. She aspired to a career on the stage, even appearing in a play in Dallas with the as-yet-undiscovered Clark Gable, and wound up being a teacher of "expression," the art of conducting your conversations with animation and grace. My only surviving sibling, my brother Frank, also trod the boards while in college.

I was pushed into command performances early—for first my older brothers and then for any company that would drop by or come to dinner—reciting from atop the dining table the suffragette speeches I picked up while, as a pre-schooler, being toted by my mother from one feminist rally to another. While at Tyler Junior College, I was a member of Las Mascaras, the drama society, and got good notices (or at least "good and noticed") for my performance as the clown Touchstone in "As You Like It."

Tyler eventually organized a Little Theater, complete with its own building and professional director. While working at the Tyler news-papers, I somehow found the time to appear in several of their produc-tions. And even though I thought my career as a Washington journalist had put my formal acting days behind me, once I became an member of the Women's National Press Club, I found myself frequently drafted into their satiric sketches about Washington life and Washington celebrities. I usually played fellow Texans like Lyndon Johnson or Sam Rayburn.

So, although acting has not played a central role in my life, it has played a persistent one, whether on the stage or in the audience—so to speak—of every press conference I attend. Maybe that's why I understood President Ronald Reagan, I feel, better than most of my colleagues.

But then, of course, compared to Mr. Reagan, I was a rank amateur.

Chapter 9

RONALD REAGAN:
HIS BEST ROLE

In over half a century in Washington, I've covered only two Presidents through two full terms in office: Dwight Eisenhower and Ronald Wilson Reagan.[1] There were a lot of similarities between the two. Both were Republicans who served eight years marked by relative peace (though both sent troops to Lebanon) and apparent prosperity (though both faced economic recessions). Both were very popular, strong against the Communists, reassuring in a fatherly way about problems at home and able to make most Americans feel that all was well. Both learned how to be President while serving as President. Both won re-election by a landslide. Both called on me regularly during press conferences—and I regularly battered both of them.

There were a lot of differences between the two, as well. And as time goes by, those differences make me appreciate Eisenhower more and more—while my opinion of Ronald Reagan doesn't change. Every President tries to show the people only those parts of himself he thinks we want to see. Behind a bland, almost dull facade, Ike hid more intelligence and desire to learn than most of us ever realized he had. Reagan showed us a mask, too, one built by his experience and ability in acting. If Hollywood had understood how talented Ronald Reagan was, they would have never let him go.

As President, Reagan was almost always as pleasant as could be. Everybody liked him. You couldn't help but like him. I know a lot of Congressmen who went to the White House muttering, "I'm going to tell him off when I get there," and then wound up doing nothing of the sort. They sat back and listened to his jokes and let themselves be neutralized. They couldn't really stay mad at him. A lot

---

[1] In fact, in the entire Twentieth Century, only four Presidents (these two, Woodrow Wilson and, of course, FDR) have had a full eight years, or more, in office.

of journalists found themselves beguiled that same way.

Ronald Reagan knew how to use his charm on me, as well. He could be extremely thoughtful. Late in 1985, when I had an operation on my hip and was in the Veteran's Hospital for a considerable amount of time, he called. The nurses went all a-twitter and said, "Get on the telephone right quick. The President's calling you! The President!" They couldn't get over it. They were just astounded. So I picked up the phone and there was Mr. Reagan, wanting to know how I was getting along. That was very nice of him—and very flattering.

It was after New Year's before I was home from the hospital and ready to go back to work. On the afternoon of January 6, the President's office called to tell me that the President was going to have a press conference that night. They asked, "Ms. McClendon, are you coming to the press conference tonight?" I replied, "I certainly am. I wouldn't miss it." They said, "If he should call on you, would you have a question for him?," to which I said, "You better believe it." Well, with that warning, I prepared hard. And Ronald Reagan still managed to give me quite a surprise.

When I got to the press conference, he had arranged, for the first time in his Presidency, for me to sit in the front row! It may have been the first time that I ever sat in the front row for a presidential conference. It used to be that if you got to the White House early, you could get a front seat. But not now. For quite some time, it's been arranged so that the biggies, the wire services, the networks and the big-city newspapers, get those front row seats. The seat with my name on it is on the left end of Row 5.

But this time, Mr. Reagan had notified the wire services ahead of time to make a space for me. He came in and followed his opening statement with this announcement:

"But wait; before taking your questions, let me extend a warm welcome back to one of your colleagues, Sarah McClendon. Sarah's been absent for a while, but she's back now, and I'm delighted.

Sarah is a true Washington institution who's seen a lot of history that she's covered aggressively and fairly. Sarah's kept several of my predecessors, eight Presidents in all, and me on our toes over the years. And I'm truly honored that she chose tonight for her first public appearance, but I had a feeling that she wouldn't miss this.

So, you see, it's not that we haven't been holding press conferences; I was just waiting for Sarah to come back!"

This was his first press conference in four months, and his tongue-in-cheek attempt to blame me for that gave everyone a laugh.

I was very pleased but confused. I could hardly believe the kindness of the tribute. I was so astounded at Reagan's words that I kept wondering, "Who's he talking about?" This was a President I had regularly taken to task for almost five years! My now-deceased dear friend, Malvina Stephenson, sitting there beside me, was stunned with pleasure at the President's recognition of me. Then Mr. Reagan surprised me once again: "And in honor of her return, I'd like to offer Sarah the first question. Don't worry, Mike," he told the Associated Press correspondent, "you'll get the second one."

There were plenty of reporters who specialized in throwing this president softballs that he could hit over the fence. But I never had and wasn't about to start. So even under these circumstances, I asked the same tough question I had planned, one I'd learned a lot about during my hospital stay.

"Oh, thank you, Mr. President. That was very nice of you, and I appreciate it", I said. Then I continued, "Sir, I want to call your attention to a real problem we've got in this country today. The hospitals and the doctors are sending the elderly sick home too soon, before they are really ready to go, and that makes a burden on their families. This all seems to be based on the Medicare payment formula, and I know that there's a fear across the land, from Gramm-Rudman,...that the Medicare payments may be reduced further." I asked if his experts couldn't find a solution.

Well, with that, the party was over. His answer, I'm sorry to say, was all too typical of his style. First he generalized: "Sarah, I can't tell you what the final decision has been on this. We have been looking at this entire program, things that can be done and should be done, and also the possibility we're looking at as to whether we can't find something to take care of catastrophic illness."

Next, he shifted the blame onto someone else: "I tried to do this when I was Governor in California, and I couldn't get any public interest in it at all. I guess everyone has a feeling that it will never happen to them."

Then, he fell back on his old favorite, the budget: "But we are looking at this and as to what we can do with regard to some of the problems that have arisen, because, as you know, the program has expanded in costs greatly. Medical care and, well, health care, generally, has been one of the highest factors in the increase in inflation."

Finally, he ended with an empty assurance: "So, I promise you, we're looking at it."

When I tried to follow up with a practical suggestion—"Well, Sir, has anyone ever thought about the fact that Canada gets her medical care with a little extra taxation but practically free? Why couldn't we start something like that?"—the President quickly dismissed it. "Well, we're looking for answers. All right, Mike," was all he said, turning to the AP man for his question. That cut-and-run tactic was pretty typical, too.

This was done so smoothly that practically no one noticed the smoke and mirrors. Reagan's productions showed a real sense of showmanship. He seemed to know just what time of day to feed news to the correspondents so it would hit prime time on television in the evening without giving them a chance to analyze it too deeply. He had a careful eye for production and props. His stage settings, whether at the White House or away, were unusually fitting. His makeup made him appear younger. His suits were well tailored. He was always careful to give supporting credits to Vice President George Bush and perhaps a bit player from Congress. He and the First Lady, Nancy, usually held hands in public. The frequent show of romance complemented the constant show of sincerity.[2]

Ronald Reagan stands high on the list of Presidents who developed a strong sense of being connected to the people out there. The people liked him because they felt they knew him and could understand him. It was obvious that his movie career had taught him a great deal. He also learned a lot about public relations during his days in World War II, when he served as a communicator to help the war effort. Though his Press Secretaries, Jim Brady, Larry Speakes

---

[2] Did President Reagan dye his hair? Though his press aides always said no to that vital question, I got the opposite answer once from a pretty good source. One day when Neil Reagan, the President's brother, was visiting him at the White House, I was among a few reporters who got him aside for a talk. Pointing out that Neil's hairdo made him look quite young, I asked, "Which of you is older?" Neil answered that the barber he and his brother used was an ace at giving dye jobs—a service he performed for both his clients named Reagan.

and Marlin Fitzwater, were all quite good at their jobs (and unusually kind to me), the President himself was still better, a real professional at handling a question thrown to him by Helen Thomas of UPI or Sam Donaldson of ABC en route to a helicopter or waiting limousine. His humorous one-liners were perfect "sound bites" for the hungry media, getting him extra coverage and endearing him to the American public.

Ronald Reagan was a natural campaigner. Because he was so excellent at relating to people in crowds, often using only one word or phrase to conjure up approving images or empathy, he was in actuality campaigning all the time. Everything he said or did seemed designed to make you like him. In that, he far surpassed anyone the Democrats could set up against him, despite how much charm candidates Carter and Mondale or Congressional leaders like Tip O'Neill of Massachusetts and Jim Wright of Texas tried to show.

The President managed to make patriotism seem like an exclusively Republican idea. He knew when to play on the heartstrings of the public by talking about motherhood, clean living, peace and national pride. He always seemed to be pushing programs for better education or cures for drug abuse and crime, but, because funding or real follow-through wasn't always in the picture, these programs actually worked best at selling the public the picture of Ronnie Reagan as a concerned, "can-do" kind of leader. He made Congress and the Democrats the whipping boy for all that was wrong with the country and took credit for all that was right. He turned "liberal" into a dirty word.

Reagan would "personally" invite citizens from all parts of the country to come to Washington (at their own expense) for White House "briefings". At these functions, 150 to 500 wide-eyed, excited visitors would spend the day hearing from Reagan's people what a fine job the Administration was doing in building up national defense, helping the small businessman, saving on spending by correcting waste and fraud and cutting down the welfare rolls and inflation at the same time. The carefully choreographed events would usually include luncheon and finally climax with a few words from Vice President Bush and then fifteen minutes of the President himself.

These get-togethers almost always had another speech on the agenda: some staff person talking about how slanted the White

House Press Corps was and how badly they were treating Mr. Reagan whenever they wrote anything that wasn't 100% favorable to him. It was Lyndon-Johnson-style news management all over again—but this time fed directly to the public. The listeners would generally go away angry at the press and ready, whether they were new converts or just fired up with the Word, to spread the Reagan doctrine to all the land: the "liberal" media needed to have their powers of access to information curbed.

Because he was so good at getting public opinion behind him and making anyone who criticized him seem elitist, wrong-headed or even unpatriotic, there were not nearly so many journalists ready to take on Ronald Reagan as the White House liked to pretend there were. I learned the risks of doing so when, at a press conference late in July of 1982, I tore into him about his refusal to release an important report he'd authorized on federal laws that discriminate against women. As Reagan and I went back and forth, arguing at length about whether the report even existed, I clearly and repeatedly accused him of not telling the truth. From the shocked reaction of the other journalists in the room, I thought I had stirred up as big a controversy as I had when I'd named the names of two high-placed security risks during a nationally televised JFK press conference 21 years before! I couldn't help thinking of the denunciations which had followed that incident, the threats of a government hearing, the Women's National Press Club calling a meeting to criticize me! But I was so furious, I didn't even care.

You see, the report over which we were arguing was the direct result of something shocking that had happened at the Republican National Convention in 1980, the convention which had nominated Ronald Reagan to run against Jimmy Carter. Actually, its roots stretched back even farther, into the administration of Jerry Ford. And I'd been there, both times.

The incident, which had, for many of us, shaken the walls of Detroit's Renaissance Center, where the convention was taking place that summer, had involved the Republican Platform. When the Platform Committee had wound up its paperwork and prepared to issue the new statement of party policy, there was a startling omission. For the first time in forty years, the Equal Rights Amendment—which had originally been introduced into Congress in 1923 and finally passed and submitted to the states for ratification in 1972—was not going to be endorsed by the Republican convention. Up to this time, no matter how conservative the Republican presidential candidate had been, the ERA had been backed by and campaigned for by the GOP all the way. With the ratification deadline looming ahead in 1982, this defection sent a signal which could be a deathblow to its chances. The ERA had always been a favorite project of the Republican leadership. But now the committee had voted to leave it out.

Like most of the women covering the convention—and many of the women attending it—I was aghast. Mary Crisp, co-chair of the Republican National Committee and a strong advocate of the ERA, was being stepped on, pushed aside, shunned. Platform Committee member Martin Anderson, a former professor at Stanford University and a staunch Reaganite, knew that as Governor of California, Ronald Reagan had always enthusiastically supported the amendment. Reagan was a moderate, just like me, Anderson thought...wasn't he? The professor decided to send a note to Reagan in his 16th floor suite, before the non-endorsement was set in stone, to see if he would, as the candidate, try to override the committee's vote. According to witnesses, Reagan looked at the note, then passed it to his wife. Nancy Reagan turned thumbs down.

And this is how the Equal Rights Amendment was written off by the Republicans and how Ronald Reagan began his long, hazardous journey to live down an anti-woman reputation. I saw Mary Crisp leave the convention. She wasn't walking out in a huff; she was being ridden out of town on a rail. She had no choice. From then on, she became a non-person, so far as her political party's leadership was concerned, though she remained a loyal Republican and is so today.

One close friend of Mary's (and just as avid a supporter of the ERA), may have felt like leaving but could not. Though she had reportedly seldom seen or heard from her father before his nomination, Maureen Reagan, Ronnie's daughter by his first wife, was needed as a show of family support. When she appeared on the main stage to hug her father in celebration, her step-mother appeared rather less than delighted. At the press conference Maureen gave, I asked about her father's decision. Loyally, she insisted that, despite the party's choice, "he will some day bring about legal justice for women."

When it became doubtful whether the ERA was going to meet the June, 1982 deadline for ratification by the states, some of the women on President Reagan's staff tried to make good what his eldest daughter had said. They went back to a study that had been launched by Gerry Ford at the suggestion of Major General Jeanne Holm, his Women's Advisor and a close friend of mine in both military and civilian life. The study, a Justice Department inquiry into federal laws, regulations, policies and procedures that discriminate against women, had been delayed by lack of funding, lack of encouragement, and other bureaucratic complications. Though the Carter Administration had supplied the needed funds and encouragement, it was still uncompleted, largely due to data held back by the Department of Health and Human Services, where many injustices had occurred in Social Security and other programs.

The women, most prominently Elizabeth Dole, then Assistant to the President for Public Liaison, her assistant Wendy Borcherdt, and Barbara Honegger, former assistant to Martin Anderson in Policy Development, wrote up an Executive Order for Reagan to sign. This order, the strongest initiative towards women's equality since Suffrage, was a way the President could still become the champion of women's rights they felt he should be. On December 21, 1981, he signed the Executive Order calling for uncovering, designating and correcting any federal laws or policies discriminatory to women. A group of women lawyers in various departments was chosen to implement the study. Assistant Attorney General Carol Dinkins, a native of Houston, was to head the panel. But she delayed and then resigned her job.

It seemed as if the report might be put back on the shelf. Although the study was to be completed and updated by all government agencies and departments, many, including the State Department, did not want to reply to it. Though a second Executive Order had required quarterly reports, the Chief Executive did not seem inclined to ask for them. When Barbara Honnegger reminded him of this, she suddenly found herself in charge of getting all the material together. She was further startled to find that her job had been moved from the White House to the Justice Department, where she found it very difficult to get anything done. When data would finally come in, it lay unread for months on the desk of the Attorney General. Barbara became so dissatisfied with this that she finally came to me and asked me to help get the report released, even in its incomplete form.

As I often did when I could get nowhere else, I called James Baker, III, the White House Chief of Staff and a personal friend from Texas. (His mother's last name was Bonner, as was my mother's, though we found out we weren't related.) I told him it would be smart for the Reagan Administration to release the report—and by all means by the June 30 final deadline for ERA ratification. By now it was obvious that the ERA, still three states short, would not get the 38 state legislatures' vote needed to make it part of the Constitution—and the Republicans would need something to cushion the blow to women across the nation. I tried every argument, saying, "Jim, this would offset the feeling that most women in this country are going to have that your boss and the Republicans sold them out in Detroit."

But nothing was released. I later found out that a Cabinet Council on Legal Policy had indeed reported on the women's legal study to the President on June 28. When I finally persuaded an assistant to Press Secretary Larry Speakes, Peter Roussel of Houston, to tell me what the report was about, he peeked in a file folder and just told me, "Sex." I should have guessed that the President would soon use the same kind of joke to try to avoid my questions.

Upset by the defeat of the ERA and outraged by the government's lack of response, Barbara and I decided to tell all about what she had been through. I would interview her in my parlor and then leak the news to the press. In mid-July of 1982, Barbara's story appeared in the *Washington Post*, prominently displayed. She was resigning from the Reagan Administration, it read, because of the inactivity in pursuing this important report.

I went to the next Presidential press conference, on July 28, and waved my hand until Reagan took my question as the last one of the day. But when I asked when he would make the report available to the press, he claimed that he had never heard of such a report, that he didn't know anything about it.

I let him know I wasn't buying that: "You got it, you got part of it. You got the first quarter of it." I named who had given it to him, where and when. He said, "No," and I said, "Yes." Then, in my worked-up state, I fumbled for a word: "It says there has been a lot of sex discr... harassment of women."

That was all he needed to get in a joke. "Now, Sarah," he said, "just a minute here with the discussion, or we'll be getting an R rating." Of course, that caused some laughter among my more nervous colleagues, as the President knew it would. But I just continued: "I hope you'll look into it and let us see the report instead of waiting to get it out for years."

He tried to deflect the issue by claiming that he had hired more women to high-ranking jobs than Jimmy Carter, and then finally recalled he had asked the Justice Department to look for federal laws that discriminate against women, but they hadn't finished their work. I told him they'd finished enough of it for us to see. He finally cut me off with one more joke, raising the imaginary sexual content of the report even higher: "I'll look into that and see what it is. But I don't recall anything that really had an X rating that ever was handed to me." When it was over, the transcripts showed that Mr. Reagan and I had gone back and forth eleven times!

The next day I found that I had, indeed, stirred up a controversy comparable to my set-to with President Kennedy—but this time, there was a big difference. Although the White House announced it had a "heavy onslaught" of calls and letters running 2-to-1 against me, I received only 65 letters that said that I was wrong, or even rude—and literally thousands of favorable comments, letters, calls and personal "thank-you"s, which kept coming in for months. And they weren't all from women. The phone call that woke me the morning after the confrontation was a man who said, "I just realized what you're talking about. I have three daughters and if we don't change those laws, they aren't going to have a chance." I was so happy to hear that he understood. As I was going down Connecticut Avenue, another man got out of a car and came over to me on a sidewalk and said, "I want to touch you." One man who wrote to say that I was "no lady," wrote back to apologize after he got my explanation that I might have been a little carried away by the importance of the issue. He sent me an embroidered handkerchief, "because it's suitable for a lady." I guess the oddest letter of all was from a woman from Alabama who wrote to say, "We should clone you!" I think she was serious.

Just as importantly (but no more or less), a large number of politicians and most of my fellow print journalists came down on my side. Rep. Charles Schumer of New York said he "was appalled not only because the President sought to evade an earnest and appropriate question but also because the President thought it appropriate to joke publicly about one form of discrimination and abuse, the problem of sexual harassment." Tom DeFrank of *Newsweek* was disturbed that other reporters laughed at my question: "Sarah's conduct can make you cringe sometimes, but she has every right to ask a question in whatever fashion she chooses. I have never bought this ridiculous argument that presidents must be handled with kid gloves." I especially appreciated two wonderful columns written by Georgie Anne Geyer of the Universal Press Syndicate and Carl Rowan of *Field Enterprises*. Political cartoonists drew pictures of me leaping at the President like a wildcat and of Reagan afraid to come out of the White House for fear I'd be there.

Helen Thomas backed me up by also demanding the report be released. The National Women's Political Caucus waged into battle on my side by issuing a statement disputing the President's claim that he had named more women to high posts than Jimmy Carter had. Even Presidential Press Secretary Larry Speakes' reaction was much milder than I had expected. He showed me some letters he wrote to people who'd objected to my question. His replies said nothing derogatory, simply that I was a person who believed in persevering until I got an answer.

Which was really all that I had done. I think that most people realized that I was only trying to make the government release a report that the people had paid for and were entitled to receive. An overdue report that could have helped people understand what women face and, if it had come out earlier, might have lessened people's fear, misunderstanding and opposition to the ERA.

I made my point, but the government still took its time. Before the week was up, the White House had leaked a story and a few pages of the report, but the sample tried to make it seem as if the problems the study was looking at were really nothing. On the *CBS Morning News*, I called the leak a lie, which it certainly was. Congresswoman Pat Schroeder of Colorado, a member of the House Judiciary Sub-Committee on Civil and Constitutional Rights, which has jurisdiction over such statutes, sent a letter to the President requesting copies of the full report and taking him to task for trying to turn it, as he did my question, into a laughing matter. "You have said you are opposed to equality with a capital E. It is now becoming clear you are opposed to equity with a small e."

When she finally obtained a copy of the report, Representative Schroeder was still dissatisfied. "I now see," she said, "why he was hiding it from everybody. They still think the major women's issue is the shortage of white gloves in this country." It took almost a year for what was now being called "Sarah's Report" to be available to the public. And when it was, it got little coverage in the papers. One broadcaster for CBS called it "cosmetic changes...just a few changes from 'his' to 'hers.'" But it was a fine report, a needed first step, even though it was not altogether complete since the State Department and some other agencies would still not admit to all they knew. I have heard it resulted in changes in the Space Administration's dealing with women. After that, women, who had been denied access by NASA, were put on an equal footing as astro-nauts. I think in time the report will have a greater effect. I hope that some day it will finally help put an Equal Rights Amendment into the Constitution.

Around the same time that the report on discriminatory laws was being held up (and the ERA was going down), Ed Rollins, an advisor to the Reagan White House, put together a 47-page analysis of why the President was doing so poorly in his ratings with unmar-ried women. Used to being popular with everyone, Reagan could not understand this problem area. This document took on many aspects of single women's lives, from low pay to fear of crime and from child care to the loneliness of the elderly. It pointed out things that Reagan had already done which hurt unmarried women—and his approval rating with them—and things he could have done to improve both areas. It said that if the Republicans weren't willing to make a lot of changes, the President could not expect to get the vote of single women. Though it seemed to recommend that the Party just write off this important segment of the voters, it surprised Reagan and did bring about some reforms.

I don't think President Reagan ever meant to alienate women. His obvious love, respect for and reliance on his First Lady made it clear he liked ladies as people. I think he genuinely felt he was looking out for our best interests, in his own protective way. When he was

Governor of California, Reagan not only supported the ERA, but signed one of the most liberal Freedom of Choice laws in the country.

But things changed when he came to Washington. The case of Patricia Bailey quickly showed how much they'd changed. Pat, a skilled lawyer, member of the Federal Trade Commission, and wife of a top Republican pollster who had helped the Reagan campaign greatly, wanted to become Chairman of the FTC. She was very well qualified and supported by Republican Senate Majority Leader Howard Baker. She was just days away from being approved. Then, in a speech to the District of Columbia Bar Association, she dared to tell a group of lawyers that the planned 50% cut in the FTC budget and 17% cut in its personnel might lead to a lessening in enforcement of anti-trust laws and a slowdown in consumer services. The Reagan budget cutters saw this as criticism, a real slap in the face. Some of them began circulating the word that, despite the GOP's about-face, Pat Bailey was still an active supporter of the ERA. Suddenly a far less experienced, almost unknown male member of the Commission was appointed Chairman.

I brought this up in a press conference early in Reagan's first term: "Is this a signal to other Republicans that if they don't go along with you on everything, you'll say 'Off with their heads'?" Reagan seemed surprised, unprepared for my question. Then, with a smile and a purr like the Cheshire Cat, he asked back, "How can you say that about a sweet fellow like me?" It got the laugh he wanted.

Reagan liked the phrase and the story so much, he took to repeating it. So did his opponents. Scotty Reston wrote a *New York Times* column about it that inaccurately said Reagan "tamed me" with that answer. Arthur E. Rowse wrote a book called "One Sweet Guy, and What He's Doing to You." Joe Glazer, a labor movement balladeer, wrote a song called "A Sweet Fellow Like Me" that goes:

> How can you say that,
> How can you say that,
> How can you say that,
> About a sweet fellow like me?
> The man with his yacht,
> Folk who don't have a pot,
> Must sacrifice equally.
> It's waste we are stopping
> By cutting and chopping,

Please don't say that I'm mean;
Now don't be greedy,
If you're truly needy,
I'll send you a jelly bean.

The President threw back his head in laughter when I called him a "sweet fellow" for inviting me to the state luncheon he gave for President of Mexico Jose Lopez Portillo. It was right in the reception line, and I'm quite sure the Mexican President didn't get the joke. But I meant it quite sincerely, because in the 37 years I'd been covering the White House, this was the very first time any President had invited me to a state affair. Presidsent Reagan could be sweet, indeed.

Like he was one time when, working late at the White House, I realized I'd forgotten to thank him for a favor he'd done me that day. Without really thinking, I called from the Press Room to the President's living quarters at nine o'clock at night. Mortified when I realized what I'd done, but too far in to back out, I asked for him. He came right to the phone and had a laugh with me about my embarrassment. He treated it like a personal call from a relative.

Another of those rare but lovely occasions when I felt close to President Reagan was during the nationwide demonstration of American solidarity known as "Hands Across America." Organized by super-manager Ken Kragen, it was a symbolic gesture to bring attention to the plight of America's homeless by having people link hands as a solid chain from coast to coast. Saying the problems of hunger and homelessness were overstated, Ronald Reagan had originally declined to participate. Since homelessness had grown considerably under his administration, this was a issue that made him quite defensive. He kept insisting there was enough food and shelter for everyone if they just knew where to look. As the event drew near, however, his daughter Maureen convinced him that the bad press he was getting for that attitude would change if he let the chain go across the White House grounds. On May 25, 1986, when Hands Across America extended across the north side of the Executive Mansion, Ron and Nancy joined in. I was pleased to see the First Couple there. Thanks to Maureen, I was there, too, the only White House correspondent present as the chain of hands was completed.

Of course, at the same time I was sharing some warm and gracious moments with the President, I realized quite well that he could do things that seemed cold and devious. Things I would take him to task for in one press conference after another, only to have him respond with a denial, a deflection, or an attack.

Things like naming a black fundamentalist preacher, Sam Hart of Philadelphia, to the Civil Rights Commission after Hart had publicly stated that he did not agree with the goals of the Commission or even believe it was needed. Reagan denied that Hart ever said that. But Hart did.

Things like pushing the Project for Democracy, a "missionary" program to spread capitalism into developing countries, and, I suspected, to test which governments we liked and didn't like, so we could have a hand in changing them if necessary. Reagan blamed the other guys, saying we were just doing what the Communists had been doing for decades.

Things like continuing to select appointee after appointee who, like Interior Secretary James Watt and Environmental Protection Administrator Anne Gorsuch Buford, had to be removed or resign under a cloud. As, both voluntarily and under fire, staff members continued to leave Washington so rapidly that the President needed a revolving door, Reagan would treat my questions as if I was unfairly sniping at their backs.

Things like cutting back Medicaid so sharply that hospitals were beginning to turn away the elderly, resulting in patients dying untreated. That time, Reagan disgustedly accused me of listening to those "demagogues in Congress" and stormed out of the room.

Even though my questions about the social, ethical and economic problems that were occurring under the Reagan Administration often went unanswered, I continued to ask them, trying to get through the President's wall of defensiveness and his refusal to face the facts. At the very least, I hoped to raise public consciousness and perhaps make others in power sit up and take notice. As one press conference drew to a close and he was preparing to leave the podium, I jumped up and said, "Mr. President, may I have one domestic question?" There had been not a single question about what was going on inside our country's borders. Reagan looked quizzically at Helen Thomas, who as senior wire services reporter always closes the conferences, and asked if there was time. Being my friend, Helen said there was. Then I asked Reagan what he was going to do about the people sleeping on sidewalk grates over the boiler rooms at various government buildings. What would he do about these homeless people as winter approached?

Of course, I already knew what Reagan's answer would be. On this subject, he was predictable. His advisors had convinced him that there simply were no really hungry people in the United States. And as far as homelessness was concerned, he believed what he had been told, that one could take the money spent annually on keeping a family in a cheap hotel room and buy them a house in any metropolitan area. He seemed irritated that I had once again brought up this sore subject—but for once the results the question got were well worth getting him riled.

The action came, however, not through the White House but through Congress. A bi-partisan House conference called to ask if I would attend, joining such figures as Speaker Jim Wright, New York Governor Mario Cuomo and Boston Mayor Flynn. Later the House voted $400 million in emergency funds for the homeless. Congress, the states and the cities could not afford to simply ignore a problem that a walk down any city street in the country would tell you was real.

It would seem that only a genuine isolation from reality could account for some of the situations into which the President's decisions, indecisions, denials or about-faces plunged the Reagan Administration. And indeed, as we move backward through his life, we can see three different ways in which such detachment from real life could have happened.

The work pattern Reagan developed in the California statehouse and "perfected" while in the White House involved delegating to others the gathering of facts—and the weeding out of any information the gatherer thinks is non-essential. In theory, this is efficient. In reality, the advisors often presented to the President only the information they thought he wanted to hear. This led to a narrowness of vision, a reliance on only those who already agreed with the administration, and at its worst, as in the Iran-Contra scandal, a tangled web of deniability.

It is clear, for example, that Oliver North and others on his staff didn't tell the President all of the things that they were doing. Only when Oliver North's operations became so widely and publicly known did Reagan apparently learn enough to be forced to demand the Colonel's resignation.

This same managerial style could also explain why the Administration sent troops to Lebanon but failed to adequately protect them against a suicide attack or why we invaded Grenada "to protect the American medical students" when, according to believable sources, the island's government had already agreed to our every demand. Not only were the press kept in the dark on the more troubling aspects of these operations, but so, it seems, were many government officials at both ends of Pennsylvania Avenue. The need to show strength had short-circuited the President's need—and the public's right—to know the facts.

A second level of isolation between Reagan and the realities of American life could have been the effect of the cartel of wealthy Californians who allegedly decided to hand-pick a president and chose Ronald Reagan for the role he was born to play.

We know that Reagan's working-class childhood and admiration for Franklin Roosevelt and his New Deal policies made the actor a solid Democrat when he first got interested in politics. After World War II, when good roles started coming less frequently, Ronnie ran for and was elected president of his union, the Screen Actors Guild. But by the 1950s his acting career got on track again, thanks to television and Big Business. He became the public relations spokesman for General Electric and other companies, and his politics got more and more conservative. He re-married in 1952, and got to know his new wife's adopted father, Dr. Loyal Davis, described to me by those who knew him as an uncompromising man with little charity for minorities or for the nurses who worked for him. Since Nancy's politics were to the right of her new husband's, no one was really surprised when Reagan re-registered as a Republican in 1962. Many, however, were surprised when he was elected Governor of California in 1966.

By then, it's said, Ronald Reagan had attracted the interest of a handful of rich men in California who were determined to find themselves the right man to mold into their own vest-pocket President of the United States. I was told all about this by a woman who was the girlfriend of one of the men and would cook for them when they gathered together. First they had small meetings in one home or another. Later on, these became full-fledged supper parties. Finally, they had Ronald and Nancy come to several of their get-togethers. They met with them and talked with them. Reagan, I am led to understand, was the fourth choice of this group of men. I hope some day to learn who the first three were. (My source, incidentally, says Mrs. Reagan always treated her like hired help.) A lot of this was also confirmed to me by a man of aristocratic, early-California Hispanic heritage who left the group because he detected racist overtones in their constant joking.

Aided by these rich friends and an uncanny ability to keep a grip on public opinion, Reagan could get away with playing "the boss," doing anything to get his way: if he didn't like what an agency was doing, he would just deny it enough funds to work effectively. By not filling vacancies, he could render commissions inoperative. He could delay things for months by simply not reading a report. He did this time and again to stymie the Equal Employment Opportunity Commission, the Civil Rights Commission, the Federal Trade Commission, the Environmental Protection Agency, and the implementation of Title IX, designed to give women full athletic opportunity in colleges. And, as the boss, he could play with the books, making us think he was improving the economy while actually doubling the national debt.

Reagan could get his way and make us love it by behaving like a king but acting like a jester. He could visit Iowa without even once mentioning the word "agriculture," and then make up for it on his next visit by posing for a cute photograph holding a little pig up close to his face.

It takes a third level of detachment to explain some of the oddest aspects of Ronald Reagan's terms in office. I may be wrong, but it seemed to me that many times there was a distinct difference between what Ronald Reagan looked at and what he saw. To be "The Great Communicator," as he was called, he had to do more than just sense what the people wanted and needed to hear. He had to be able to put himself in their place. But he was such a natural actor he seemed to feel he could do this by looking at their surface instead of looking into their hearts. I think he saw people not as they are, but as they would be if he were going to play them. I don't think he ever quite figured out the difference between real life and reel life.

The ability to shift from one reel to another might explain why we so often saw different versions of Reagan at the same time. One character would be a decent, compassionate man and the other a stubborn, tightfisted one. It was as if he was playing both the James Stewart and Lionel Barrymore roles in "It's a Wonderful Life" and kept switching back and forth. He made budget cuts that were supposed to help the family paycheck by reducing income supports for the neediest families. He came out for strong oversight in the Department of Defense, then did nothing to stop a group of contractors who allegedly made over $80 billion in profits by colluding to get around competitive bidding. And sometimes it worked the other way: Reagan said he was opposed to spending federal money on job training, then came out for it strongly and took credit for getting it passed. He originally said he would abolish the Departments of Education and Energy, then allocated money and manpower to strengthen them both.

Ronald Reagan was so good at playing parts that he seemed to assume that everyone else must be, too. The same skills that made him successful in Hollywood—and, at one level, successful in Washington—served to insulate him from many of the groups and individuals whose lives he would affect as President Reagan. There is no doubt in my mind that he wished to give the people of America everything he thought they needed. But he never seemed to see a man in a wheelchair as really that much different than the character he played in "King's Road"—the one who got his legs cut off and cried out "Where's the rest of me?" One is flesh and blood. The other is a symbol, who, if he costs too much, can simply be written out of the story. The actor who plays him can get up out of the chair and go find some other way to earn his keep.

How else can you explain a genuinely kind, genuinely good-natured man who took some of the actions he did while he was President? Perhaps he listened to the advice of his staffers, to the advice of out-of-touch legislators like Senator Jesse Helms of North Carolina, or to the advice of the Republican National Committee, a group which wielded far more power than it should have during those years. Though these things he did were little heard about, they badly hurt a lot of Americans. One was that Reagan cut off almost 500,000—half a million!—disabled people who were entitled to be given some payment from the federal government to keep them alive, as they couldn't work. Reagan just seemed to think that they should get up and go to work, that they could go to work. So he cut 500,000 off the list.

Well, this put quite a few of these people in the worst trouble of their lives. Disabled centers from Maine to Arizona didn't know what to do for them. They didn't know how to overcome a system that had suddenly turned its back. The people didn't know if they could appeal to anyone or not. A few of them gave up and committed suicide. Some were denied medical attention and died natural deaths. And many of them finally found the only help they could because of a woman in North Carolina who kept trying to get their problems in front of Congress.

For some inexplicable reason, when hearings on this were finally held on Capitol Hill, the names of the disabled people who testified that they were hurt by Reagan's actions were not kept on a roll, as they should have been, so people could go back and refer to them. So there was a hard time putting together and getting any real organized help for these disabled people. With everyone dropping the ball, it was an unmitigated disaster for Congress, the White House and the nation, but one that surprisingly few people in the country heard about.

To make things worse, it came out, much later, that Reagan had also cut off funds for around 500,000 needy children. All this from a man who got angry with me when I said his Medicaid cuts were letting elderly people fall through the safety net, who honestly believed himself when he said he will see to it that no one falls through the safety net.

How do I evaluate a man who could flash a dazzling, honest smile even as he, without malice, knowledge or intention, hurt our country in ways from which we may not recover in this century? I think that, to the extent which he inspired the average American to believe in our possibilities, he was good. But his record shows that we would have been better served had we elected a man who knew more about government than Reagan did. To echo Jim Wright's rueful words, "He played the role of President superbly."

And in a strange way, that was his glory as well. No president in decades had been as excellent as Ronald Reagan at smiling confidently and dechilling the dignified atmosphere of White House events, unbending stiff-backed visitors with a joke or a homespun anecdote. He acted out the President as a charming, informal, confident and strong individual. Strong enough to shrug off even bullets, it seemed, joking all the way through his recovery from an assassination attempt, the wounds from which, we later learned, could have killed a far younger man.

Though at times it seemed the world was laughing not at Reagan's jokes, but behind our backs, we loved the show our President was putting on and voted overwhelmingly to give our star a sequel of four more years. And sure enough, during this second feature, a sort of "RONBO II," our allies—and our enemies—started seeing the image as reality, as well.

When the "Evil Empire" began to crumble, Ronald Reagan was perfectly cast to take on the role of tough but forgiving victor, willing to welcome Mikhail Gorbachev to break down the walls and enter a new world, the same world Reagan had mastered, where perception is everything. In that world, President Reagan's accomplishments are clear to see. And the greatest of them all, his stewardship over the beginning of the end of the Cold War, comes directly from the fact that Ronald Reagan saw the presidency—and made us see it, too—as his best role.

ROSWELL, NEW MEXICO, 1947;

AMERICA, 1996:

In 1947, the McClendon News Service had the El Paso Times *among its clients. Back then, the* Times *was the largest paper serving New Mexico and part of Arizona, as well as the far west of Texas. So when a strange story out of Roswell, New Mexico reached Washington DC, I showed up to cover what has become, to many minds, America's greatest "cover-up."*

I'm sure you've heard the story, but if the government had just been straight with us, you probably never would have. It would have stayed the kind of item found buried in the pages of the local newspaper, not the stuff of endless media speculation, pseudo-documentaries and TV movies.

In mid-June, some odd debris was found on a ranch near Roswell, New Mexico. When, later that month, a pilot in Washington state reported an encounter with nine glowing disks that "skipped like saucers" across his flight path, the ranch manager in New Mexico told the local sheriff about the debris he'd found. The sheriff called the Roswell Army Air Field. On July 8, the Roswell Daily Record *headlined an Army press release saying they had recovered the wreckage of a flying saucer. Within hours, the military changed its story: the debris which they had confiscated was merely a lost weather balloon.*

Over the years, this incident has mushroomed into a national obsession. Except for the widespread skepticism over the "official explanation" of the Kennedy Assassination, there is probably no subject on which more Americans doubt our government is telling us the truth. Rumors have spread like wildfire that not only is the government hiding physical evidence of alien visitations but that they even have some of the alien visitors themselves, dead or alive, stowed away under top secret security.

It wasn't until years later that Washington offered a more convincing explanation of what had occurred and why the government had issued first one and then a second cover story. Back in 1947, so they finally told us, the military was conducting Project Mogul, in which high-altitude balloons equipped with odd-looking radar reflectors were launched to detect not only Soviet nuclear experimentation but Soviet attempts to spy on our nuclear facilities at Alamogordo, less than two hundred miles from Roswell. Trying to keep Project Mogul secret, the government's clumsy stories had only succeeded in sowing the seeds of a nationwide belief that not only do flying saucers exist but that our government is covering them up.

The lesson is clear—though Washington doesn't seem to have heard it. When the government tells lies, the people come to expect lies. When the government covers up, the people come to expect cover-ups. When the government shrouds its activities in secrecy, it is only under-standable that the people will supply their own explanations, no matter how far-fetched they may seem.

Secrecy in government is at the root of many of our nation's problems. Secrecy in input encourages mistakes in decision making. Secrecy in finances is a feeding ground for corruption. And every instance of a mistake or misdeed that's been shrouded in secrecy leads the public to imagine a hundred—or a thousand—more. They're not necessarily wrong.

I'm very worried about the failure of Washington to understand the seriousness of this credibility gap between big government (them) and little people (us). My office is perhaps better informed on this sub-ject than most news organizations. Just as people from around the country call and write me asking for help, people are not afraid to con-tact me about their concerns, real or imagined, about where our gov-ernment is headed. They often have no contact with, or trust in, their elected officials, and do not know how—or are afraid—to call govern-ment agencies and make inquiries. Most of them have a feeling it would do no good to try. Somehow, though, they feel they can come to me with their worries. They call here because this office is independent of the big networks, wire services, big business, or organizations with any agenda. I do give consideration to every call or letter. My address and phone number are in the Washington directory.

The people I hear from in this way appear to be of three differ-ent types—those who are individually concerned about the future of our country on a moral or intellectual level, those who have personally felt the sting of government injustice, and those who have gathered into organizations of protesters, including that worrisome phenomenon of our age, the militias. Though most of these correspondents and callers are conservative, some are liberal and a growing number are quite radical.

What are some of the fears that these people share with me? There is a growing belief that the "New World Order" means world gov-ernment and that our nation is about to turn its powers over to the United Nations. There is speculation that the military bases which are being closed in the name of redundancy are being fitted as prisons, not for criminals, but for citizens.

I am told there is already in existence a national police force that searches and seizes homes, persons and property without legal jus-tification, and that secret panels of judges are trying people without the opportunity to defend themselves or to even know their accusers. Some point out that the U.S. is importing large shipments of weapons from the former Soviet Union and ask why.

With the fall of the Iron Curtain and the end of the Cold War, the fears we once focused upon our external enemies have turned inward. What we have learned from revelations about the misuse of power by the government is that the government itself can threaten our liberties. The media is increasingly filled with speculation and accusations about how the U.S. is misleading its own citizens, hiding information that we should know and covering up actions that should alarm us.

The nasty way in which politics has lately been conducted doesn't help, either. What begins as a disagreement along party lines becomes an ideological split, which, in turn, gets exaggerated into a moral (and sometimes, even mortal) standoff. Americans are increasingly seeing each other as leftists or rightists, elitists or rubes, patriots or traitors, rationals or paranoids—but not as fellow human beings. We are losing our ability to see in shades of gray. The only thing we seem to agree on is that government has become our common enemy.

What is the answer to America's intensifying battle with itself? I think it lies in the understanding of one simple fact: the opposite of speaking is listening—it is not just waiting impatiently for a chance to speak again. That goes for individuals, for groups and for the government. We must recultivate the lost art of calm discussion and real communication. Whatever you may think of my friend Ross Perot, when he spoke about our need for "town meetings," he was right. And all we need for those meetings to happen are 1) people who are as concerned about what the other person has to say as they are about their own opinions, and 2) a large supply of facts.

Two current forums that pass themselves off as person-to-person communication have not been helping the situation. Most radio talk shows are more concerned with getting ratings than getting at the truth, and their opinionated hosts specialize in shouting down anyone who disagrees with them. They are usually just preaching to the choir, reinforcing their listeners' biases and patting them on the back for agreeing. In a similar way, the "Information Highway" promised by the Internet often seems more like a detour when it comes to getting to the truth. Certainly the potential is there, but it's sometimes hard to see it among the abuses like bulletin boards and chat rooms that present themselves as open discussions but chase off anyone who disagrees with the prevailing opinion. Over the air or through the modem, folks are getting the wrong information and passing it along as if it's gospel. And the sermon that's being preached is predominantly anti-Washington.

If this country is to survive, the people must feel connected to their government. Without this, I do not believe the United States, this great experiment in democracy, can go on. At a time when the developing nations of the world, which look up to the U.S. as an example, are more and more seeking to model their governments upon ours, we seem increasingly convinced that we are losing our democracy.

There are, of course, efforts underway to turn this negativity around. I know of several ongoing or upcoming projects in this direction. The cable network C-SPAN, a public service created by America's cable television companies, is a wonderful example of uneditorialized public affairs coverage of both government and civilian gatherings. First Lady Hillary Clinton's syndicated newspaper column, "Talking It Over," is a responsible attempt to bridge the gap by providing solid facts and sound thinking. Martha Roundtree, a communication giant who started "Meet the Press" and other television shows in her career, is quietly working on a television show to give people answers. She calls it "Stand Up, America." Former Republican Senator Bill Brock of Tennessee, who now lives in Maryland, is launching, with associates, a communications campaign to spread understanding and truth about government. The Creative Coalition, founded by actor Ron Silver, continues in its attempt to use the name-value of celebrities like Susan Sarandon, Robin Williams and the Baldwin brothers to attract interest to bi-partisan forums of political figures discussing issues like "Money and Politics: Are Dollars Buying Democracy?" And then there are, of course, Nader's Raiders—and Mr. Perot, that little fellow with a giant love for America, who seems determined, in one way or another, to open up the U.S. government for inspection.

My own ongoing contribution to shining a little light on the government is the McClendon Study Group, which meets bi-weekly at the National Press Club. It centers around government activities that have been misunderstood, either through a lack of information or, in some cases, secrecy of purpose. It is open, free, to all who wish to attend and the speakers over the years have included Marita Lorenz, former mistress of Fidel Castro and an admitted CIA operative; Peter Djinis, Director of Financial Enforcement for the Treasury Department; Floyd Brown of Citizens United, who produced the infamous Willie Horton commercials; and Edward Gonzalez, Director of the U.S. Marshals Service, which, among its activities, now operates casinos which have been taken over by the government. We have even heard from Richard Hoagland, the man who popularized "The Face on Mars" and who believes that NASA is concealing evidence of ancient, Biosphere-like structures on the moon. Among our more faithful members are a Constitutional expert, a congressional staffer, various government bureaucrats, a leader in Perot's Reform Party, several whistleblowers, two activist/taxi drivers and a conspiracy expert working on Kennedy's murder.

But all these efforts will be meaningless unless the government takes on the primary responsibility to clean up its own image. How can our elected officials make us feel involved in and in control over the work they're doing? People are generally ignorant of what government offers and how it is organized—and any attempt to learn is usually neither encouraged nor encouraging. The ways people are offered access to their government just don't work. So many who do make the effort to contact Congress or the White House get no answer or one that merely patronizes them. The only people in government most citizens see face-to-face are unresponsive, unelected bureaucrats who create red tape rather than cut through it. The Freedom of Information Act is often just a waiting game, and finding what you're looking for can cost both time and money. It can keep people on the hook for five years and then not give any answers. Administrators often reply by saying, "Due to the right of privacy, the government cannot answer your inquiry." There has got to be a better way.

Ignorance and disinformation fight the truth on more levels than one. Many people leave the watchdog process to someone else because they feel their education is inadequate—they don't believe the government is theirs to watch. They think that they would have no effect even if they did express themselves. Many in government who do not want them to interfere make light of their efforts. But while timidity in the face of intimidation has become the normal route, the truth is that one man or one woman can make a difference.

An idea that this one woman has tried to push is the notion of a "Truth Court." When there's a disagreement waged before the public, the people are often given two very different sets of statistics or so-called "facts." This, quite naturally, leads to myths and rumors. I believe that whenever we are given radically different versions of the "truth," we must have a body of investigators, trusted by and acceptable to both sides of the issue, search out what is really correct. This process should be used whenever there is a fight between the Democrats and Republicans, when government agencies get embroiled in feuds (as, say, the State Department and the Department of Defense have been known to), or when an outside group or individual disputes the information we are being given by the government. I have written about this and mentioned it to President Clinton several times.

Another idea is one that Eugene McCarthy came up with while he was running for the presidential nomination against Lyndon Johnson in 1968. Eugene told me that if he became President he was going to have regional Vice Presidents. Perhaps he was joking when he said he would make me Vice President for Texas and the Southwest, but his notion struck a chord of truth in me. The government not only needs a greater understanding of the needs of the various regions of our country—but a greater connection to them. McCarthy's concept can show us the way.

I think that the time has come to set up a series of regional centers where inquiries can be taken and answers given, determining the truth or falsity of all the rumors, myths and reports that flourish when people feel the government is for insiders only. Our President and Congress should get together and create a plan to establish these places where a literal dialogue between the government and the people can take place. Getting past their own conflicts to work together on this would be a great first step in the right direction. In these regional sub-capitals throughout the country, people would be able to meet their Congressional representatives and administration officials face to face.

Still another idea came to me from an anonymous member of an audience which was listening to me speak. As a long time observer of our government at work, I am frequently called upon to talk to one organization or another. One time when I was making my usual speech about things that were going wrong in government, a man from the back of the room arose and asked, "Lady, can't you tell us about anything good in government?" I was startled. Of course I could. And from then on, I did.

Whether what you have to tell them is good or bad, Americans appreciate hearing the truth about their government. It is only in this way that they can understand and do their part in helping to improve it. That is why I believe that at each of these regional centers, a bureau should be established to send reliable speakers to any group requesting them, speakers who could be depended upon to tell the truth. Perhaps the speaker's bureau should depend on people with no direct connection to government. People who have no agenda, no reason not to tell the truth. People whom the public feel they can trust, people they have trusted and people with different points of view that they admit to freely and openly. Speakers could be paired, one from either side of an argument, so that the things upon which they do agree could be more readily depended upon as fact. Perhaps we could even take a trick from the Creative Coalition's book and use celebrities as a draw.

I know the power of person-to-person communication in bridging the gap between a government and its people. I was once invited to Finland as one of a group of American women journalists. The native reporters of this small country could not write their criticism of Communism or tell how much they despised the Soviets because of the precarious situation between their government and their Russian neighbors. If the wrong words were written, the Bear might easily lumber across the border and devour Finland whole. We were there to learn the truth and tell it to the world for them.

As a longtime supporter of women in the military, I took the opportunity of a speaking tour of Germany to report a few truths regarding the little-known duties that they were performing abroad. At a time when women's responsibilities in the Army were generally assumed to be strictly clerical or nursing, I interviewed female intelligence officers who were stationed in the woods, relying upon only themselves to maintain and repair all their sophisticated tracking and communications equipment. Many men were surprised to learn that, and many women told me they felt proud to know it. On another trip, this time to Alaska, I met Air Force women doing similar work in isolated outposts, monitoring whether Soviet military aircraft were violating American airspace. These women were being trusted with decisions that affected the balance of peace.

Here in America, I have tried to use my speaking engagements to help the many military bases I've visited understand how to develop closer ties with the local communities and the media. At the Strategic Air Command headquarters in Nebraska, the commander asked me, "What is wrong with us? Why is it people in the media criticize us?" As I had at other bases, I suggested that each officer look up some member of the press, introduce him or herself and personally explain the problems faced by and goals desired by the military. Most of them said they did not know any civilian in the media, had never been interviewed by one and felt hesitant about approaching them. "Have a cup of coffee and get acquainted," I urged.

I see my unofficial position as a liaison between my countrymen and my government to be an honor, so I take it quite seriously. I feel most conscientious people would. Even if—and when—it hurts. In October 1985, I needed a hip operation but kept putting it off, because of one speaking engagement after another. Finally, I realized as I stood at one podium giving a luncheon speech that it was not just my devotion to duty that was keeping me there. My hip had locked up, and I simply couldn't move. They carted me off to the Veterans Hospital where they unbent me, put me in a body brace, plopped me into a wheelchair and, at my insistence, got me to my evening speech by 6:00 PM. The doctor made me commit to the operation, but I told him it would have to wait until mid-November, since I had one more speaking tour to make. "You'll have to speak to them from a wheelchair," he told me. "I think they'll understand," I said. I had the surgery after returning from Alaska, where I had toured by small plane, speaking to Vietnam Veterans—some of them in far worse shape than I was.

Sometimes telling the truth can hurt, but getting the truth out is worth it. It is, in fact, the only way in which our country can heal itself in order to survive this age of increasing skepticism. Mistrust grows best in darkness, which is exactly what we get when questions are not honestly answered—or remain unanswered.

Chapter 10

GEORGE BUSH: UNANSWERED QUESTIONS

The mark a President makes on American society can stretch far beyond his time in office. Many ex-Presidents add to their record of accomplishment after leaving the White House. There is, of course, a wealth of experience and know-how which can be shared with—and should be sought by—his successors. But there is often even more: away from the pressures and the partisan fighting, presidential retirees often display qualities that they didn't show—or we didn't notice—while they were in office, abilities which can serve the country in many ways.

Look at our living ex-Presidents. In an age when we need reassurance that the federal system works, Gerald Ford has become Washington's ambassador to the American people, a symbol that even the highest levels of government don't need to be inaccessible. Jimmy Carter's "ambassadorship" ranges even farther: he seems ready to go wherever he's needed, whether it's refereeing the world's problems or building houses for America's poor. Ronald Reagan has withdrawn from public life, but not before he wrote a brave and eloquent letter which touched our hearts and raised our consciousness to the problem of Alzheimer's disease.

And then there is George Bush. The reception he and his spirited wife, Barbara, got when they appeared at the 1996 Republican Convention in San Diego shows that the Bush following is still large and enthusiastic. And there are said to be even more who admire him in foreign countries than here in the U.S.: families in the Persian Gulf, I'm told, still hang pictures of George Bush above their dining tables. Millions around the world love our former President George Herbert Walker Bush.

But how many people actually know him? Except for a limited number of interviews and some high-paid appearances before high-power groups, our last President seems to have kept a fairly low degree of visibility in the three and a half years that he's been out of office. His family and associates seem to have closed around him like a circle.

I have followed the career of George Bush since he first came to the House of Representatives in 1966 as the first Republican to represent Houston. I admired the fact that, despite its unpopularity with his constituents, he voted for the Civil Rights Act. And I recall when, in 1970, he announced that he would give up his seat to try again to become a U.S. Senator (as he had, unsuccessfully, in 1964), I practically urged him, through my questions, not to leave the House. I could not understand why he would want to do that. I thought he was risking a career which could go far. I have a profound respect for the House, and his membership on the House Ways and Means Committee put him in a seat of power from which Speakers and Vice Presidents have come. Little did I know that George Bush had other ways of climbing that high—and still higher.

Though he did lose that second Senate race, the GOP was not about to let him go. Instead, George Bush became the utility player on the baseball field of Republican politics. The very next year, President Nixon appointed him U.S. Ambassador to the United Nations, the first in a series of various jobs of increasing importance Bush would take on under Nixon and Ford. As Watergate heated up, he left the U.N. to get involved in partisan politics, taking over the chairmanship of the Republican National Committee. For almost two years, Bush battled loyally for Nixon but was, at the very end, one of those who advised him to resign. President Ford sent Bush to China to head the U.S. Liaison Office in Beijing, and then, at a time when it was under quite a bit of fire from Congress, Bush took over as the top man at the Central Intelligence Agency.

Between 1971 and 1975, George Bush had received four major appointments in two administrations. While he did not stay long in any of them, each seemed more exciting and more powerful. At the time, we all just supposed that he simply received this series of appointments. Now I wonder how actively he sought them—and the experience and influence they gave him across the wide range of government affairs. I also wonder how significant it was where he wound up at the climax of that four-step climb.

I have always found George Bush a mystery. He is a many-sided man who, it seems to me, operates on at least two distinct tracks. One personality is as straight, friendly and helpful as a Boy Scout. This George Bush is kindhearted and humorous, sensitive to others' needs and thoughtful in the extreme. Then there is another side that he doesn't show as often—the inflexible, stubborn, secretive hard-liner. This was, I think, the Bush of the CIA.

I have heard that his year as Director is just the tip of the iceberg when it comes to his involvement with the intelligence community. His connections to and associations with the CIA, so it's said, are long and deep. If so, then Bush is excellent at keeping his cover. I think more people know that he hates to eat broccoli than know of his history with the CIA. It's been written in a number of places that those in intelligence gave him the code name "Ice Pick." I can only wonder why.

There are persistent rumors that George Bush became part of the intelligence community as far back as his college days in the late 1940s. It is said that his father, banker and later U.S. Senator Prescott Bush of Connecticut, and an uncle who was an early member of the intelligence community, persuaded him to join while he was studying economics at Yale University. He was, after all, already a decorated war hero, shot down as a pilot over the Pacific. He had received the Distinguished Flying Cross and three Air Medals.

But, as it often seems, the more I hear about George Bush, the greater the mystery becomes. Former Representative Thomas Ashley, a Republican from Ohio and a classmate of Bush's at Yale, recalls that George was always very independent, making up his own mind, regardless of advice from several uncles among the Yale alumni. And after he graduated, with Phi Beta Kappa honors, his life did not, at least at first, follow along a path that points to involvement in the shadow world of intelligence.

Despite the family's assumption that he would follow his father's footsteps into the New York money market, George took Barbara, whom he'd married during the war, and moved to the west Texas town of Midland, where he went to work for an oil company. In Midland, they lived off his income. For a while they rented rooms from a woman who, they discovered, had numerous callers throughout the night. They quickly moved. One tiny house they lived in is now part of Midland's public housing project. A far cry, indeed, from the White House.

In two years, he and a partner had opened a company trading oil leases and royalties, and by the mid-1950s, he was president of the Zapata Offshore Company and on his way to becoming a millionaire in his own right. Between here and the mid-60s, a few more rumors emerge. It's been said, for example, that Zapata, which developed new oil-drilling equipment, was sometimes used by the intelligence community for exchanging information and gaining access to foreign lands. And I have personally seen a letter in which FBI chief J. Edgar Hoover wrote that on the day after John Kennedy was assassinated, a Mr. George Bush contacted him to ask for a briefing about the expatriate Cuban community in the United States. He told Hoover he was a CIA employee acting as a liaison with the Cuban-Americans. When I brought up this letter to the Bush staff, they told me that there had been another man in the CIA named George Bush, which I found out was true. But when I checked with that man, he said, "I was there at the CIA for just a short time and I had nothing to do with Cubans. I assure you that I don't know what you're talking about." So I was left with...just more mystery.

Finally Bush became involved in politics, serving in both elected and appointed positions. After all he did for Nixon as Chairman of the Republican National Committee, I think he was probably disappointed when Ford chose Nelson Rockefeller to be his Vice President. In 1980, Bush waged a determined run for the GOP presidential nomination, but finally asked his delegates to support Reagan. There was a push to put Gerald Ford on the ticket as Ronald Reagan's running mate, but at the last minute, supporters convinced Reagan that with a former President in the V.P. slot, he would be only half a President. Bush got the nomination instead.

One particular memory of George Bush as Vice President vividly brings back to me what I consider to be his two sides. Once, as I started across West Executive Avenue, the lane between the White House and the Old Executive Office Building, the Secret Service barked at me to get back on the curb. I was a bit put off, but then heard a quiet voice from the back of the limousine nearest me say, "How are you today, Sarah?" It was George, and the Secret Service was simply warning me to watch out, as his car was pulling out in a caravan leaving for the Capitol, where he presided over the Senate. His smile sweetened my disposition that day. But in the days that followed, I grew frustrated, as the heavy security with which he always seemed surrounded began to cause the other reporters and myself delay after delay. I could not remember it having been like this with other Vice Presidents as they came and went.

In 1988, George Bush seemed a natural enough choice to continue the policies of the Reagan era. Though his picking Indiana Senator Dan Quayle as his running mate put a momentary glitch in his 1988 campaign to succeed Ronald Reagan, George Bush coasted to victory on the themes of peace and prosperity and by pinning the Democrats with the American Civil Liberties Union and Willie Horton. Those who'd expected someone less dynamic to follow in Reagan's footsteps got a much more scholarly and sophisticated politician than they had imagined. I think both the public and the press were caught off guard.

Whether timing his announcements to gain support in the polls or springing a surprise to draw attention from a failure, Bush's moves were those of an expert. Despite my qualms about image control through media control, I could not help but admire how good he could be at it. Take, for example, this short "lecture" he gave the press following a rather turbulent session:

"My *modus operandi* is to be pleasant with you people when you ask me irritating questions, and that isn't always easy. But I think you'll have to give me good marks for having done that. I think being pleasant is the way to do it and keeping your sights set on the major issues facing this country, challenging the Congress to move."

In the course of just three improvised sentences, Bush manages to be not only sharp but self-effacing, and then, for good measure, reminds us what an uphill battle he has against the real culprits: not us—the press—but Congress!

Sometimes it seems as if George Bush and I confronted each other almost continually during his press conferences while he was in the White House. It was often adversarial, with him on one side and me on the other. But as longtime acquaintances, he and I had started off on quite good terms. During the campaign, when *Newsweek*, rather stupidly in my opinion, had run a cover picturing him as a "Wimp," I wrote a column saying that the last thing George Bush would ever be was a wimp. He took the time to write me a nice thank-you note from his campaign plane, and later, Barbara wrote one, too.

Don't forget, though George was born and raised a

Connecticut Yalie, he thinks of himself as a Texan. And we Texans do stick together. In fact, like Lyndon Johnson, George Bush seemed intent on filling Washington with more than its share of Texas talent. There was, however, one big difference in the way he went about introducing his appointees into government service. While Lyndon used to label his cronies as being from McLean, Virginia, Bush didn't hide the fact that he liked having Texans around. In fact, I remember South Carolina's Senator Ernest Hollings arriving at a party at my friend John Sherman Cooper's home in Georgetown, fresh from a confirmation hearing for Robert Mosbacher as the new Secretary of Commerce. Spotting me, Hollings said, "S-a-a-arah, I thut Jawrge Bush said 'No moah Texans!'"

Maybe I was the Texan George Bush had had enough of. By his seventh news conference, we had begun the sometimes jovial, often hostile interplay that would define our relationship. One reason for the press conference was to introduce his new Secretary of Defense, Richard Cheney. I wanted very much to get in a question about whether the new man would be able to maintain our troop strength. As usual, the President had concentrated on questions from those in the front. Since my assigned seat is in the seventh of eight rows, it looked like he would never get to me.

Bush had already established some rules: be seated quietly well in advance of his entry and, when attempting to pose a question, merely raise a hand—without shouting "Mr. President!" But since I am short, he could not even see my hand, so I had taken to standing and waving my arm. Bush had said he should give the folks in the back a chance, and at least one reporter had voiced his loud agreement. Still, Bush did not give us a chance. Time was running out. Finally, I dared to shout the forbidden words. He ignored me the first time and answered another question. When he was through, I shouted again. This time he cupped his hand to his ear as though to say, "Do I hear a familiar voice back there?" The ensuing exchange went like this:

"Mr. President—"

"Now, [Press Secretary] Marlin [Fitzwater] tells me that that was the last question, but out of respect for Sarah McClendon, who is persistent, but who- I will make a new announcement of press policy, Sarah. The squeaking wheel will not always get the grease in life, and the loudest voice won't always get recognized, because it isn't fair to the others... And I will continue to try, but I cannot identify people—I don't think it's fair to the others—who stand up and yell while others sit and raise their hands. But I don't mean to be pedantic about this or in some lecturing mode, but you and I have known each other a long time, and so this is the last time that I can succumb to the tendency to go to the loudest or most frantic wave. I can't do it, and it's not fair to calmer souls. But, Sarah, have you got a question?"

That got laughter.

"I want to know if-"

"We've known each other so long, I can address her in this forthright manner. Yes?

"And I thank you very much. And I wanted to ask your new man what he feels-"

"Go ahead."

As he said that, he pushed Cheney to the podium, gave him a "good luck" shrug and, with a wave to the assembled press, fled out the door. There was a great deal of laughter at his performance.

In response to my question as to whether there would be enough funding for recruitment, pay and benefits to stave off a military cutback, Dick Cheney replied, "Sarah, those are very important questions, but they really are the kinds of things that I should not discuss until I have the opportunity to appear before the (Senate) Committee (for confirmation)..." Then he, too, left.

When it was over, Helen Thomas of UPI came over at once to give me a reassuring pat on the arm. Several others said, "Don't feel badly," but it was clear that I had been reprimanded. Haynes Johnson of the *Washington Post*, however, was cynical: "Don't tell me you felt hurt about that—you couldn't buy that attention." And since it had gone out on satellite on CNN, I got some surprising responses. My granddaughter, who was studying in Israel, called to ask, "Are you all right?" So I guess Haynes was right: It's not everyone who can get lectured before the entire world by the President of the United States. My real regret was that I had not gotten an answer.

As I'm sure both he and I expected, this was not the last time I got a lecture or a reprimand from President Bush. In his excellent book, "Call the Briefing!," Marlin Fitzwater, Press Secretary to both

Reagan and Bush, recalls another incident where I came out somewhat less battered. As Marlin recalls it, President Bush, exasperated at me, said, "Sarah, I won't take your question until you sit down and ask it in a dignified manner." But as I pointed out, "You won't answer my question if I ask it in a dignified manner, Mr. President."

Bush's reply to that was, "I'm not going to answer it now," so I told him, "Well, I'm going to keep on asking it." Marlin says that by that time, he and the entire press corps were getting edgy, knowing neither of us would back down. Some reporters started saying, "Just answer her question, Mr. President," and Bush finally did, in a thoroughly peeved mood. When the President himself recalled this incident to me, he said that I was the one who blinked, sitting down before he took the question. But my recollection matches Marlin's: "Sarah had beaten another president into submission."

No matter how rough they got, I preferred the arguments to the times when the President simply wouldn't take my questions. I remember how frustrated we all were by Bush's photo opportunities. Since they had been introduced by Nixon, the practice at these events was that the President would not take questions. Like his predecessors, Bush would, when he wanted his picture taken with an official or diplomat, allow about 70 still and video photographers and lighting technicians in, along with a few broadcast journalists and one or two print reporters. Unlike his predecessors, Bush would, I felt, sometimes tempt the reporters into thinking they might get in a question or two.

Once when I was in the pool of reporters invited to watch President Bush greet the Prime Minister of Bangladesh, I tried to ask a question. President Bush interrupted to explain to the visitor what I was doing. "You see, this lady is a newcomer here," he said. "She has only been around here for about 40 years, and she does not know the rules." Even Helen Thomas, who was regularly asked to the photo ops because of her wire-service status, would, when she tried to ask a question, usually get a little lecture about the "no question" policy. I think at these times, away from the front row seat and the courtesy afforded her by press conference tradition, my friend understood how I felt when my attempts to ask a question were ignored.

On another occasion when I was a pool reporter, we were in the Cabinet Room just prior to their meeting. With all the departmental Secretaries and other staffers sitting around the long table, I asked the President a question which he did not want to answer. He replied, "We can't answer your question now, Sarah, but we still love ya." Though I couldn't get an answer, I didn't pass up the opportunity to reply, "Well, I'm glad you still love me," as we were all marched away from the room by our "handler" from the White House press office. The President did, however, get in the last word that time: he soon sent me a picture of the event, inscribed by him with the words he'd used to send me on my way.

I think that President Bush looked forward to our tangles, because he continued to call on me at press conferences with surprising regularity. Some of my colleagues said that this was because he could usually depend on me to change the subject. That speculation had come up during the Reagan years as well. If Bush had bad news to report, I was told, or was facing a troublesome question from someone else, he felt that calling Sarah would get him off the hook. The heat of our exchanges could be depended upon to make the rest of the conference fade in the public memory. If this was his strategy, I decided, then it was my responsibility to make sure my questions were not only on point but that I would not let him use them—or me—to avoid his responsibility to keep the public informed. There were enough unanswered questions in George Bush's life to let him get away with vague answers during his press conferences.

So if a question was important, and I'd felt the President had danced around it, I might ask it again, in a stronger fashion, at the next press conference. Take, for example, the weeks before the Gulf War. As the crisis that Iraq had begun by invading Kuwait continued, I made sure that President Bush would clearly state whether he would seek the permission of Congress before going to war in the Persian Gulf. As he complained, over and again, how unwieldy Congress was when it came to decisions, I kept bringing up Section VII of the U.S. Constitution, which says that Congress shall have the power to "declare war and make rules concerning captures on land and water. To raise and support armies... To provide and maintain a navy. To make rules for the government and regulation of land and naval forces." As so often before, I felt a President needed reminding of those words which they apparently found so hard to understand. By November 30, 1990, my exchange with George Bush had expanded to this length:

"Sir, why do you seem to be avoiding the people's representatives having an opportunity to talk on this and to express their opinion? You know Congress, and yet you're avoiding it. And you know that the Constitution gives them power not only to declare war, to provide the money and to say their things about what shall be done with troops. That's the Constitution. Yet you seem to be avoiding that. The experts on Capitol Hill say that what you have done by pre-notification, calling two or three members and saying to them, "We're on the way," you've already made the decision, you're just notifying them, that's pre-notification; that's not consulting with Congress. They say you should sit down and have a back-and-forth with them-"

"Yes, but-"

"-and I will remind you that when (Rep. Thomas S.) Foley (D-Washington] speaks as Speaker of the House, he may be Speaker of the House, but he sure as hell doesn't represent Florida or Texas."

"Well, now, Sarah, therein you brought up the—properly brought up the dilemma I face. There are 435 members of the United States Congress. There are 100-"

"Well-"

"May I finish, please? There are 100 members of the United States Senate. Each one has a view as to what I ought not to do. And that's fine. They have the power under the resolution of adjournment to come back 20 seconds from now, and to take a voice, to stand, to take a common position. If they want to come back here and endorse what the President of the United States has done and what the United Nations Security Council has done—come on, we're ready. I'd like to see it happen. But what I don't want to do is have it come back and end up where you have 435 voices in one house and 100 on the other, saying what not to do, and saying—kind of a hand-wringing operation that would send bad signals. I welcome these hearings. We are having hearings. We are consulting. I've told you I'm consulting. I'll be honest with you. I cannot consult with 535 strong-willed individuals. I can't do it, nor does my responsibility under the Constitution compel me to do that. And I think everyone would agree that we have had more consultations than—than previous administrations."

"Sir, we have a majority rule in this country, and you seem to be afraid of it."

"No, I am not afraid of it at all. We have a tripartite form of government, and I know my—I know my strengths and I know the limitations on the presidency. This is an interesting debate, Sarah. [Laughter] And—and I know my limitations. And I know what I can do, and I know what previous presidents have done. And I am still determined to consult the extra mile. This is an interesting debate, Sarah."

"Well, sir, you seem to give—you and Jim Baker give the other countries a chance to talk, and you give the United Nations a chance to talk, but you won't give the United States people a chance to debate with you."

"Well, now, that's an absurd comment, Sarah, from a bright person like you. That is absolutely absurd. They're holding hearings. They're talking. They have the power under the adjournment resolution to reconvene this minute. Some in the House want to come back now. Some want to talk about it later on. Some in the Senate want to come right back now and immediately endorse what the president has done and what the Security Council resolution is, and I'm for that. But some don't, and so consultation is going on. Please do not assign to me improper motives. We're—they're talking right now. They're having endless hearings by endless experts up there, each one with a slightly different view. And that's the American way. And that's fine. And I know what the responsibilities of the president are, and I am fulfilling those responsibilities."

And with that, he ended the press conference. As argumentative as it may have seemed, at least I felt that I'd gotten the President to commit himself on the issue. I considered it an accomplishment to get it on the record.

Bush's record was a departure from that of many presidents. He dared to do things many others had not done. In my search to understand this complex man, I have found that his friend Thomas Ashley is a useful guide. College companion, fellow member of the House and close advisor to Bush during his presidency, Ashley now practices law in Washington. He obviously admires his friend very much and feels he is underrated by many Americans for a number of reasons. "George did not toot his own horn like a lot of others did," Ashley explains. While Vice President, he was in the shadow of a very popular and flamboyant President. But we in the White House press room were often given to understand that it was the sharper, better-educated Bush who was making strategic decisions while Reagan was enjoying naps—especially on Wednesday afternoons.

There are still some pages in the Bush record not filled in, like, for example, just how loose a cannon Oliver North was. Or how much Vice President Bush's advice and expertise figured in the Reagan decision to invade Grenada, ostensibly to rescue some 300 young

Americans who had gone there to study medicine when they failed to get admitted to medical schools here. And given his wide-ranging background, it is certainly probable that President Bush knew that General Manuel Noriega had, at times, been on the payroll of the CIA.

My ever-questioning attitude towards President Bush was, in many ways, stimulated by how complex and, at times, contradictory his actions seemed. While the Gulf War was a triumph in many ways for our country, looking back at its roots never fails to wrinkle my brow. Under the Reagan and Bush administrations, both Iran and Iraq built up their weapons supply from U.S. stockpiles. Before, up to and to some extent during the Gulf War in the Middle East, U.S. suppliers of weapons were still allowed to sell arms to Iraq. When I questioned him about this, Bush was scornful and refused to acknowledge the fact.

For some time, Bush had been working on the Iraqi leader, Saddam Hussein, hoping to win his favor and keep him from losing in a war with our mutual enemy, Iran. In the long run, though, Iraq was using Bush to gain weapons from the U.S. Saddam actually took billions from the U.S. Agriculture Department under the guise that it was needed to buy food for women and children, when in reality orders for food were transformed into orders for weapons.

When Saddam Hussein invaded Kuwait, Bush reacted quickly. Saddam was threatening to corner the world's oil supply and raise the price, Bush said, which would cripple the economy and way of life in the U.S. and other nations. To save Kuwait's oil from being used as a high-priced ransom, Bush strongly lobbied our allies to join in a unified opposition to the occupation. Thomas Ashley insists that Bush did not act because of his former oil connections. "It was because he understood the important part that oil plays in the economy of the world."

Then, as Bush supporters point out, the President had the good sense to leave the actual running of the war to the Pentagon. He did not try to run it from the White House, a mistake its other occupants had made in Vietnam.

The war was soon over. There were only 150 U.S. casualties from combat. Bush was very relieved; he realized that if Iraq could keep Kuwait, it would have eventually invaded other countries, such as oil-rich Saudi Arabia. As a result of the Persian Gulf War, the close alliance between the U.S. and the Saudis, which had existed from about 1950, has become stronger than ever.

Amazingly, the Persian Gulf War didn't cost the U.S. any money. It was paid through arrangements Bush made with other countries who were our allies. Bush was successful in getting them to agree to this. General Brent Scowcroft, foreign affairs advisor to Bush, says this is the first time the U.S. has fought a war free of costs and without incurring major debts to carry into the future.

Perhaps President George Bush's greatest contribution to the nation during his presidency was the way he organized this international coalition of heads of state. It was maintained by frequent telephone calls from one head of state to another in time of crisis.

The record shows that Bush was unusually active in military and international affairs, from the Middle East to Central America. Bush became known for the "swift response" style we saw in the Persian Gulf and Panama. James Baker, Bush's Secretary of State, said the President's decisions in this regard should be "the textbook of what to do in a military and diplomatic crisis" such as Iraq's invasion of Kuwait. Bush showed the way for others to follow when, in the future, a big country tries to take over a smaller one. When, after he had left the White House, Bush went to Kuwait, he received an overwhelming welcome from a grateful people.

President Bush's supporters also note his outstanding handling of the United Nations. His work in the Security Council was adjudged by close Bush associates as actually helping the organization fulfill its original purposes for the first time. Out with the Cold War went the Russians' customary practice of vetoing a more active role for the UN in world affairs. Bush was instrumental in setting up the peacekeeping forces in Somalia, an observation mission for Iraq and Kuwait, and negotiations between Morocco and Algeria. During the Bush period, White House dealings with the UN ran smoothly and there was a general feeling of accord, with many unanimous decisions.

Bush is generally recognized as having made two notably excellent appointments. One was Richard Cheney, as his Secretary of Defense, and the other, Colin Powell, as the Chairman of the Joint Chiefs of Staff. But even Bush's supporters differed greatly on the wisdom of his naming Clarence Thomas to the U.S. Supreme Court. Ashley says that Bush was impressed by Thomas' record in the legal profession and also by the fact he was one of the few qualified black judges who was both a Republican and a conservative. Bush not only named him but sent cohorts into the Senate hearing to lobby with both Congress and the press for Thomas' confirmation.

On the home front, Bush anticipated the "Contract with America" Republicans. He had aspirations for reforming the welfare program and had held numerous conferences on this with governors at national meetings. He was also concerned with crime control and had campaigned on a platform of criticizing Congressmen for taking large contributions from special interests when running for re-election.

There are at least two ways in which the influence of George Bush is still felt by the present administration. He kept control over decision-making in the Justice Department in the same way that President Lyndon Johnson once did: getting career people who had been political appointees to take a lower pay grade and become civil servants. Because of their experience and their connections, seventy percent of them stayed on into the Clinton years. Many in Washington say that the decisions in today's Justice Department are being largely influenced by them. I have met people who tell me that when they call the Justice Department to speak to an aide to the present Attorney General, Janet Reno, they get a call back from a Bush appointee.

The second way in which Bush's influence remains is through a surprisingly cordial relationship with President Clinton himself. The two have been friendly since 1988, and despite the apparent bitterness of the 1992 campaign fight, I have heard that Bush has, since then, been quietly giving his successor advice about decision making. This "standing in one party and reaching over into another" is not uncommon between former and current Presidents. In this instance, considering George Bush's world view, it is not even that surprising. The effect of Bush's involvement in both the Clinton and Reagan administrations will be studied, I have a feeling, for a long time.

Given his command of world politics, why was Bush a one-term President? By the 1992 election, the focus had shifted from Bush's international successes to his less successful record at home. Burdened by Ross Perot's unexpected strength, a declining economy, and his failure to keep his pledge of "No New Taxes," George Bush seemed out of touch with the immediate concerns and needs of the average American. Stories were circulated about his amazement over such everyday concerns as the price of cereal or common facts of modern life like item scanning and the Universal Pricing Code. About his declaring April as Recycling Month—in a document dated April 20. About how his Secret Service guards, seeing wires when they x-rayed a gift package that had arrived in the mail, shot to death a pair of electric socks. I think, that having in some ways already served three terms as President, he was simply tired of government. But before Bush left the White House, he did some tidying up: in the last weeks of his administration, he issued pardons to six Reagan-era officials who had been under investigation for up to six years for their alleged connection to the Iran-Contra Affair.

Does George Bush miss Washington? I think he might. As he said in a message sent to an 85th Birthday "Roast" thrown for me, attended by 500 friends and aired on C-Span: "I never thought I would say this—and I'm sure you never thought you would hear this—but it's possible that I miss you." If he misses the likes of me, he must miss Washington, too.

The mark a President makes upon American society can stretch far beyond his time in office. The mark a President makes upon history can stretch far beyond his lifetime. I suspect that, with increased perspective, history will write George Bush and his presidency in letters larger than we now can realize. I think the world beyond America may already sense this. But despite his many accomplishments, I, for one, remain a little mystified about this President and his legacy. I like George Bush, admire much of what he accomplished and sincerely appreciate his kindness. In fact, I wish he'd give me an interview. There are still a couple of questions I'd love for him to answer.

WASHINGTON, DC, 1944-1996:

Every once in a while, as I walk up the driveway towards the White House on my way to a press conference or a briefing, I suddenly think to myself, "What are you doing here?" This isn't just some place where I show up to do my job. Inside these walls, there's history being made, decisions that affect not only every citizen of the United States but every country and person around the world. It is a focus of power unlike any other on the planet. And for 52 years, I've had the responsibility—and the honor—of dragging my aging bones up that White House driveway, sometimes every day. Sometimes in a wheelchair, sometimes with a walker, sometimes with my canes and a pair of good tennis shoes with a little tread still left on them.

I am still there because the people need a direct channel to their President. The presidential press conference is perhaps the closest our government comes to that. The President meets regularly with his Cabinet, consults with Congress (or at least its leaders), talks with representatives of business and the bureaucracy—but when he speaks to the people, it's usually with a carefully written speech or a few well-thought-out sound bites as the text. As representatives of the people, the press has a duty to make that a two-way conversation.

Currently, some two thousand people have active press passes to the White House. Each of them has been cautioned not to represent anything other than the media, no special interests of any kind. Each of them is investigated by the Secret Service for security reasons. Each is fingerprinted and must wear a special press pass, with their picture on it, to get in the gate. Special arrangements may be made, from time to time, to get others in for a special press conference or for temporary coverage, especially if a reporter's from out of town. But they, too, have to supply special information.

It was President Truman who turned the presidential press conference into an event where reporters could sit down, balance a notebook on their knee and actually write down the answers to their questions. At the request of the White House press, Truman also extended the conferences to last thirty minutes. Eisenhower was the first President to allow actual quotations from the conferences to be used and the first to allow edited sections of the conferences to be broadcast or shown in newsreels. President Kennedy allowed live television coverage. While Eisenhower had asked reporters to give their names and affiliation, there was concern that in a live broadcast, we might become prima donnas. But it was tried out for a while. President Nixon covered over the White House swimming pool and built the press center in which we work today. (We think it's still there and wonder if some day some administration will press a button and the entire White House press corps will fall in.) Ford was the first to officially allow follow-up questions, though some of us had gotten them in with earlier Presidents.

The presidential press conference, now listened to by millions worldwide, is indeed an all-too-rare opportunity for the President to learn what is going on in the nation and the world. It is a rare occasion in which people's problems, if known by the reporters, can be taken right to the top without going through intermediaries or channels.

In the past, when formal press conferences were given in the East Room of the White House, around 300 reporters would attend. President Bush, who held more frequent press conferences than any president before him, usually liked to hold them on extremely short notice in the smaller briefing room, where there are about 70 seats for the 150 to 200 reporters and photographers present. When it gets this crowded, people with assigned seats are almost completely overshadowed by the people standing in the aisles along the sides. It can be hard to work when there are bodies leaning over you. Not all reporters with White House passes can get in there. The 70 seats are assigned by brass-plated names. I have one on the aisle in the next-to-last row.

The President usually starts with a statement, then calls on either the United Press International or Associated Press reporters, alternating each time for the first question. The other wire service gets the second question. Then the President calls on the broadcast networks. Each of them gets a question. Then he goes to the big newspapers: the New York Times, Washington Post, Los Angeles Times. Big chains like U.S. News and Knight-Rider always get in, and usually, so do the Baltimore Sun, Boston Globe, and Miami Herald. It is extremely difficult to get the President's attention in that crowded, brightly lit room. The President can see the front rows quite well, but he often forgets about the people in the back. They have a hard time getting recognized. Sometimes I will remind him that we are back there.

The form in which questions are put to the President is important. At times, the question may be used to get a reaction from a President. It may be used to educate him about government, as we sometimes needed to do during Mr. Eisenhower's administration. A question may ask the President to explain his purposes or a new policy. It may inform the President of something going on in his administration of which he may be entirely unaware. It may ask about something he is not reporting to the public—or make the request that he do so. The sad thing about White House press conferences is that so many questions just lay there without being answered. But I always say that whether we get the answer or not, if we can just get the issue before the public, on the record as needing an answer—even if it did not produce the hoped-for results at that conference—it was well worth it.

The custom of asking follow-up questions has cut down the number of reporters who can get in a question during the 30-minute time limit. But they are necessary. Presidential answers are by no means always clear. Most reporters tape the conference as it unwinds, and so does the government. The conference is taken down by an official White House reporter and recorded, usually by the Army Signal Corps. The transcript of the presidential press conference is a valuable reference document.

As senior wire-service correspondent, my longtime good friend, Helen Thomas of UPI, always closes the conference with the traditional phrase, "Thank you, Mr. President." Then there is the aftermath. Before the room has cleared, several network television correspondents climb up on chairs so they can be seen above the heads of the departing reporters as they give a summary and analysis of the press conference.

During the press conferences, visitors are not welcome. There simply isn't room. Because I am persistent about getting answers to my questions, there are times that I don't feel too welcome there, myself. But I am merely following the advice given to me long ago by one of the best presidential press secretaries ever. When the White House Correspondents' Association posted a formal report criticizing me by name for loudly exerting energy in striving to get recognition at press conferences, I sought out Joe Laitin, who had been on the press staff of several Presidents. "Joe," I asked, "how should I act to get recognized at press conferences?" He replied, "Any way you can, Sarah."

Before the White House assigned regular seats to reporters, I learned to get to the press conferences early so I would get a seat close to the president. There was a man who always tried to sit by me, Ben Cole, from an Indiana paper. He'd say, "If I sit next to you maybe I'll be recognized." In over a year, he never was. A number of other reporters claim this story as theirs, but only Cole actually did it. The others would just push and shove me.

Though things may not be as physically formidable at the daily press briefings, they can be even more of a roughhouse, verbally. Not as many reporters show up when it is merely the Press Secretary or another spokesperson giving out the news and taking questions. The presidential conferences may be the star attraction, but I believe the American people would find the transcripts of the daily press briefings very interesting. At times the wit is quite prevalent. As Larry Speakes, one of Reagan's Press Secretaries, once told us, "Everyone wants to be a comedian." The press briefings are our daily grind. Sometimes the speaker will read long passages out to us, and we'll get a little tired of listening. I remember one reporter interrupting a long transcript of a presidential meeting. "If you really want us to take this drivel down," he said, "you've got to go slower."

Since the spokesperson would usually rather tell us things than answer our questions, these press briefings can be a constant fencing match. It's really too bad that the public cannot read these transcripts. I think they should be made available like the presidential ones. Some pages might be boring, but much of it reads like a comedy or a truly lively drama.

Let's take a look at how the Press Secretary operates. It's an important job that can make or break a President. He or she is the conduit between the President and the public. How well the job is performed affects how well the public is informed. To do it well, he or she must have both a free flow of information and access to everything that's going on in the White House: new programs and plans, ongoing situations, and all the meetings, even the secret ones. Reporters can tell in a minute if the president is letting a press secretary get on the inside or not. If not, then the press has no use for the answers they receive.

There are times when highly important questions are handled by Deputy Press Secretaries, Assistant Press Secretaries, Acting Press Secretaries or just plain assistants on the press relations staff. The title of the spokesperson is not as important as the issues they present in what are sometimes critical situations.

Some Press Secretaries stay for years. Men like Steve Early for President Roosevelt, Jody Powell for President Carter, Pierre Salinger for John F. Kennedy. Jim Brady was not there long before he was shot in an assassination attempt on President Reagan. For a long time Brady held the title while recuperating, with Larry Speaks as Acting Secretary.

The life of the presidential Press Secretary is not an easy one. Pierre Salinger had the saddest task, arranging the funeral for JFK. Ron Ziegler was President Nixon's secretary at a time when things were so dramatic and so secretive there could be little direct communications with the President. Jerry terHorst was rated a highly capable person but only stayed in the job a brief period, resigning because he was kept in the dark about Ford's intentions to pardon Nixon and so misinformed us.

I knew and liked a whole gamut of press secretaries. There were Joe Short and Roger Tubby during the Truman time. While Joe Short was Press Secretary, his wife, Beth Campbell Short, was covering Washington as a reporter. When Roger Tubby and I appeared together, years later on a Hoffstra University press program, he told of the many crises he experienced as an Assistant Press Secretary to Truman. James Hagerty, Press Secretary for President Eisenhower, was the best I ever dealt with. He understood my reasons for asking the questions I did. Pierre Salinger became a rather famous figure in his own right, working in Europe for the ABC network and writing several books.

Lyndon Johnson was blessed with George Christian, a real professional who, better still, actually understood the President. Christian was always gentlemanly and helpful. George Reedy, a wire service man, found his job at the White House so burdensome that he begged to be relieved, but Johnson refused. Then George found an excuse—his sore feet—and Johnson had to acknowledge that. Bill Moyers was a strong interpreter of Johnson's mind. Joe Laitin, an old pro when it came to being press spokesman for government agencies and Cabinet officers, came to help out the Johnson press office through a crunch. He accompanied Lyndon on overseas trips, acting as spokesman to the foreign press. Also assisting during this administration was a straight-talking cattleman from the Southwest, Lloyd Hackler, and youthful Tom Johnson, who rose in the business later to head several big newspapers and then the new enterprise which changed news coverage in the nation, CNN.

The Nixon press team were also many and varied. Herb Klein, who'd been his Press Secretary as Vice President, was, as the President's Director of Communications, frequently quoted as the official line. His deputy, Gerald Warren, was expert at obtaining answers for querying reporters. I found them both quite helpful. Murray Snyder was a thorough professional. Ron Ziegler, who came up with the term "photo opportunity," took a lot of the heat for Nixon during the Watergate years.

Under Nixon, Ron Nessen showed sympathy for the Vietnam vets, being one himself. But for Gerald Ford, he became a sharp critic of Congress, denouncing members by name. After Jimmy Carter's term, Jody Powell opened his own public relations firm, with Mrs. Ronald Reagan's former press secretary, Sheila Tate, as partner. Larry Speakes finally apologized to Barbara Honegger for calling her a "Munchkin" in front of me when she exposed the Reagan team over their non-release of the government's discrimination study.

Under Presidents Reagan and Bush, Marlin Fitzwater displayed his previous experience in other departments of government. He played it straight with the press—and kept their respect and warm good will. He tried to serve the press as well as the Presidents and in doing both, served the nation. I only wish he had been able to provide more answers and had not had to say "I do not know" so often. The Bush people did not tell him all they could. Once the administration made him take back an answer he had given to me about a vital question simply because the affected weapons manufacturer howled in protest.

Republican Ann Whitman was a Deputy Press Secretary who occasionally acted as Press Secretary, the first woman to do so. Later, under President Clinton, another woman Press Secretary, Dee Dee Myers, had the full title. She expressed herself well in an admirable voice, but she could have received more support from her boss. The male reporters were needlessly hard on her, I guess because she was a woman and they are accustomed to dealing with men. They also ran out George Stephanopoulos, who had a hard time with the press and who left to go back to his more comfortable job of advising President Clinton. Mike

McCurry, Clinton's current man, requires all the diplomatic skills he learned at the U.S. State Department to pacify hard driving reporters who now combine the stubbornness of a bulldog with the investigative determination of a J. Edgar Hoover. But in a soft voice, McCurry is riding the herd, staying in the saddle.

This is not an easy job. It is not glamorous. Press Secretary Marlin Fitzwater's secretary Natalie Wozniak suffered a heart attack. She did not return to the job. Former White House Press staff usually land jobs in quieter, less stressful departments of government. On some occasions they are hired by industry wanting to learn more about how to operate with the White House.

I have maintained friendships with many of these men and women for whom I occasionally made life hard. When I told dear Joe Laitin I was writing this book, he said the title wasn't quite right. He says "Mr. President! Mr. President!!" sounds as though I had to repeat myself to get the President's attention. "One was always enough," he reminded me. And Marlin Fitzwater loves to kid me by saying that he told both of his Presidents that "It makes no sense to ignore Sarah. She's like a gall bladder stone. The longer you wait, the more painful it gets." No wonder I like these people.

There were times when the White House press staff made me feel as though they were working to help me get out the news. And there were times when they were a more formidable border between me and the President than the White House fence. It wasn't exactly "them against us." Since I run a one-woman news service, it was usually more like "them against me." My daughter Sally had served as my copy girl and assistant (which was how she met Lyndon and Lady Bird Johnson's two girls), but when she reached age 22, she announced she was retiring from the newspaper business. So my most frequent allies in my day-by-day battle for the truth have been the long string of interns who have passed through my office, often on the way to bigger and better things.

It is impossible to remember all of them. Looking back, I wish I had kept a log. I could have had a lot more but I did not always want them around, I confess. At times we meshed well together, but there were times we didn't. I hope they all benefited from the experience that I tried to give them.

My first intern was a banker's son from my home town of Tyler, Texas. He was Abe Pounds, Jr. He was polite and learned easily. But he was surprised to learn that in Washington, he had to wear a coat and tie to work.

Eileen Shanahan, who worked with me for a brief period, was later to write a letter in my defense to the editor of the New York Times. It was important, as she was breaking precedent as a staff member by writing a letter to the editor. The editor gave her permission to do so. It was a defense of me on behalf of herself and the NY Times *Washington Bureau* members after the Times had written an editorial criticizing me for a question I had asked President Eisenhower. I'm grateful to Eileen.

Francie Bernard was one of my favorites. She would probably be running the El Paso Times today—with me as her Washington bureau chief—if her grandfather, who owned the Times, had not decided that Francie and her brother, Bruce, who stood to inherit it, were liberals. He sold the paper to Gannett to avoid leaving it in the hands of his talented, energetic grandchildren. When Dorrance Roderick, the editor-owner, asked me if I would take Francie under my wing if he sent her to Washington, I think he wanted to get her out of Boston, where she had been reporting for an underground newspaper. I was not sure I wanted this, but he said, "You two get acquainted," and so we did. After one day of going about with me she said what a lot of others have said, "I'm worn out." But the truth was that Francie was already a reporter, and I did not have to teach her. That is why I am sorry that Francie left journalism for art and is now a painter.

Another intern was Donna Smith, who today covers the White House and Congress, reporting on the Federal Reserve Bank, international trade, and, at times, tax matters. Her by-lines go around the world, distributed by Reuters. I am very proud of Donna when I run into her in the White House news room these days.

I remember our first meeting. It was near dusk when she knocked at my door. She had driven in from Michigan in an old car which nobody thought would get her to Washington. She had been referred to me by a former colleague then working in Detroit. Donna meekly asked my help in finding a job. She was on her way to a friend's in the Washington suburbs, someplace difficult to find, especially at night. I do not know what prompted me to ask if she was hungry. She was, so I gave her dinner. Then I asked if she would consider living in my small extra bedroom and receiving a small monthly salary in return for working for the McClendon News Service. She said yes and stayed with me for over a year before she left to go to the Sorbonne in Paris. In that time, she covered a lot of stories for me in the Senate and House. She had a quiet way of going about her job, attending strictly to business—despite the fact that her beautiful red hair caused quite a sensation among the men in the press gallery.

Roberta Oster and her pal, Kara Swisher, approached me when they were undergraduate students at Georgetown University and told me they would like to be guided by me in journalism. These two, with all the nerve one can imagine, approached the president of Georgetown and told him they wanted a journalism course. Since there was none then at the University, they asked him to put me on for a weekly guidance session in putting out their school newspaper, the Hoya. I went *there one night per weekend for a year, tried to teach some journalistic ethics and tactics as I judged copy and advised editorially. It eventually led to Georgetown adding some training in this respect. Kara is now a very good writer for the* Washington Post.

Roberta went right from following me around in the White House press room to New York City. A friendly CBS staffer offered to introduce her to friends in the big city. At first she was a telephone switchboard operator at NBC. From there she went on to work for all three networks at various times, including being Jessica Savitch's confidential secretary when Savitch died (and refusing to disclose Jessica's secrets to the hungry press). Roberta now works as a producer for "NBC Dateline." She observes, researches, reports, interviews and assembles segments on individuals and groups with causes and problems. She provides an overall production that impresses the public as well as her bosses, who may send her to Belgium one week, to a prison the next, and, in the third, to interview "special needs" children who face adoption. I was honored when Roberta produced a recent segment on me for her program. It must have been effective; I know that hundreds of people have written me since, many asking me to take over their problems.

There have been a number of other interns. Sonja Hillgren, now president of the National Press Club, worked with me when she was looking around for a job. She found a good one. Kate Quick came to me from the staff of Dr. Donna Allen, my editor and printer. Kate was amazingly efficient and productive. She has held jobs in several states since then and sends me letters of appreciation periodically. Joan Shaffer provided me with valuable assistance in reporting news from the White House.

Matthew Tate Felling is one of my most helpful assistants. He came straight from graduating in Journalism at college in Boston, en route to get a master's degree in Journalism at the University of Missouri School of Journalism, of which I am a graduate. He writes exceedingly well, a natural gift, but rather more formally than I do. Over the five-month period in which I wrote this book, Matthew often covered the White House and Congress and attended some press conferences for me. I predict great things for him in journalism.

It has been a rewarding experience to have interns. It has been even more rewarding to have two very special friends among my colleagues.

The top print journalist in my book is Helen Thomas, chief of the UPI Bureau at the White House for many years. Helen's support of me and my right to ask questions—whether they meet the approval of other White House correspondents or not—has always meant a lot to me. When others might smirk and say let's get on to some other subject, Helen would drop by my seat in the back of the press room and whisper, "That was a good question and ought to have been asked," or she might just tap a beat of sympathy on my arm as she goes by. In recent years, she and I have often appeared on the same program or panel. These days, it often happens that I am called on to introduce Helen when she is getting an award for her journalism and vice versa.

Helen came to the White House during the Kennedy administration. Though they were from competing wire services, she and Frances Lewine of the AP formed a sort of partnership: when the Press Secretary failed to fully answer a question from one of them, the other one would ask it again later in the press conference. Helen asks clear questions and is never satisfied with cloudy answers, but she manages to frame her objections in a more diplomatic way than I do. A frequent member of the pool which gathers in the Cabinet Room before they close the meeting, she is usually the only one to get some real news.

Helen broke the ice of several of the most prominent journalistic organizations. One was the Gridiron Club. When Helen got into the Gridiron, the first woman to be admitted to membership there, she was criticized heavily by some women who said "You are just allowing yourself to become a token." Helen's reply was, "Someone has got to go first," so in she went. She was a real door opener for women in many other ways, as well.

My favorite broadcast journalist is Sam Donaldson. He can be sharp. He has asked questions that provoked presidents into giving answers they had tried to avoid. He can be humble. He used to read aloud to his colleagues in the press room from the critical letters he had received. And I think I know where he got both of these characteristics. Sam once bought his aged mother a pipeline to water her chickens on the farm, but she turned it down, preferring to continue by hand. You see, the Donaldsons are independent. But she was interested in how her boy was doing at the White House. Did I know him, she asked me when I was speaking in New Mexico. In fact, wherever I have spoken I get asked, "Do you know Sam Donaldson? What is he like?"

I can tell you that he has one of the quickest, brightest minds on the air. He can always come up with just the right question. He has a natural gift for improvised humor, as well. In fact, everything he does seems spontaneous, not planned or concocted. In the last few seconds of David Brinkley's Sunday broadcast, Sam can cut through the confusion of all the other panelists' overlaid arguments, sum up the issues and bring some conclusive sense out of the discussion. His sharp wit and piercing analysis of public issues put him on the cutting edge of television journalism.

Over the years, my relationships with many of my fellow news gatherers have been as turbulent as those with my eleven Presidents. But, as with the Presidents, when all is said and done, I have a great deal of respect for most of them. CNN's Larry King has become the foremost journalist in broadcasting with a unique approach: he gets the most newsworthy guests and then actually lets them talk. Other broadcasters I admire, even though they are not my colleagues on the White House beat, include Peter Jennings and Ted Koppel of ABC and Bob Schieffer at CBS. When CBS anchor Dan Rather worked at the White House, he and I would shout at one other at times, but in his book, "The Camera Never Blinks," he was very kind to me. I miss seeing Maurine Dowd of the New York Times working in the White House press center, but I still enjoy her columns. Bill Plante of CBS and ABC's Brit Hume are thoroughly enjoyable co-workers and, like most of us who cover the White House, I greatly appreciate the help of Al Sullivan, who is there almost all day, covering the President for the United States Information Agency. We are all members of the same profession, and any of us who are worthy of the job have the same goal in mind—making government understandable, accessible and accountable to our readers, listeners and viewers.

I'll tell you a secret, though. There are times that the last thing in the world I want to do is to go to the White House and endure another press conference. It has nothing to do with the fact that I'm 86 years old and have been at this same assignment for over 52 of them. No, it's always been that way.

When I was a young mother, I wanted to stay home with my baby daughter. With no father in sight, she deserved more than a part-time mother. As she grew up, Sally would talk to me about leaving Washington or at least going to work at some 9 to 5 job here. I always told her it was an investment in our future to pursue my career—but she wished I had more time for her, and so did I.

She did have compensations. Living in an Auntie Mame-style household filled with everyone from top government officials to colorful characters right off the streets. Being swept along to political conventions in Chicago and Los Angeles, where she'd be the darling of the press corps. Having Congressional pages and Presidents' daughters as her playmates and the Capitol as her playground—even climbing around up inside the dome!

But even now, with Sally the mother of a grown daughter herself, I wish I had the time to stay at home and read a good book. To talk to a visitor or be one. Even to write checks to pay the bills.

It's not that I'm complaining. I know I'm very fortunate. As an independent, I am not subject to the limitations that reporters working for a chain or network have. I have always been my own boss—or, as one of my employers, Frank Mayborn, once said, "Nobody's your boss." I know how many people would like to have had this job—and I know that anyone who spends as much time as I do at the White House cannot expect to have a normal life. I think it is essential, though, that one never loses the common touch. That goes for me as much as it does for the Presidents I have known, from FDR to Clinton.

Chapter II

BILL CLINTON: THE COMMON TOUCH

I think that Bill Clinton may go down in history as one of our really great Presidents. Not so much for his political skills or his record of achievement—though he certainly has the desire, and, I hope, will have the time, to improve both. No, the reason I think he will be remembered and admired has to do with the genuine sincerity with which he treats people. Every time he speaks, he has a way of connecting with everybody in the audience. They all feel as though he is speaking to them personally. It's not the same kind of charisma as Roosevelt or Kennedy, but it is charisma nonetheless. Roosevelt's came from power, Kennedy's from charm. Bill Clinton's allure comes from the unmistakable feeling that he genuinely likes you.

He makes use of this strength in the enormous amount of time he spends with regular people, not just high-ranking officials. At practically every event, you see him going into the audience, often for thirty or forty minutes and sometimes even hours, to shake hands and speak with everyone. People are amazed that the President is actually among them. When he played the saxophone on television, some journalists wrote that he seems to have the appeal of a rock star. I think it's more like a charismatic preacher at a tent meeting; some folks become euphoric at the very opportunity to meet, speak with, and be close enough to actually touch him.

Although he is often criticized for being ten or twenty minutes late to his next appointment, it is because he spends that extra, unscheduled time with the crowd that came to see him. In his concern to meet every American he can, he's been known to accidentally slight a politician, official or other VIP. The amazing thing is that in all the times I've seen Bill Clinton go into an audience, it's never once seemed forced or contrived, like a big act put on by somebody who's trying to score points by being a regular guy. I think Clinton does it because he really enjoys it.

I sensed how different things in Washington might be on the day after the 1993 Inaugural. During their first official day in the White House, the new President and First Lady extended an open invitation to everyone to come to the White House. Our new First Family, along with Vice President Gore and his wife, Tipper, remained available for eight or nine hours, greeting thousands of people who took the opportunity to drop by.

This was the first time a president had been so available to the public since Andrew Jackson's day.

I think it is a genuine shame that this same President who threw open the White House gates on the very first day he lived there has now had to increase security like no President has before. One madman fired into the grounds, and another crashed a plane just short of the building itself. The legacy of hostility the government has been bringing upon itself for decades has now gone so far that this most outgoing President I've known can't be as open as he wants to be in his own home. But he hasn't let it stop him, or even slow him down. His energy seems relentless, and it's good for us that it is: I think more people in this country have been able to voice their concerns directly to this President than to any other.

Whether in Washington or on the road, he is always listening to what Americans have to say. He has frequently brought large groups to speak with him in the White House or on its majestic lawns. He gathers people who should be talking together: teachers and students, health care workers and those in need of health care, businessmen and those who would like to start businesses but do not have the means or opportunity to do so. He has brought into the mix, in groups or as individuals, the entire range of American voices. For the first time in decades, Native Americans of every Tribal heritage were invited to come and make public the needs of their people, who often feel forgotten. President Clinton seems to sincerely want an American Reunion in a family reunion atmosphere.

I am sure that most of his visitors—or those he visits—come away from meeting Bill Clinton feeling that he actually listens, understands and tries his hardest to act upon the concerns of everyone he talks to. I understand that during his administration the White House has received up to 15,000 letters a day, four times the amount of previous modern presidents. He answers as many of them as he can personally and sees everything that goes out over his signature.

The first time that I saw Mr. Clinton was at a labor meeting. He was campaigning for the Democratic nomination at the time, and like most of the Washington press, I didn't know all that much about him except that he was supposed to have had an impressive record as a two-term governor of Arkansas. We only spoke a few words at that time. When I next saw him, he had come to Washington as the President-elect, to plan for his upcoming administration. I waylaid him in the lobby of the Hay-Adams Hotel, where I had heard he might be showing up. Sure enough, he did.

When I introduced myself, it turned out he knew more about me than I expected him to. He told me, "I know very well who you are. I have been watching you all of my life at the press conferences, Mrs. McClendon." With a little shock, I realized that this President was still two years from being born on the day I covered my first presidential press conference. I mentioned that he would be the eleventh President I've covered, and he replied, "Well, I hope I'll be a good one." I said, with some conviction, "Well, I'm sure you will be."

My optimistic prediction has only partially come true. Though I still think he's been "a good one," Bill Clinton's first four years as President have been, at times, a study in frustration—for him and the country, too. Winning with a campaign built around a "new generation" of leadership, Clinton promised to turn around the economic recession and come up with innovative domestic policy. And Clinton felt ready to make some big changes, right from the start. In addition to the enormous job of getting the economy back on track, he dove right into the social problems facing our country. He ran into some problems of his own right away.

Even during the campaign, I don't think Clinton got the kind of support he needed from the Democratic party. After George Bush won the Gulf War in 1991, a lot of major Democrats announced they weren't going to run against him in 1992. His poll numbers and approval rating were so high, it looked as though he was a sure winner. When Bill Clinton stepped in to take him on and actually won, I think some folks like Sam Nunn and Dick Gephardt were sort of disappointed. Any ambitions they might have for the White House were going to have to be postponed, maybe until the next century. This may have been one reason why Clinton, after only weeks in office, found himself facing a surprisingly hostile Congress.

The Democratic National Committee wasn't as much help as they could have been, either. I don't think they shared Bill Clinton's vision or came through for him as strongly as they should have. His campaign was well-organized and well-financed, but that was his own doing. He kept back a lot of money from the early campaign days to spend in the national race. In comparison, it seemed to me that the DNC efforts were poor and frail.

I don't think the communications between the Clinton administration and the Democratic National Committee are fully straightened out even yet. For months I had been getting a dozen faxes a day from the House Republican Conference, calling Clinton a liar and saying that he's giving out false statistics to justify his positions. And the Democrats were doing nothing to answer these charges, which were being sent out to journalists all over the country. I called up the DNC and asked whether the Democrats had any intentions to start protecting their President. Well, some time after that, they started sending out two or three statements a day, but nothing like as many as the Republicans were putting out. I'm told that one thing that threw the DNC off stride and caused them to be fluttery is the new primary system where there are so many more elections in the states. Well, I don't know why they couldn't get over that pretty quickly, if they wanted to. I will say that their national press secretary, Joe Lockhart, seems to be doing a much better job lately.

The Clinton administration made some of its own problems, too. Forgetting the lessons of the Carter presidency, they seemed to suffer a spell of "Outsider's Disease." Like Governor Carter had before him, Governor Clinton brought to the White House an inexperienced staff that not only required job training but lacked know-how about how this city works. They were well-meaning but young, unorganized and without guidance. Leading the staff was the President's boyhood best friend Mack McLarty, an affable and kind Arkansas CEO with zero experience in national politics or the ways of Washington. The communications staff especially seemed tied up in concerns like who got what title or office space. By the time the administration got things together and learned from their mistakes, there had been some real damage done to their ability to work with Congress.

There seemed to be a leadership vacuum. The White House was unable to control the congressional agenda even though both the House and Senate were being run by Democrats. It was kind of schizophrenic. Here was a Democratic President in a stand-off with a Democratic congressional leadership and the end result was the kind of gridlock we'd grown used to with Republican Presidents. The failure to gain the cooperation of Congress hurt or killed many of the administration's most ambitious ideas.

For example, the Clinton Health Program went down in flames. Congress resented the fact that the President had put First Lady Hillary Rodham Clinton in charge of the task force. She had been rather secretive about the plan, preferring to release it all at once rather than have it dribble out in little bits. The trouble was that she didn't ask for congressional input. They saw that as a slap in the face. When the plan turned out to be long and overcomplicated, the Democrats used that as an excuse not to support it. The Republicans didn't need any excuse. And one must remember that there were many millions of dollars from the health insurance industry spent to defeat the program, efforts from an industry that stood to lose profits had the health program gone through. Seems to me like the same old story: once again business and government had a fight, but it was the people who lost.

It's also important to remember that during the first two years that they were in Washington, the President lost his mother and Hillary lost her father. Losses like that, so close together, certainly added to the pressures of the office.

Some people at the White House have started referring to those first two years as Clinton's "first administration." Labeling them like that puts those years behind them, which I can understand, considering they were pretty much a fiasco. Despite good progress with the economy and a lot of other achievements that often go unrecognized, Clinton's popularity rating sank to its lowest. On top of his inability to control his own party, Clinton was faced with a Republican minority in the U.S. Senate which, under Bob Dole, filibustered and blocked every major piece of legislation supported by the White House. Sure, that's politics. That's maneuvering with the 1994 mid-term elections in mind. That's either good or bad depending upon your own position, of course. But what it added up to was that this President was not able to pass any but the most broadly supported measures, like the Brady Gun Control Bill.

This state of affairs disgusted me, because legislators of good will and good intentions from both sides of the aisle were stymied by squabbling between their own leaders and between their leaders and the President. Clinton, of course, must take his own large share of the responsibility for this sorry situation.

I suspect Bill Clinton knew the 1994 election would be bad, but I doubt that he thought it would be as bad as it turned out. It was a shock: for the first time since 1954, Republicans gained control of both houses of Congress. They also won the governorships in a majority of states, including seven of the eight most populated ones.

But then came Bill Clinton's big surprise. Handed a mandate by the people, the "Republican Revolution," under the leadership of the new Speaker of the House, Newt Gingrich of Georgia, began to find how hard it can be when the shoe is on the other foot. Now that they had a legislative program that they had promised the voters to put through, they were the ones on the spot. They soon began to find that sometimes life is easier as a minority party.

Bill Clinton now began what his people like to call his "second administration." He had learned enough from his first two years to avoid the kinds of mistakes that had made them so troubled. He was finally able to make clear that not everything was as bad as some were saying. The effects of a rising economy were beginning to show. Deficit reduction was progressing as planned. And now that he could take the role of the noble opposition, he played it well.

The more extreme the Republicans seemed, the more Bill moved to the center. The more contentious they became, the more presidential he demonstrated he could be. As his battle for a second term drew near, I could sum up his achievements in the headline story of my bi-weekly newsletter, "Sarah McClendon's Washington Report," dated July 19, 1996:

CLINTON A DIFFERENT TYPE OF PRESIDENT

The Presidency has been broadened by Mr. Clinton from the high summitry of war and peace, international trade and foreign policy to include such matters as abuse of women, teen-aged pregnancy, youth gangs and even school construction. While these matters may seem local or personal, they require federal help through legislation and federal money, which justifies his interest. His actions extend a helping hand to those living with the problems in homes, communities and the job world. As I see it, the people appreciate his help. If many of these issues can be solved, then the people would have more time to devote to such issues as simpler, better tax plans, solving inflation, and scientific research for health and business.

Mr. Clinton has taken on a lot more than he had to. I think this is what he means when he says "we need change."

He is the first President I have seen to bring to the dignity of the White House East Room the reality of abuse of women. He had two such programs. He included a wide assortment of bureaucrats who must deal with the problem.

Other problems he has worked on are: the Family and Medical Leave Act, which was not his solution alone but which could not have passed if not for his enthusiastic support. Tracing guns to keep them out of the hands of children. Improved child care. Increased funding for collections for child support. Increasing the minimum wage to help poor families to buy a little more food for the table to stave off the hunger that exists daily for one of every four children.

When one passes a federal building in Washington these days, one is likely to see a fenced-in area with playground equipment for the children of mothers who work in the building.

He introduced the 1-800 telephone number so that violence against women could be reported. He put 100,000 new policemen on the beat to prevent crime. He introduced Operation Safe Home to fight crime in public housing. He created and signed Student Loan Reform, saving students and taxpayers money. He brought more pre-school children into the Head Start program by increasing funds to allow for more students and for improving teaching facilities. He supported the Safe and Drug Free Schools Act. He increased the safety and availability of mammograms for women and increased funding for breast cancer research by 65 percent.

He made it possible for many students to get credit toward college by working in community programs through Ameri-Corps.

Also for women, he increased lending through the Small Business Administration and provided extensive business skills training. He increased federal contracts for women in federal procurement. He established a White House Office for Women's Initiatives and Outreach. Forty-two of his Presidential appointments were women. He named the highest number ever of women to judicial posts.

After Mr. Clinton established the system whereby guns used in crime can be traced—an effort to keep them out of the hands of children—a whining White House reporter asked if this was being done just because this is election year, adding that she had never heard of it before as being in the Presidential realm.

She was right. This is an extension of the President's role.

Bill Clinton likes to think of himself as a People's President, and when you look at the impact that he has had on these "smaller," more people-oriented problems, his record of achievement improves considerably. He is well on his way to earning that name.

Let's look at one of these efforts in a little more detail. I think one of the best things that he did was to establish Ameri-Corps. This is an organization of young people who work hard at civic tasks, anything that needs to be done for the community at large. In exchange, they get tuition credit for college. This has proven to be very successful and productive. I've talked with some of these young men and women. They were quite downcast when they heard that the Republicans wanted to eliminate funding for their organization altogether. But the President somehow saved it.

He has also snatched from the ashes of his health care program a major bipartisan victory: in August of 1996, he signed into law the Kennedy/Kassebaum Health Insurance Portability and Accountability Act, which guarantees that a worker changing or losing a job can take with them and renew the job's health plan.

Certain aspects of Bill Clinton's personality deserve further study—because, like a two edged sword, they cut both ways. His standing rule, for example, is not to get into feuds with people. Wonderful in principle, but a damn nuisance at times. Heaven knows you can't please everybody every minute of the day. He is quite skilled at arguing when the situation presents itself, but he will try different ways of problem solving instead of confrontation. He does not want to be anybody's enemy and hates to hear you talk badly about anyone, especially one of his appointees. He will fight you over that.

Because of this, he can't bring himself to fire people on his staff, despite the recommendations of his associates. He's been told several times that some of his staffers are ineffective or weak, but he keeps them on anyway. Though some have been let go or encouraged to move on, it's not the President who breaks the news to them.

Remember that it was his Vice President, Al Gore, who he appointed to oversee the initial downsizing of all federal government institutions. During the first eight months of the Clinton administration Vice President Al Gore did just that: meeting with supervisors and the workers themselves in countless government agencies, he asked them directly what they believed could be done to save money and shrink costs in their department. I was impressed that Gore chose to go directly to the workers and bottom level managers, not just to the top brass and high level officials of these agencies. It worked. Gore fulfilled their promise to shrink government substantially (and fulfilled a Clinton/Gore campaign promise, as well) by reducing the Federal work force by 240,000.

With this reduction, the White House staff, too, was cut by twenty percent. This didn't go over too well with many of the press, who began to experience difficulty in trying to get daily schedules and perform our regular duties. This was especially apparent in the early months of the Clinton administration. During the transition, many receptionist and secretary spots were not filled with paid employees but interns. Interns, interns, interns...and more interns!

Clinton increased the amount of young unpaid volunteers working in the White House substantially over any other administration. In a given period, as many as several hundred might be brought in. Not only were they not paid, but they had to arrange for their own room and board while in Washington. They were just happy to get the chance to work at the White House.

Because of the unusual amount of young people that were brought in, my daughter, Sally, who has a way with words, renamed the White House "Camp Clinton." The interns do tasks that are sometimes menial but always important: copying, filing and working in the mail department. You can find them in the media office, the First Lady's office, the Vice President's office and most everywhere where sensitive information is not readily available. Many young people from all over America have been given the opportunity to work in the White House for a few weeks or a summer under Clinton's expanded program. But nevertheless, it still gave the press corps a little aggravation while Washington adjusted to the increased numbers of interns coming into so many departments.

Downsizing the federal government took up most of Al

Gore's first months in office. This former Senator from Tennessee followed in the footsteps of his namesake father, who had also been a Tennessee Senator. Al Senior recently told me that his son has a certain chemistry with Bill Clinton that makes them natural partners. Gore has become the conscience of the Clinton administration, always pushing his pet issues of safeguarding the environment, stopping the import of narcotics, and, of course, reducing the size of government and making it more efficient. Clinton backs Gore fully on these issues and many more and allows his Vice President an amazingly high profile, an exceptional thing for a president to do.

But, then, it was exceptional that Clinton chose Gore as his running mate in the first place. When he did so, back in 1992, he defied the conventional wisdom that says a presidential ticket needs balance. You know: North needs South, Industrial needs Rural, Big Personality needs Background Support. Instead, they almost seem like twins, both white, moderate, Southern Baptist Baby Boomers. (Try saying that three times fast!) In addition, both men have strong, outgoing personalities. Unlike most every President who preceded him, Bill Clinton is not afraid to share the spotlight. He surrounds himself with strength...and has always tried to.

Bill's brother, Roger Clinton, tells about the day his big brother brought home Hillary Rodham to meet their mother, Virginia Kelley, for the first time. Roger was only 15 back then. When the couple walked through the door, he and his mother were very surprised. This girl from Yale was not the kind of woman Bill had dated in his high school and undergraduate years. She was really different. No make up. Thick glasses. Rather shapeless brown hair. After a few awkward moments, Bill excused himself and took his mother and brother into the tiny kitchen. There he said, "Look, I want you to know that I've had it up to here with beauty queens. I have to have somebody I can talk with. Do you two understand that?"

Yes, folks, Bill likes Hillary for her mind. And so do I. Though either one of us, I'm sure, would be quick to admit that she just gets prettier every year. Sure they had problems. Who hasn't? But for each of them, this is still their first and only marriage. Betsy Wright, Clinton's former Chief of Staff from the Arkansas years says that any man who fought as hard as he did to keep his marriage going deserves a medal. It is obvious the Clintons are closer than ever, despite gossip and personal attacks that might have wrecked weaker people.

There are a lot of misconceptions about President Clinton. For instance, he is much stronger on foreign policy than people realize. He's made a lot of friends for the United States overseas. He has visited Russia many times and his jovial friendship with Boris Yeltsin has helped the Russian President and perhaps prevented the return of Communism to that struggling nation.

One of Clinton's last trips before the 1996 campaign began in earnest was to Korea and Japan. Many people thought he made the trip to capture headlines. But going to Korea right then was important. North Korea was threatening the border and acting like they were building atomic bombs again. Clinton was determined to do something about this. He went to South Korea to talk to the President. He talked to the people in South Korea, reassuring them that they could depend on our support. Continuing on to Japan, he worked on our worsening relationships over trade. In each country, he was assessing a critical situation, getting vital first-hand information and representing our country's strength.

Then there's the fact that he did not serve in the Vietnam War. There are still a lot of people who think that means that he's anti-military, weak on our nation's defense. I think there is no question in the world that Mr. Clinton has great patriotism and understands the need for an adequate defense for this country. I am a veteran and I'm tired of all this talk about our President having been a draft dodger. It wasn't that he didn't love his country. He thought that there were other things that he could do for his country with his life—as did many others on both sides of the political fence, many of whom went on to serve their country in public office.

I think the fact that Bill Clinton was never in the military actually makes him feel that he should be stronger on defense than he would otherwise be. He has made it a point to back the military and honor our veterans and their rights. He initiated a White House breakfast on Veteran's Day in November and Memorial Day in May. On the 50th anniversary of W.W.II he brought together all the leaders of the veterans' organizations and their wives from across the country for a breakfast at the White House. They did not usually get such attention.

Clinton has had to overcome the advice of some staff members who don't see veterans as a top priority. Sometimes Jesse Brown, the Secretary of Veteran's Affairs, has had to fight some of those in the White House for his budget. But Clinton has protected veterans all the way and sees that they're well cared for.

He has certainly gone to work on the World War II Memorial. A man from Ohio came to town and discovered to his horror that this city, of all places, did not have an appropriate monument for World War II. He went to his Representative, Marcy Kaptur, and told her about this. She sponsored the legislation which Mr. Clinton signed to enable the World War II Memorial to be built. The President named an advisory committee of 12 people, and I am deeply honored to be among them. I have my signed Presidential commission on my living room wall. He came and helped us with the dedication of the site. It will honor not only the veterans, but the spirit of cooperation and purpose, both here and around the world, that brought us to victory. I continue to work very hard on the plans for the memorial, and President Clinton continues to be our greatest supporter.

I like William Jefferson Clinton very much. I have great faith in him, as a man who will bring about change and whose leadership seems well suited to lead America into the future.

Having seen most of this century, I know I'd feel comfortable if the man leading us into the next was a person-to-person President, with the common touch.

TYLER, TEXAS, 1910-1929;

WASHINGTON, DC, 1944-1996:

There is a story about how John Quincy Adams became the first President to be interviewed by a woman journalist. As it goes, a reporter named Ann Royal came upon him skinny dipping in the Potomac and sat down on the river bank, right on top of his clothes. She refused to move so he could leave the water and get dressed until he'd answered her questions. Not having been there at the time—I'm old but not that old—I have no way of knowing if the story is true. But I can tell you this: what she went through was nothing compared to some of the things I've had to do to establish my journalistic credibility in this tough town.

Last year, I ran into my old friend Liz Carpenter at the White House gate. She was going in to give President Clinton a report on the Council for Aging. I was headed out after a news briefing. We stopped to chat for a while—after carefully locking our wheels. You see, we were both in wheelchairs at the time.

My life has locked up with Liz's at frequent intervals. She had just begun reporting here in Washington when I left the Army and joined the Washington press corps myself. We became rivals for clients when we both worked in the Press Building. She was Lady Bird Johnson's Press Secretary during Lyndon's White House years. Facing the same parental problem, we had campaigned together for a tax provision to let women who worked deduct the expense of hiring a baby-sitter. Now, as we sat there, discussing the upcoming celebration for the 75th Anniversary of Women's Suffrage, we reminisced about our very earliest connection: my mother and her aunt, Birdie Robertson Johnson, had been companions in the fight for women's suffrage, not an easy task in east Texas in the 1910s. I remembered Liz's aunt well; as a young child, I was brought along by my mother to rally after rally at which the two of them spoke.

Liz and I were among the pioneers of another fight for women's rights: the struggle of women journalists for the same rights and respect as their male counterparts. We both had offices in the National Press Building and were both denied membership in the National Press Club. We've both been president of one of the "distaff" organizations to which women were long relegated: she at the Women's National Press Club, I at the American News Women's Club. I'd like to think that one result of our fight for credibility was that Lyndon Johnson now trusted women reporters. When he needed to address the nation for the first time as President after that horrible return flight from Dallas on Air Force One, he asked Liz to write the speech. I was very proud of her excellent work in that critical time.

I've always been an organizer. When I returned home from college, I organized a group of my friends in Tyler into a literary club. The organizing bug must have bit me hard. When working in Washington, I noticed that many of the newswomen were not getting to meet, see or talk with top officials. Even if one was part of the group interviewing an official, he might well direct the story toward the men and never bother to talk to her. So I brought together a group that was exclusively newswomen. I asked an experienced reporter of considerable talent, Helene Monberg, who at the time had her own bureau, to assist me with these meetings. We usually met in the office of the person we were interviewing. We had Senators, House members, Cabinet members, agency heads and other people in the news. The one rule was that these sessions were on-the-record. If the person being interviewed squirmed and asked to talk off the record, I did not permit that. This was serious newsgathering, not a chat.

At the same time, there was a group of male reporters who had their interviews off the record. In their sessions, the information was always given as "background," meaning that although the reporter might use some of the information divulged, the person being interviewed could not be quoted. Men reporters would often tell me that you cannot find people in Washington who will agree to keep the interview strictly on the record. Guess again, boys.

My group's greatest moment came when I asked J. Edgar Hoover, director of the Federal Bureau of Investigation, to give us a press conference. Much to my surprise, he agreed to do so. I learned later that it was perhaps his second press conference ever, and certainly the first one with women. He was not known for talking with the press. I think his staff was surprised, too. We went to his office in the Justice Department. During the session, Mr. Hoover sent out for his annual report. When it came, he read from it. Apparently it had received no media coverage before we came, and he wanted us to hear it. The session dragged on. It eventually lasted for two hours and 45 minutes.

One of our members did not think the session would be interesting, so she did not attend. But later, after all the hullabaloo and front-page news that emanated from this press conference, she was fired by her New York newspaper. Another member was in the bathroom when the session heated up.

In an attempt to make things more interesting, we began to ask Mr. Hoover some pointed questions. When someone brought up Martin Luther King's assertion that the FBI was not only hard on blacks but discriminated against them in hiring, Hoover said, "He is the most notorious liar in the country." Hoover decided he wanted this statement to be off the record, but we agreed that we would be the only ones to use it and not discuss it with other reporters.

The news quickly hit the fan. The next morning at 6:00, I was awakened by a telephone call from the New York Post, wanting to know all the details. There was a storm of coverage in the eastern press. Ironically, my wide-spread papers thought it was too much of a national story for me to write my own version, so I was denied the scoop.

Martin Luther King heard about it, and publicly vowed that he would come to Washington, take J. Edgar Hoover on personally and make him apologize. But nothing like that happened. Dr. King came to the Justice Department to see Hoover, yes, indeed. They went into a room together. I stood outside the room, waiting for the result. But Dr. King never appeared. Finally, I was told that he had gone out another door and had left the building without giving a statement. He had apparently been silenced.

I was told that Hoover probably let Martin Luther King know some of the things he and his men had developed about the civil rights leader by stalking him and spying on his conduct. As we later found out, Hoover seemed to think that Dr. King was a Communist and an adulterer. The FBI chief may well have threatened to release those accusations and any evidence he might have had to back them up.

King, however, did not seem to suffer as much damage from this incident as Hoover did. In 1969, it was made public that the FBI allegedly put illegal wiretaps on King's phone, among many others. After his death in 1972, Hoover's files became notorious. The King incident was one of the first major cracks in Hoover's reputation. I felt proud that I helped reveal some of his misuse of power.[1]

Another activity in which I take pride is my long-term crusade to

---

[1] In 1971, Representative Hale Boggs, Democrat of New Orleans and Majority Leader of the House, made a powerful speech on the House floor. He said that the FBI, under the direction of Hoover, had been spying on members of Congress, as well as encroaching on the privacy of citizens. Despite the prestige of his office, Boggs was widely criticized for making that speech. He was accused of being under the influence of liquor, drugs or mental depression.

When one re-reads the speech, however, one can clearly see that it is a Jeffersonian-type masterpiece on the right to privacy. It is an insistence upon one branch of government officials staying out of the private lives of other officials who might otherwise be intimidated.

The attacks on Boggs were carried on by friends of Mr. Hoover. What we have learned of Hoover's activities since his death lends credibility to Boggs' charges, yet denunciations of Boggs, not Hoover, continue to this day in certain areas. Most who criticized Boggs, though, look at things in a different way. Some wish there had been a more thorough investigation of Boggs' death, which occurred only a few weeks later in the mysterious disappearance of an airplane in which he was flying over Alaska, where he was helping another Democratic congressman's campaign. It should also be remembered that Boggs served on the Warren Commission.

eliminate stag events which exclude women to the detriment of their careers. I started doing this in Texas, when, as a reporter in Tyler, I dared to go to cover an oil field barbecue for 400 men. I did not stay very long.

I worked for years to try to get the bi-weekly luncheons for visitors of the Texas delegation at the US Capitol opened to women. My friend, former Speaker of the House Jim Wright, recently wrote about it. Maybe you should hear it from his point of view:

> Another episode that stands out in my mind involves Sarah's persistent crusade to open up the weekly Texas delegation luncheon to allow women guests. That luncheon traditionally was an all-male bastion, one of the few remaining enclaves of masculine chauvinism on Capitol Hill. Sarah led the fight to break down the sex barrier.
>
> Each Wednesday, she would station herself at the door to the Speaker's dining room through which members entered for the weekly luncheon confab. "When are you going to come to your senses and open this up to women?" Sarah would demand. It became a little embarrassing to some of us who had a constituent guest in tow. Finally, on one of those alternating Wednesdays when we observed a members-only rule, Jack Brooks and I announced that we thought it was silly to insist on the men-only rule. After all, we didn't tell dirty stories! Jack and I decided between us that on the next Wednesday open to invited guests, each of the two of us would bring a woman guest.
>
> Mouths flew open in astonishment as I walked into the room with Leonor Sullivan, a highly respected woman member from Missouri. Upon seeing Jack and me ignoring the time-honored barrier, Kiki de la Garza went across the hall to the public dining room and found a woman of his acquaintance to bring back into the meeting as his guest. After that, the men-only rule was dead forever at our delegation luncheon.
>
> And it was a good thing. Soon thereafter, Mrs. Lera Thomas was elected as a member of our delegation from Houston to succeed her late husband, Albert Thomas; a few years after that, Barbara Jordan joined the delegation. It would have been doubly embarrassing to have had such a rule that excluded a distaff Texas colleague. Lucky for us all that we had discarded the antiquated old rule before this happened—thanks to Sarah McClendon.

When, in 1990, the Texas delegation lovingly threw me an 80th birthday party, I think every speaker brought that story up.

I may have bugged my fellow Texans by standing by their meeting room door, but I actually picketed the Gridiron Club over their men-only membership policy. Senator Hubert Humphrey, the speaker that night, begged forgiveness for crossing our picket line. And then there was the time I got out the word that Washington's Convention and Visitors Bureau Annual Party was going to be a stag affair, with 900 men in attendance and no women. That was before D.C. had its first woman mayor.

Even closer to my heart was the battle I fought to help my fellow newswoman Jessie Stearns. Jessie, who had served overseas for sixteen months in the Pacific in World War II, wanted to get into the Veterans of Foreign Wars, a large organization which is active in national political campaigns. As a veteran with service overseas, Jessie should have been eligible, but the group was still all male. But the same determination that she'd shown in the war won out for her again. I remember how delighted I was when a spokesman from the VFW Convention in Dallas called me to say that they had voted women veterans in. Jessie was the first female to become a member.

This was not a fight I was waging for myself, since I had spent my war service first at the Pentagon, telling Congressmen and the public about the WACs, and then as a public affairs officer with the Army Surgeon General. But I have always saved my best efforts for my fellow female veterans. I feel I owe them that, since it was in the Army that I really learned to be proud of women. After I saw little women back those big trucks into alleys to deliver food to the mess halls or saw them take a hose and stand out in the freezing cold, spraying down an ice-covered truck, I knew that women could do anything.

But we were constantly being questioned. The inquiries from Congress showed a great deal of skepticism about a woman's ability to be a good soldier. Did the nation's needs justify the presence of women in the service? Were we strong enough for heavy work and capable of withstanding hardships, both mental and physical? Should the Army keep us on in peace time? The answers were yes, but still, for years both during and after the war, we had to prove ourselves. Once the Army sent out a number of prominent lay women as a board of review to test the adjustment of women to military life. I think they believed the all-female board would recommend that Army life was just too much for women. But not a single one of the women on the board recommended disbanding the WACs.

I have continued to campaign for my successors in olive drab by serving as a member of the Defense Advisory Committee on Women in the Services, or DACOWITS. Each time I've served on this committee or attended a program, I come away with a renewed understanding that the military needs the female point of view every bit as much as women need the respect a military career can bring.

I served on DACOWITS with Sandra Day O'Connor, the first woman to be named to the U.S. Supreme Court. She was very busy but attended our sessions whenever she could. Her legal perspective was useful with the problem we were evaluating: the fact that sometimes when a case of sexual harassment or even rape was reported, the military authorities would not even set up a court martial to try the accused. In the Marine Corps, in particular, they might simply dismiss a man from the service. To the Marines, you see, that signified the worst punishment a man could have—to not be allowed to continue as a Marine.

The mood at DACOWITS is not always so somber. At the opening of one semiannual session, we heard from Admiral Elmo Zumvalt, then Chief of Naval Operations. One issue touched upon was whether women should serve long tours of duty aboard Naval vessels. I asked him what he thought about women at sea. "I always think about them," Admiral Zumvalt replied, "especially when I am at sea." He said it so sweetly, I don't think anyone there took offense. He did a great deal for women, including having them assigned as Navy flyers.

I'm not saying that flying a jet is a more important role for a woman than managing a household. I'm saying that any qualified woman who wants to fly a jet—or manage a household—should be able to do so without any restrictions based solely on her gender. I cannot remember a time since I've come to Washington that I have not been involved in one crusade or another aimed at breaking down sexual barriers. Very few of them have directly affected my livelihood. But one injustice I faced simply because I was a woman was so damaging to my ability to function as a journalist in this city that it was never far from my thoughts. For 27 years, I campaigned to become the first female member of the National Press Club.

It was not as though I did not belong to a professional journalists' organization. In fact, by 1960, I was president of a very fine one, the American News Women's Club. The ANWC was organized over 50 years ago as a club to give closer access to office holders, both male and female, unusual personalities, persons of accomplishment or any other VIPs. The club fashioned its charter on that of the National Press Club, with active and affiliated, or associate, members. The ANWC and the Women's National Press Club were rivals, with the latter claiming to have stricter rules for eligibility. As soon as I arrived in Washington as a uniformed public affairs officer, I was given guest cards to both clubs. I worked hard for both and often appeared in the annual program of skits given by the WNPC.

It was during my presidency that the American News Women's Club finally arranged to buy the first permanent club house in Washington for women journalists. The two women's clubs had each assembled committee after committee trying to get a club house. I had been part of that search for years. I thought it was essential for our events, for which both clubs had always had to rent rooms. But we always met with disappointment. May Craig, a prominent woman journalist who covered the White House with me, once told me, "No women's press group in Washington could ever obtain a club house of its own, nor could it maintain one." I remember telling her, "We'll see."

I located a beautiful home for sale at 1607 22nd Street, NW. But the responsibility of buying and maintaining it stirred up controversy. Such a big project frightened many of the members. After a lot of infighting, I finally won approval for the purchase—just before my term in office ended. I won by one vote, that of Mrs. Charles Cabell, an associate member and my loyal supporter. My successor signed the papers and closing on the house.

Today the club house remains in our possession and in use. It's permanence was increased by the recent donation of an elevator to gain access to the second floor for activities and to the upper floors for tenants and management. The club house has been the scene of receptions for prominent persons as well as our regular speakers on professional pursuits. The club is often rented and used by other organizations in Washington honoring women. First Ladies are honorary members.

Why, then, was getting into the all-male National Press Club so important? No one can imagine the hardship of being kept out unless one personally has experienced it. More than many other newswomen of that period, I suffered because I was working in that very building. It was embarrassing, to say the least, when I needed to contact my own boss, Bascomb Timmons, and he would be unavailable, since, being an active member of the club, he was upstairs at the bar or in a luncheon meeting. Later, when I was operating my own news bureau, I needed to contact various members and speakers and prominent guests almost every day. The best tips on new jobs or new clients, on changes or resignations at the bureaus, on a newspaper being sold or closed, came from that bar upstairs. The latest information often meant career progress for members.

I worked in the building almost every night until 11, but even if it was cold or snowy or rainy outside, I could not go upstairs to get a hamburger. To get into the club, I had to be accompanied by a member. Maybe I knew one close enough to take me and maybe I did not; most of them were married. I could not even take little Sally, when she was a child, upstairs to the annual Christmas party. Each year we would see the children of members coming up in the elevator for these events as my daughter and I would be going out of the building. She didn't understand why she wasn't allowed to go up and see Santa like the others. And frankly, neither did I.

I couldn't even rent office space in the building unless I shared the office with a member. And the offices were small. Sometimes the men I had to share with were loud and messy and listened to my conversations with others.

Once I lost a good account over this. I was sharing the office at the time with two male journalists. I sat between the two in a small area with a desk and a chair and a few files. In walked three men, the publisher, editor and business manager of the Beaumont Enterprise, a good paper with a wide circulation area in Texas and Louisiana and one with which I had a history: it was the last paper I'd worked for before joining the Army. Much to my embarrassment, there was no place for the visitors to sit and little room for them to stand.

Since her husband Les was a member, Liz Carpenter and he had just moved into a roomy, freshly painted office down the hall and had applied to represent both Beaumont newspapers. The Carpenters already had Enterprise's rival the Beaumont Journal, a vacancy which they had learned about through me.

To crown it all, this was just before Christmas, and I had arranged for Sally to come downtown to see the Santa Claus parade. She was sitting on my lap when the men arrived. It did not look at all professional. The visitors decided they would have a better organized, two-correspondent agency with the Carpenters. I lost the Enterprise, although I had far more knowledge of its needs and had provided a massive amount of copy for them.

The Press Club bar was a place considered sacred. Women visitors to the club could go with husbands and boyfriends to other sections, but not the bar. I learned one day that a Texas candidate for the U.S. Senate, Thad Hutcheson of Houston, was holding a press conference for Texas reporters in the NPC's club bar. I telephoned the club, but no one would call him to the phone. So I went to the front desk and hammered with my fists on the counter, yelling and screaming until the men from the bar ran outside to see what all the commotion was about. Hutcheson came, too. I told him that I was covering his visit to Washington and could not go in the bar. He had not known about the exclusion of women and agreed to continue his press conference outside the bar, so that I could listen.

India's Gandhi and the Soviet Union's Krushchev had much to do with breaking down the barriers for women. They both had heard of how women were kept from participating in Press Club events and both refused to come there to hold press conferences, unless women could be admitted too. We could stand or sit, though there were seldom any seats, in the Press Club gallery but could not ask questions of the speakers. When Cabinet Secretary Oveta Culp Hobby of Health, Education and Welfare addressed the club, she insisted that women be admitted to the luncheon. We were allowed to sit at the meeting, not for the luncheon but for the speech only.

I brought up this situation to President Jack Kennedy, at a White House press conference. I asked him if he would keep his Cabinet officers from speaking at the National Press Club, since women reporters who covered these officials were excluded from the luncheons. Kennedy looked stunned. He had not known about the restriction. He indicated that he did not agree with the exclusionary policy and would take my request under consideration.

Finally the club had a president, Don Larrabee, who tried to do something about this. He brought the matter to a vote after overcoming great objections, including threats of resignations by officers and members. How he got it to a vote, I do not know. It was that difficult.

When the club admitted its first black journalist, I decided I would formally apply for a membership, thinking that if they were beginning to become less exclusionary, they might take in a qualified woman. I filled out a formal application and had legitimate members sign it to sponsor me. The club, after some time, was asked to acknowledge receipt of my application. They said they had never received it. I had to go so far as to bring forward a Western Union messenger to prove that the application had been delivered and received.

In 1971, I learned that Esther Tufty, a deceased member's wife with a guest card admitting her to certain areas of the club, was about to get into the club as a full member. She had kept this quiet as she wanted to be the first female member. After all my applications and efforts, the club officials had not even notified me of the plans to admit women. Twenty-seven years after I had first attended a press conference in the Oval Office, I had to fight my way into being one of the first group of female journalists to be admitted to the National Press Club.

It had taken me so long to get in, that when I finally made it to the children's Christmas party, I took my daughter—and my granddaughter, too.[2]

In later years I ran for an unexpired term as vice president of the National Press Club against three men. I was elected by a plurality. It came as such a surprise to the members that they immediately changed

---

[2] Four generations of McClendon women have worked hard for greater equality for women.

First, Annie Bonner McClendon made speeches throughout east Texas seeking support for the passage of the 20th Amendment, which gave women the right to vote.

Second, Sarah Newcomb McClendon accompanied her mother on these trips, learned points from her to use in future speeches, news stories, columns and broadcasts as the battle to pass the Equal Rights Amendment continued.

Third, Sally McClendon MacDonald headed a federation of women's organizations in Canada which reviewed and rewrote legislation to give more rights to women. Today, at every level of government in Canada, there is a minister with the responsibility to examine every law to see how it impacts on women's rights under the Constitution of Canada. Today Canada affords its women more rights than women have in the U.S.

Fourth, Allison McClendon MacDonald studied women in Middle Eastern Countries and women in Islam. She is writing her thesis on this subject for her Master's degree from Tel Aviv University. Later, she worked briefly at the White House in the Office of Women's Initiatives and Outreach. Today, she heads the administrative staff of the Women's Studies Department of George Washington University and will pursue further studies of women as she seeks her Doctor of Philosophy degree.

the rules so that elections with similar results would not happen again. During my four month term, I put out press releases notifying the members that we were about to lose our license to serve food because of the condition of the kitchen and that we were losing liquor by night because someone was taking booze from our storage to sell in another bar. I was censured by the board, which had apparently not planned to let the members know the true condition of affairs. I think I was a fine vice president. It seems to me that raising a little hell when it's called for is part of the job description.

Breaking down barriers for women can have its ironic side, too. Sometimes, it seems, you can be too effective a motivator for your own good. When Rep. Margaret Heckler was a freshman Republican from Massachusetts, the American News Women's Club invited her to speak, along with other new members of Congress. Arriving at the club house, she came up to me and said "Do you recognize me?" I replied that I was afraid I could not recall having met her. She said, "Well, you ought to... You're responsible for my being here."

When I asked her why, she said, "You came and spoke to us in Massachusetts and you said that there ought to be more women running for Congress and participating in the political process. As a result, I ran for Congress against the incumbent, and I won!" Little did I have in mind when I made that speech that she would run against and beat one of my good friends, Speaker of the House Joe Martin.

Still, I accept appreciation where I can find it, and if a few old friends suffer as I inspire new ones, I guess I'll have to learn to live with it. Because whenever I see a barrier, there's something in me that itches to knock it down.

Sometimes, it seems, I can inspire old friends as well. I was very flattered when at a "Tribute to the News Women of Washington," Katherine Graham, Chairman of the Board of the Washington Post, said, "I am a real admirer of the grit of Sarah McClendon. She is a woman who made it long before the barriers came down... In that unmistakable twang of hers, she kept the backs of uncounted Presidents firmly against the wall."

I may have knocked down barriers for women, and put Presidents against the wall, but if I do my job right I hope there will always be an open gate for me at 1600 Pennsylvania Avenue:

"Sarah McClendon does not have to climb a fence at the White House or fly a plane into the White House grounds to get the attention of a president. They have been answering her questions, although warily at times, for many years."

— Hillary Rodham Clinton

Thank you, ma'am. I never turn down an invitation from a First Lady.

Chapter 12

THE FIRST LADIES: INSIDE THE FENCE

For our nation's First Ladies, being inside the White House fence can have a double meaning. It means they are close to the seat of power, perhaps the major influence on the man who is both their husband and the President of the United States. But the Executive Mansion can also be a prison.

All of the First Ladies have had a hard time. According to research conducted for the Smithsonian Institute by Edith Mayo, nearly every First Lady had at least one major project on which she worked, hoping to bring about some reform in government or improvement in the lifestyle of the people. On nearly every one of these, there was controversy, with various groups expressing their support or objections. Some of the early First Ladies were treated very harshly, but none as harshly as Mrs. Abraham Lincoln, or our present one, Hillary Clinton.

ELEANOR ROOSEVELT

Eleanor Roosevelt received a great deal of criticism. As with many of the First Ladies who would follow, her energy and determination frightened many Americans who could not understand it. She worked in her own office, largely under the direction of her husband, President Franklin D. Roosevelt, who, appreciating her keen mind and compassionate heart, asked for her help. Since he was disabled, she did much of his traveling, keeping in touch with the sights and sounds of the twelve turbulent years through which he served. As his surrogate, his ambassador, she was loved and hated for his strengths and flaws, as well as her own.

The wife of one President and the niece of another (Theodore Roosevelt), Anna Eleanor Roosevelt set a precedent herself: no other First Lady had ever been as famous in her own right.

She gave speeches throughout the country and wrote her observations for the newspapers. In 1933, she held, for a group of newswomen, the first press conference ever in the White House by a President's wife. Many other press conferences, for women reporters only, would follow.

Eleanor Roosevelt was a woman of large vision who knew that small problems count, that the nation cannot be strong while so many are troubled and weak. She received an enormous amount of mail from people who, like her President, needed her help. Case by case, she would contact the appropriate government agencies to see if the situation of the family who wrote her could be solved. She set an example of activism on a person-to-person level that other First Ladies have followed. She showed how to handle problems by using the right federal agencies. Today, this kind of hands-on problem solving can be found on Capitol Hill. In the office of each member of Congress, there are case workers who, in theory at least, carry on the spirit of Eleanor Roosevelt.

In theory—because in practice, there are few among us who can measure up to Eleanor Roosevelt's indelible style. There's a story I love about Mrs. Roosevelt during her last days, told by a woman who was her secretary and who helped handle her never-ending volume of mail. Though Mrs. Roosevelt was very frail, she continued to try to answer it all. One night, the secretary knew that Eleanor was not feeling too well. But it was cold and late, and Mrs. Roosevelt told her, "Honey, go on home and go to bed. You're tired." So she went home, but as she prepared to go to sleep, she happened to look out the window of her residence hotel. Below her, on the sidewalk, a little, bent-over figure, huddled up in her jacket, was walking through the snow toward the mailbox. There had been one last letter, in which a man was asking the government for money he needed badly, and Mrs. Roosevelt knew it needed a reply. So, she answered the letter herself and took it that night, out through the cold, alone, to the mailbox.

BESS TRUMAN

On the surface, at least, Bess Wallace Truman could scarcely have been less like the First Lady that preceded her. Mrs. Truman separated herself almost entirely from public affairs. She held one press conference, shortly after her husband had become President—mostly to say that she wouldn't be holding any others. Someone on her staff said that Bess didn't even like shaking hands in a reception line. I observed this to be true.

While Harry Truman was in the White House, Bess Truman spent months back home in Missouri. It was clear he missed her very much. He was devoted to "his Bess" and consulted her, whether in person or by phone, whenever he had a decision to make. Sometimes he would mention that he had spoken about an issue with "The Boss." Though she had much to say against his running for re-election, she seemed to feel it was for his good—she thought a loss would devastate him.

Mrs. Truman did have an intimate group of friends in Washington which she had made when she served as Harry's secretary while he was in the Senate. And away from the White House, she could be warm, gracious and friendly. As an honorary member of the American News Women's Club, she came to a surprising number of the receptions and programs which we regularly held. She would bring her daughter Margaret with her to these mostly afternoon affairs. The two were quite accessible as they sat and talked with us, spending time with club members and their guests.

I think perhaps Bess Truman was simply a woman of her times. The war had been the kind of crisis in which everyone pitches in to help. After it was over, a lot of Rosie the Riveter types felt it was time to get back to "normal," which to most women those days meant back to domesticity. By rejecting the role of First Lady, Bess Truman may just have been coining her own version of one of her husband's favorite sayings. The way Bess Truman turned it around, it went, "If it's too hot for me, I'll get back in the kitchen."

MAMIE EISENHOWER

As an Army wife for thirty-seven years to a high-profile military man, Mary Geneva Dowd Eisenhower grew used to being on display to groups of influential people. She stood by her husband and was very devoted to him. She weathered the sad moments, like when she heard about Kay Summersby, in silence. If she suffered, she never showed it publicly. Instead, according to her friend, Ruth Butcher, wife of Ike's Naval aide, Mamie treasured the letters her husband sent her from the front.

She acted more forcefully when her rival for Eisenhower's attentions was his assistant Sherman Adams, who was monopolizing his time on the campaign trail. We all said "Good for Mamie!" when we heard she'd moved Sherman out and herself back into Ike's hotel suite.

As First Lady, Mamie had only one press conference that I recall. Some of the men were allowed to come to that, as well as the women. She didn't particularly like the press and she didn't particularly enjoy answering questions. She was quiet and dignified and avoided publicity when she could.

Mamie suffered from some affliction which made her dizzy. Some people attributed this to a drinking problem. But I believe it was medical. She was a darling woman, very feminine, likable and charming. She spent a lot of time with his friends, a group of military wives. They would have long luncheons at Washington's Mayflower Hotel. I'm told that after these extended lunch breaks the waiter would have to come around and decide who owed what on the check. They could never quite straighten it out themselves.

Mamie thought of others and could be very generous. She donated a shampoo board to a house for widows of military men which, I understand, is still being used today. But, as with so much else in her life, she kept her good works private and low-key. Like Bess Truman, she was not a conspicuous First Lady. Unlike Bess, however, she never seemed to reject the role.

JACKIE KENNEDY

Jacqueline Bouvier Kennedy brought an aura of glamour to the White House that no one had before. She had an aristocratic background, a fashionable education, a handsome, dynamic husband and two beautiful young children. She was a painter, an art collector and a linguist. And she had been a working girl, a member of the press. No wonder the country loved her.

Jackie came from a family of educators, considered more intellectual than Jack's. Her family is credited with organizing the educational system for the state of New York. It troubled her that her parents were separated, and she dined with her father whenever she could. She attended Vassar, the Sorbonne and then, here in the District, George Washington University.

When Jackie worked as the old Washington *Times-Herald's* "Inquiring Camera Girl," she was respected and liked by her co-workers. I knew several who had worked to train her in news photography, and they were unanimously approving in their remarks about her. She was considered friendly and approachable, on their level, with none of the distance you'd expect from someone whose mother was part of the Newport, Rhode Island society scene. It was while photographing in the Senate that she met Jack Kennedy.

I think Jack cared deeply for Jackie when he married her. But he had a very male libido, a way of looking at sexual relationships that was far different from women, who tend to be faithful and consider sex tied to love. It must have been a brutally cruel blow when she reportedly found a piece of a rival's underwear in their bed.

The Kennedy public relations machinery was used to publicize every good thing Jack or Jackie did. The press noted how valuable she was in France and Germany because of her élan and language skills. And she received raves for her good taste in looking over the furniture in the White House attic and bringing out pieces of great renown to place in the state rooms. She not only "did over" a number of rooms but took the country on a televised tour to show what she had done. The media went wild.

She did not let the Kennedy children become too central a part of the public image. She was an excellent mother and gave considerable thought to Caroline and John Junior's schooling and playmates, while limiting their media exposure to preserve as normal a childhood as possible.

At a luncheon for the press which Jackie hosted, she graciously addressed us, but her voice was that famous "whisper" that often kept her from being easily understood. I did not care for the whispering voice, but I suppose it added to her elusive charm.

Jackie apparently did not want to go to Texas with Jack on that final, fatal trip. It was clear to my friend, reporter Jessie Stearns, who was watching as they descended the Grand Staircase of the White House the night before, that they had been arguing. Jessie said they continued the "discussion" as they greeted the guests at the last state dinner the Kennedys would ever hold. But Jack prevailed and she went. He wanted her with him because she was popular and could do him great good in a state where he was not that well liked; the people wanted to see her as well as him. The argument must have stopped somewhere along the way. I have heard that they seemed unusually loving once they arrived in Texas.

I'll never forget Jackie standing with a crowd of staffers on the platform as she exited *Air Force One* at the end of the journey carrying her husband's body home. She looked so forlorn with that dried blood splattering her skirt and hose. She had not changed her clothes. She did what I think she should have done—she stayed with the body.

But there is now some doubt as to whether the ambulance into which she was ushered was the one really carrying the President's remains. She went directly to the Naval Hospital at Bethesda, but rumor has it that the fallen President may have been taken to Walter Reed Hospital for doctoring of the exit wounds before arriving at Bethesda for the autopsy. Later, the public was often told that Mrs. Kennedy, along with the Kennedy family, wished that people would stop investigating the shooting of her husband. She apparently figured it could not bring him back and would possibly do more harm than good to the nation. She felt it best to put it behind us and move on.

She gave us an indication of her own determination to do just that when, wedding Greek shipping magnate Aristotle Onassis in 1968, she became the first widow of a president who'd died in office to ever remarry.

LADY BIRD JOHNSON

One of the First Ladies who became particularly well known throughout the nation is Claudia Alta Taylor Johnson. You know her as Lady Bird. She got the nickname when she was two. The family cook noticed she was as "purty as a lady bird," and because it was true, the name stuck.

Lady Bird was a vital partner in her husband's presidency and provided a number of its successes. Like him, she brought a wealth of political experience to the White House. She was intensely loyal and useful to her husband, supporting his ambitions by organizing her own campaigns in his behalf from his earliest political days. She also helped manage his broadcasting and ranching interests back in Texas. As a Congressional wife, she ran his office in 1941-2 when he asked for a leave of absence to join the military, the first member of Congress in World War II to enter active service. She remained active in his office from then on, escorting more visitors through the Capital than any other political wife.

She filled many important roles as First Lady, sharing both the public affairs responsibilities and the social duties. But there was one particular cause that she completely made her own. Today Lady Bird is known and loved wherever a wildflower blooms. In fact, she instilled into many a love of beautification, which had never been thought about in an organized way before she took up the cause. She brought beauty to our city and others: in the areas surrounding those ugly public buildings, there are now the rainbow colors of flowers and the green of healthy grass. She brought beautification into a campaign against ugly parking lots and bare ground. She fought for scenic highways. Her ideas have become part of legislation. Today, she has sparked an industry of beautification and heads a national center for the study and promotion of flower growing.

She has always filled her personal life with beauty and order, as well. She is an exceptionally neat and clever housewife. I was shocked when I opened a linen closet at the LBJ Ranch while I was visiting there once and found printed labels for "Double Sheets" and "Single Sheets," which were all in neat piles. It was a great example of organization. The menu, preparation and service of her meals were always excellent, as well.

One memory of Lady Bird that stands out is when I overheard her counseling her two teenaged daughters. Since the First Lady had to travel with the President, the girls were about to be left behind once again in Washington. She knew they were both sorry to see her leave. So as she was waiting for the airplane to take off, she called home to have one more conversation with them. I heard her say, with the simple earnestness of truth, "Remember, you are loved." I think those were just the right words to give a sense of security to two teenagers, who need it at that time in their lives.

I could tell how much the girls loved her when, for one Mother's Day, I became her surrogate. Lynda Bird was spending the weekend with Sally, and when Sunday morning came, presented me with a lovely bouquet of flowers. I've often wondered how a First Lady feels. At that moment, I had some idea.

Years before, there had been another moving moment when I felt a special empathy with Lady Bird. I happened to be in Lyndon Johnson's congressional office when he received a moving telegram from his wife. I did not yet know either of them that well and was amazed that he would read the telegram to me. Lady Bird had had a miscarriage, as I recall, and was understandably depressed under the circumstances. She was thinking of not going further in the political life, of dropping out altogether. She had to decide whether she was coming back to Washington or not. As Lyndon read the telegram aloud, his face lit up with love and joy. She had decided to plan her life along with his, to work beside him in politics or anything that might come up. She was coming back to Washington. I don't think many people ever knew about that telegram. And certainly, few ever have had it read to them by Lyndon Johnson himself.

PAT NIXON

I remember the first time I ever saw Pat Nixon. It was when Richard was Vice President. He was on his way into the chamber to preside over the Senate. Outside in the corridor, he spoke briefly with his wife. Then he went in to oversee that imposing body of lawmaking power—and she sat down in a nearby seat and began to write out a long list of things she had to do, much like you or I would. I had to smile at how sometimes to a Washingtonian, nothing seems all that impressive.

After that, I saw Pat many times around Washington and elsewhere. She was always in the background, listening to her husband or waiting for him to speak. He would introduce her at the end of a conversation, and she would say a few words of greetings and then simply stop. She believed in only one spokesman in the family, and that had to be him. She was there to back him up and to show her support, always with a smile. Though Thelma Catherine Ryan Nixon had been her husband's active supporter since he had entered politics, she never stepped on his lines or took his spotlight.

During the few times that she was presented without him, some of us reporters would try to get her to talk more and to answer questions about the President. But her answers were always short and careful, hardly the stuff to get headlines from. Not until the latter part of his presidency, when Watergate was in the air but had not yet become a public scandal, not until then, did Pat Nixon begin to speak with the press, answering more questions and encouraging us to talk with her. This was usually done in the standup session in the Blue Room of the White House. It was never a formal, sit-down press conference, but we would get more to quote from her in this way than we ever had before.

Mrs. Nixon seemed not only quiet but traditional. I'll never forget the expression on her face as she stood by her husband in a receiving line at a White House reception one afternoon. Senator Ted Kennedy and his first wife, Joan, came down the receiving line. Joan was wearing one of the first of those newly fashionable "see-through" blouses, and Pat was simply unable to keep the shock off of her face.

To some extent, I think we all underestimated Pat Nixon. It wasn't until later that I learned that she had, in her quiet manner, accomplished quite a lot. She had, for example, held the White House door open to more and larger groups at afternoon receptions than any other First Lady. She refurbished more rooms at the White House than Jackie Kennedy did but without Jackie's flair for publicity. She had been a gracious and dignified representative when accompanying her husband on his historic trips to China and the Soviet Union. She helped raise the visibility of women in the military by putting women Marines into the ranks of the Marine Corps band, which traditionally plays for all White House functions.

She also brought to the nation's attention a remarkable and important letter which Mrs. Abigail Adams wrote to her husband John Adams while he was away in Philadelphia with the Continental Congress. Mrs. Adams' letter had not been greatly heralded until after Mrs. Nixon put it in the Smithsonian for everyone to see. In the letter, Mrs. Adams warned her husband that if he and his colleagues who were writing the U.S. Constitution did not recognize women by giving them their rights, the women would eventually demand them.

Pat Nixon may have been quiet, but she knew what she was saying. I'll just bet that if Richard Nixon had listened to her more, he would have served his full two terms.

BETTY FORD

My first recollection of Betty Ford was sitting with her as a guest at the Congressional Club for a luncheon. The Congressional Club is composed of wives of members of the House and Senate. They have their own club house, where they have lovely luncheons and programs with speakers. Women reporters are always pleased to get an invitation. We know that we'll not only enjoy the meal but pick up some tidbit or hear some scoop from the Congressmen's wives.

But on this day, Elizabeth Bloomer Warren Ford was actually seeking to pump me to get more information. She showed great interest in public issues but didn't feel she knew enough about what was going on behind the scenes in the House and Senate. She was looking for an insider's view on the legislation that was being debated at the time.

I got the impression that her husband, Jerry Ford, didn't have enough time to explain to her what legislation he had moved through on the floor each day. He was the Minority Leader of the House then and the ranking Republican Member of the House Armed Services Committee, which had control over the programs and the authorizations for the entire military defense of the country. I saw that Betty Ford's desire to know more about the issues was genuine, and I appreciated her interest so much more than that usually shown by congressional wives.

Of course, she probably never had an idea that someday she would be a part of all of this, in a place where decisions are sometimes made in a far more direct way: the White House. Once she became First Lady, her interest in politics became more active. I especially appreciated her endorsement of the Equal Rights Amendment, something we would not get from the next Republican First Lady. Her devotion to her husband, then and now, is clear. It is regrettable that she had the unfortunate experience of hearing about the attempt of a woman in San Francisco to try to kill her husband before he called to tell her himself and assure her he was fine.

Betty Ford was always exceedingly cordial, easy to get to and to talk with. Her natural grace was a reminder that she had been a serious student of dance, working with the famous Martha Graham troop in New York City. I don't think many of us realized that she was having serious back pain and was under medication for this. Nor did we realize that the regularity of her medications were leading to a dependency and further problems down the line.

It is gratifying that the strength of character and determination that we all could see were not only enough to get her past her struggles, but to make her name synonymous with recovery. Her activism in this and other areas of health care are a true inspiration. Her Betty Ford Clinic for the treatment and recovery of victims of alcohol and drug abuse has, I feel, accomplished as much good for people as some Presidents' entire administrations.

ROSALYNN CARTER

I think that it tells us a lot about Rosalynn Carter that when she arrived in Washington, she still wore many of the simple clothes which she had made herself. She made her own inauguration gown! Her portrait in the White House is done with her wearing that gown.

I think Mrs. Carter was a very genuine, sincere person, a real helpmate to her husband. They remain close partners. I remember hearing Mrs. Carter say that she often waited around: no matter what she was doing, she dropped it in the late afternoon, hoping that Jimmy would call from the office and they could go for a walk together, where he would discuss with her the problems and issues that he'd been working on that day.

Rosalynn brought something unique to the Carter White House: a keen understanding of how government programs affect people. She seemed at home in every state. The daughter of a seamstress, she'd worked as a postal clerk in backwoods Georgia and knew things about life and people you don't learn in Washington. Mrs. Carter knew what it was to work for a living in a town with limited opportunities for business and culture. Yet her background produced a person who proved essential to carrying on a successful nationwide campaign for the Presidency of the United States.

As First Lady, Rosalynn built upon the assets that had proven so effective during the campaign. She became her husband's staff advisor, his special emissary to the people and his confidential messenger. He arranged for her to attend Cabinet meetings. Her special efforts on behalf of the mentally ill made the nation conscious of the need for greater federal investment in research funds and more loving care.

She carried the White House to the people, much as Eleanor Roosevelt did, when she went on speaking tours and special missions to the troops fighting wars overseas. Like Eleanor, Rosalynn would come back with a fistful of requests for special attention in areas where government had broken down. These requests, along with those pouring into her office by mail, were swiftly forwarded to the proper departmental offices with instructions to act upon them. Many a citizen felt renewed faith in government because of her.

Rosalynn Carter depended a great deal upon her public relations advisors. The first time that I ever saw her, she was hesitant to talk to the press. She was always trying to keep her remarks off the record. Anyone who knows me, knows my opposition to that. She turned to her public relations person to ask her if she could speak. I said, "Mrs. Carter, we don't want to know what she thinks. We want to know what you think." I didn't have success with that approach because Mrs. Carter remained very, very cautious.

Like her husband, I guess Rosalynn Carter feels that actions—and activism—speak louder than words.

NANCY REAGAN

I think Nancy Reagan will go down in history as one of the most loyal First Ladies, ever. Her devotion to President Ronald Reagan is the kind of love story that rivals any motion picture either one of them ever made.

Because of her desire to protect her husband, Nancy Reagan was, more often than people realize, a sort of "Acting President." She does deserve a lot of credit for the way that she guarded the President's health. She certainly knew every detail of his medical record and carefully watched over his well-being. Some say that there were times when he was not feeling well or lacking energy that she actually stepped in and acted for him. Though he was never as ill as some sitting Presidents have been, Ronald Reagan surely benefited from the strength and political sharpness with which Nancy analyzed and often achieved their mutual goals. I don't believe the public knew how powerful she was or how many crises she may have spared the government. She had a lot of very practical, very good sense. There's no doubt about that.

When it came to a person's character and aptitudes, the First Lady had keen discernment. She could tell if someone was a true friend to the Reagan White House or not. If any staffers were not, she got rid of them. She managed this through phone calls. She often managed it through investigations. She seemed to be able to find out almost anything that she wanted about people under consideration for appointments to the Reagan administration. She would inform the President of what she learned and offer her advice.

There were, of course, many sides to Nancy Reagan. One was her wonderful sense of style. Another was her wit and intelligence. A third was her inventiveness when it came to entertaining.

She was an elegant person who wore beautiful clothes from the top designers. Whether she paid for them, whether others did or whether they were donated remains a question. It is probable that the designers provided them in order to have the First Lady wear their clothes. She certainly showed them to good advantage.

Like Jackie Kennedy and Pat Nixon before her, Nancy Reagan refurbished a good portion of the White House—and she did it without incurring government expense. She cleverly raised funds from outside contributors to pay for this expensive work. She informed the public that there had been contributions made to the effort, but did not always let us know exactly who the contributors were.

Nancy Reagan had a great sense of humor, which could be either warm or cutting. She had a very interesting series of luncheons outside of the White House with a varied and sundry cast: news people, authors, anyone interesting whom she wanted to know better. When she first came to the District, she did not know very many people in the Washington community. She knew that making contacts and becoming known would help integrate the Reagan White House into the Washington scene in a way that, for example, the Carter White House never did.

I certainly did not think it was very First Lady-like for Nancy Reagan to suggest Rosalynn Carter move out of the White House before the traditional transition period. Mrs. Carter was very hurt by this. I, too, thought it was unnecessary, divisive and certainly not the best way to move into the most important house in the land.

Still, Nancy Reagan could be cordial. She had the press in for annual reviews of the Executive Mansion Christmas decorations. These events would be the one time when she really mixed with reporters. Her Christmas decorations were always charming. Once she had Ed McMahon, of talk show and sweepstakes fame, playing Santa, and everyone—including each reporter—was required to sit on his knee and tell him what we wanted for Christmas. I still have my photograph from that White House Christmas! To this day, I optimistically search my mail for that million dollar sweepstakes prize I asked for.

I admire several of the Reagan children. Nancy's step-daughter, Maureen Reagan, a daughter of the President's first wife, remains a good friend of mine. She helped me a lot with my contacts to the White House, giving me information when I needed it and helping me to get in on things. I enjoyed working with Ron Reagan, Jr., who shows real talent as a television personality. I appeared on his late night show, which had far greater substance and honesty than most. I was disappointed that it did not stay on the air longer.

I also appreciate that Nancy Reagan's daughter, Patti Davis, came to see me in California once. We had a long talk about the Reagans, whom she was not getting along with at the time. I sensed in this dear girl a great loneliness and a feeling that she was left out of many things. I could tell that this was preying on her mind. She did love her parents, very much, and wanted to get along with them, but she simply couldn't agree with her father's political stance and her mother's control over the family, which she alluded to in her writings. While she certainly had a right to her own views, she was deeply unhappy about the family split.

I think the fact that Patti has finally made up with her parents is a gratifying story for both the Reagan family and the American public. I'm sure Nancy is delighted because for her, loyalty comes first.

BARBARA BUSH

Barbara Bush was one of the most likable people to ever live in the White House. She laughed a lot, and people laughed with her. Her wit was, and still is, a frequent delight to her listeners.

She was always very friendly and had a way with words. She could be intimate in three words and make friends instantly. She outdoes her husband in that respect. She had an amazing sense of aptness, fitting into the crowd or rising to the occasion as needed. Once, when the Texans were honoring George Bush at a huge reception during an inauguration—I forget which one—he and she came forward to the platform, up some high steps. She stumbled against one of the stairs, cutting her foot against the metal riser. She rose, continued to the microphone and just laughed it off, saying, "I fell for you." She gave a nice little speech of thanks. Then they had to call for a doctor, as she was really bleeding by that time.

I remember a time when I covered a reception that she was having at the White House for the Daughters of the American Revolution. When I mentioned that I also happened to have been a member of that organization for over fifty years, Barbara, without missing a beat, said, "You don't look it, Kiddo!" Her wit was not only quick, but kind, since I was, at the time, in my early eighties!

Not that there couldn't be a little sharpness to this witty woman. She didn't always approve of the media—and she always spoke her mind. I was the recipient of her criticism once or twice myself. I remember one incident when I was at the White House for a reception she was giving for the American News Women's Club. As usual, she took great interest in everyone as they came down the receiving line, talking with everyone as she shook hands and, from time to time, making a quiet comment about someone coming up. I overheard the tail end of something she had apparently been saying about me. I just caught the word "...troublemaker." When she realized that I had heard her, she seemed a little embarrassed. But since I consider that particular comment to be the next thing to a compliment, I laughed, and so did she. She immediately covered the awkwardness by asking me, "Where did you get that pretty hat?" It was a big, wide-brimmed, bright green straw hat that I've cherished. She said, "Turn around here and let's get our picture taken together with you with that hat on." I've always said that she was light on her feet.

Mrs. Bush had her own personality and she stuck to it. She never altered it to suit her prominence as First Lady. She was determined to be her own self, free from any kind of affectation. Barbara had a very distinctive way of dressing. She usually dressed in full skirts and nearly always wore a three-strand choker of pearls. Though her white hair made her look older than President Bush, she refused to dye it. Her "take it or leave it" attitude contributed to a picture of confidence and competence.

It was clear that as First Lady, Barbara Bush believed in herself and her husband, in his ability to guide the nation, her ability to back him up and their love for one another. He, in turn, appeared to have great faith in her and an appreciation of the sharp, lively and very human face she put on his administration.

HILLARY CLINTON

I think Hillary Rodham Clinton has been one of the most unjustly treated public figures of our history. She is the victim of a political scene which has fallen into a divisiveness and partisanship that sometimes borders on sheer hate. I have, at times over my long years in Washington, been accused of bashing a President or two with whom I didn't agree. But I'm just a miniature poodle compared to the pit bulls who are going after the First Lady. Her critics in politics and the press have created a system of double standards by which she can do no right. Her best and most generous efforts are looked at as somehow suspect.

Take the 1996 Republican Convention, for example. A great fuss was made over Mrs. Clinton's best-selling book, *It Takes a Village.* Or at least its title, since it seemed pretty clear to me that none of those who were trashing the book apart had even bothered to read it. This book, subtitled *...And Other Lessons Children Teach Us*, explores the full range of children's issues, an area which Hillary has studied with great care and one in which she has been active all her adult life: she has worked for the Children's Defense Fund in New England, founded the Arkansas Advocates for Children and Families, and, as First Lady of Arkansas, introduced the "Arkansas

Home Instruction Program." She has also served on the boards of children's hospitals.

She is far more expert on families and children than most of the people who criticize her in Congress or the press. As a mother, daughter, advocate, attorney, professor, advisor to national organizations and now as First Lady, she has been concerned with the fact that our nation's relationship with its young has been twisted out of shape. We have gotten away from the age-old values which our country and societies around the world have found necessary to bring up children to be physically and emotionally healthy. Instead, we ignore the young ones' needs and then fear the adolescents they grow up to be.

Hillary Clinton's book is a call for a return to values. But apparently her critics think they have a monopoly on values. They smirk, "It doesn't take a village to raise a child, it takes a family!" They don't understand that what Hillary is talking about is creating a back-up system for the family, a community that understands that it's in its own best interests to support each and every family's efforts to raise its children.

And look at the raves the Republicans gave Elizabeth Dole for taking a wireless microphone and going out into the crowd to speak. Can you imagine what those same people would have said if it had been Hillary putting on such a strong, emotion-packed show? I admire Elizabeth Dole, who once told me she developed her strength after encountering terrible discrimination at Harvard Law School, where male students would come up to her and say, "Don't you realize that you're taking the place of some male student who deserves to be here?" and one professor would only let the women speak on one day of the term and then only after each had to recite an original poem. Hillary encountered similar prejudice, I am sure, when she attended Yale Law School. But when she tries to show strength, she is accused of being pushy, of trying to take over, of running the country behind the President's back.

Hillary Clinton has not tried to take on the government or alienate the Washington old timers. She has merely seen her role as First Lady to be an active one, in the spirit of Eleanor Roosevelt. Like her predecessors, Hillary Rodham Clinton brings to the role her own special talents, experience, style and interests. She sees the fact that she is First Lady as a chance to make changes and reforms and, particularly, to protect women and children.

She has supported her husband's policies and has been excellent at interpreting them to the public. When the President made health care one of his earliest priorities, he appointed the First Lady to head his Task Force on National Healthcare Reform, honoring her for her knowledge of the subject and for her desire to help. The proposal the task force put together was, unfortunately, long and complicated and assembled in a lot of secrecy, without consulting Capitol Hill or the bureaucracy, so they felt left out and resentful. Though it failed to pass Congress, both the Clintons learned much from the effort and will, undoubtedly, work in the future to bring all Americans a proper health care program.

What's been overlooked in the blizzard of criticism is that Mrs. Clinton is a warm-hearted, personable woman who is quickly liked by almost everyone she meets. She is one of the best speakers I've ever heard. Though she speaks without notes, she is organized and extremely well poised. She has shown, with great dignity, that she can preside over meetings of both men and women. She has often met the press and shown those who are willing to listen that she is more open minded than she is given credit for. She believes in talking to the press and has been very nice to them, including this reporter.

The First Lady gets along unusually well with the wife of the Vice President, Elizabeth "Tipper" Gore. Early in the administration, when Hillary appeared on *Larry King Live*, Tipper called the show to express her support for her dear friend, the new First Lady. She gave us a good clue to Hillary's strength when she said, "She keeps herself focused on the vision she has for making life better, and that is what keeps her going. She does not dwell on herself or the petty slings and arrows that come at her. She keeps the big picture in line."

Hillary Clinton is loved by almost everyone who really knows her. She is greatly admired by advocates for families and children. She is very popular with the crowds who come to see her at her book signings. In fact, polls aside, I'm convinced her fans outnumber her critics. We're just a lot more quiet and polite.

Being First Lady is a lot like walking on a tightrope. She has to be both strong and weak. She has to be there for her husband and yet be regarded as independent. The First Lady cannot be too independent, however, or we tend to not like her. And she can't be too dependent, or we tend to not like her.

Being First Lady is a balancing act that must be performed with skill, grace, intelligence, courage and humor. Come to think of it, so is the Presidency.

And so should be the job of covering it.

EPILOGUE

Citizen Journalist is a mission I took for myself. It offers the best opportunity to serve one's country, the people and the public interest. It has been a privilege to have lived this life. I thank God for it. At 86, I still cannot wait to get out of bed each morning and start living it some more.

Here's the reason I get up and go to work: I believe that people in this country owe allegiance to the United States, and the government, in turn, should protect the people, especially those who cannot help themselves. This system depends on communications. Without them, it will break down.

When they wrote the Constitution, our founding fathers thought the people would be informed and keep watch on government. We have lost that concept. Each of us ought to give some serious thought daily to making the U.S. government a success. To me, that means participating in government, to make it work at all levels.

What the U.S. needs urgently is leadership which generates confidence. Our leaders must stress openness, not secrecy. The country is in great stress, abounding in rumors and fears. A sense of unity is required for the country to succeed, to set an example for the world. Our citizens fear the concept of too much power and wealth in the hands of the elite. We keep watch constantly against monopolies, concentrations of abusive wealth and interstate controls. This fear of hovering control has existed since the colonists first came to America. The concept that "He who eats, must work" has been around since Jamestown.

Our Presidents and Congress must announce goals and discuss the programs to achieve them, not set them up and wait for endless battering and gridlock. Is there not some way to achieve cooperation? I feel we need a national list of priorities, built on voters' choice.

Here is my own list of priorities: health care for all, including preventive medicine; making women full partners in society; free education for all; an absolute block against the import of narcotics; no guns allowed in homes, businesses or cars; a nationwide list of job opportunities for the unemployed; mandatory training for jobs; an end to costly, surplus, untested manufacture of weapons; a stop to sales of combat arms abroad; a start toward manufacturing for peace, not war; elimination of homelessness; classes in parenting; scientific application of psychiatry to prevent abuse of others; stopping all secrecy in government agencies.

A long list, you say! But these changes would bring a better lifestyle for all citizens and help assure our country's survival. Such goals can be accomplished through communications, and journalism is the most expedient way of accomplishing this. We need more questions asked by enterprising reporters. Presidential press conferences provide the clearest channel of communications from the lowliest citizen who wants answers to the President of the United States. They can insure democracy.

Operating independently is the best outlet, but I realize that all cannot operate the way I have. I have been privileged to use print media, radio, television, lectures and publishing. I have never sought the spotlight; I have always tried to focus it on the truth. If this girl from East Texas has sometimes seemed to shine, it is from the reflection of the issues I have brought to light.

When I told Joe Laitin, a dear man and one of the best Presidential press secretaries that I've known over all these years, that I was writing this book, he sent me a story that he insists I put in. Here is what he wrote to me:

> When I accompanied President Lyndon Johnson to the northernmost reaches of South Korea, the last stop of the Korean railroad, I was besieged by a bevy of beautiful teenaged girls, undergraduates at a nearby college, who asked if I would point out Sarah McClendon. "Don't you want to meet the President?," I asked. No, they said — Sarah was their heroine and role model; that's why they'd skipped school that day. Well, Sarah hadn't made this trip, but it wasn't the first time she'd upstaged a President of the United States. The look of disappointment on their faces has stayed with me all these years. Their parting words, without waiting to greet the President, were, "Tell Sarah to keep up the good work."

I'm trying, girls, I'm trying.

INDEX

look more mature. Or they may be pressured by friends to try just one hit. From reading this book, you know how addictive crack is. Just one hit could really mess up your life.

There are many ways that you can avoid crack and other drugs. You can hang out with people who don't do drugs. You can avoid places where you know drugs will be used. Most of all, you have to be strong. Let people know how you feel about drugs. If they say: "You're afraid!" you can say: "Yes, I am afraid. Messing with crack is stupid! I'm not risking my life for any drug."

If you think you might have a problem with drugs, from alcohol or tobacco to cocaine or crack, you should get help. Talk to your parents. Be honest with them and ask them to help you get treatment. You may want to show them this book. If you are worried about talking to your parents at first, you can still get the help you need. There is a list of organizations in the back of this book that can give you more information on drug abuse and help you find a treatment program to get off drugs.

What should you do if you suspect that a friend has a drug problem? From

54 reading this book, you know the signs to look for in a crack smoker. He or she:

- changes friends
- doesn't care about work or school
- loses weight
- can't sleep
- can't concentrate
- gets angry easily
- runs out of money quickly

If you want to, you can share what you know about crack. Your friend may not have correct information. Be sure you talk when your friend is not high.

You can also be a good listener. Let your friend express feelings and tell you about problems.

There's something else you need to know. Sharing information will help. But this person needs professional help.

If you want to help your friend, don't lend money. Don't go to places where there will be drugs. Invite your friend to drug-free places.

You can also talk to your friend's parents. Let them know what you think. Don't worry about snitching on your friends. In the long run, you will be helping.

Reading this book is a great start toward avoiding the dangerous road of drug dependence. Studies show that the more young people know about the dangers of crack, the less likely they are to use it. You've learned that crack can mess up your body, damage your brain, and ruin your life—even kill you. You can choose a bright future by choosing to stay off drugs.

Glossary—
Explaining New Words

chemical dependency A disease that causes a physical need for a drug. Without the drug, the person suffers withdrawal.

cocaine A stimulant drug made from the leaves of the coca plant.

crack A highly addictive form of cocaine, made by mixing it with baking soda and water.

depression A state of feeling sad and alone.

ether Liquid used to freebase cocaine.

experimenting Trying something out, such as drugs, to see how they feel.

freebasing A dangerous process of mixing cocaine with ether so it can be smoked.

gateway drugs Drugs such as alcohol, tobacco, and marijuana, that can lead to the use of harder drugs such as cocaine and crack.

hallucination Hearing, seeing, or
feeling things that are not real. Can be
caused by drugs like crack.

heroin A strong, physically addictive
narcotic.

overdose A deadly or toxic amount of
drugs.

paranoia An unreasonable feeling of
distrust. Thinking that everyone is out
to get you.

prostitution The act of engaging in
sexual relations for money.

purifying Mixing coca leaves with acid
or kerosene to make cocaine powder.

reproductive system The sex organs of
the male or female body that allow
people to create children.

stimulant Drug that speeds up the work
of the body. Cocaine and crack are
stimulants.

tolerance When the body becomes
accustomed to a drug. With tolerance
a body needs more and more of a drug
to get the same high.

withdrawal Painful symptoms, such as
chills, fever, trembling, cramps, or
convulsions, that occur when an
addict stops using a drug.

Where to Go for Help

Hot Line Numbers
- Cocaine Anonymous National Referral Line: (800) 347-8998
- The Cocaine Hot Line: (800) COCAINE (262-2463)
- The National Institute on Drug Abuse: (800) 662-HELP
- Narcotics Anonymous: (818) 773-9999
- Teen Help: (800) 637-0701
- Youth Crisis Hot Line: (800) 448-4663

Support for Families
CocAnon Family Groups
P.O. Box 64742-66
Los Angeles, CA 90064
(213) 859-2206

Nar-Anon Family Groups
P.O. Box 2562
Palos Verdes Peninsula, CA 90274
(310) 547-5800

National Families in Action
2296 Henderson Mill Road, Suite 300
Atlanta, GA 30345-7239
(770) 934-6364
Web site: http://www.emory.edu/NFIA/

59

For More Information on Drugs
American Council for Drug Education
164 West 74th Street
New York, NY 10023
(212) 595-5810 ext. 7860
(800) 488-DRUGS

Cocaine Anonymous
World Service Office
P.O. Box 2000
Los Angeles, CA 90049-8000
(310) 559-5833
National Referral Line: (800) 347-8998
Web site: http://www.ca.org
E-mail: cawso@ca.org

National Clearinghouse for Alcohol and Drug
   Information
P.O. Box 2345
Rockville, MD 20846
(301) 468-2600
(800) 729-6686
Web site: http://www.health.org

For Further Reading

Easy to Read

Adint, Victor. *Drugs and Crime*. New York: The Rosen Publishing Group, 1994.

Ball, Jacqueline A. *Everything You Need to Know About Drug Abuse*. Rev. ed. New York: The Rosen Publishing Group, 1994.

Berger, Gilda. *Crack*. New York: Franklin Watts, 1994.

Berger, Gilda. *Patty's Story: Straight Talk About Drugs*. Brookfield, CT: Millbrook Press, 1991.

Carroll, Marilyn. *Cocaine and Crack*. Hillside, NJ: Enslow Publishers, Inc., 1994.

Friedman, David. *Focus on Drugs and the Brain*. Frederick, MD: Twenty-First Century Books, 1990.

Harris, Jacqueline L. *Drugs and Disease*. | **61**
New York: Twenty-First Century
Books, 1993.
Hyde, Margaret O. *Know About Drugs*.
4th ed. New York: Walker Publishing
Company, Inc., 1996.
Madison, Arnold. *Drugs and You*. Rev.
ed. Englewood Cliffs, NJ: Julian
Messner, 1990.
Shulman, Jeffrey. *Focus on Cocaine &
Crack*. New York: Twenty-First
Century Books, 1991.
Turck, Mary C. *Crack & Cocaine*. New
York: Crestwood House, 1990.

Challenging Reading
Edwards, Gabrielle. *Coping with Drug
Abuse*. New York: The Rosen
Publishing Group, 1990.

Index

64 | ### About the Author
Rodney Peck is a graduate of Central Michigan University. He worked with the America's PRIDE program in drug prevention and education for four years. He then joined the Peace Corps in Belize, Central America, where he was assigned to a drug education program for two years. His work in drug prevention (especially with young people) has taken him to Canada, the U.S. Virgin Islands, and throughout the United States. Rodney is currently living in Memphis, TN, pursuing an acting career. He continues to stay informed and to talk about the dangers of drugs.

Photo Credits
Cover photo © Frank Fischer/Gamma-Liaison; pages 2, 6, 12, 17, 20, 22, 27, 40, 46 by Stuart Rabinowitz; pages 30, 35, 38, 42 © AP/Wide World Photos; page 50 by Stephanie FitzGerald.